Dante and Medieval Latin Traditions

Dante and Medieval Latin Traditions

PETER DRONKE

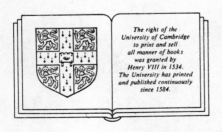

The right of the
University of Cambridge
to print and sell
all manner of books
was granted by
Henry VIII in 1534.
The University has printed
and published continuously
since 1584.

CAMBRIDGE UNIVERSITY PRESS
Cambridge
New York   New Rochelle
Melbourne   Sydney

Published by the Press Syndicate of the University of Cambridge
The Pitt Building, Trumpington Street, Cambridge CB2 1RP
32 East 57th Street, New York, NY 10022, USA
10 Stamford Road, Oakleigh, Melbourne 3166, Australia

First published 1986
Reprinted 1987

Printed in Great Britain at the University Press, Cambridge

British Library cataloguing in publication data
Dronke, Peter
Dante and Medieval Latin Traditions.
1. Dante Alighieri. Divina commedia
I. Title
851'.1   PQ4390

Library of Congress cataloguing in publication data
Dronke, Peter.
Dante and medieval Latin traditions.
Bibliography: p.
Includes index.
1. Dante Alighieri, 1265–1321 – Knowledge – Literature.
2. Dante Alighieri, 1265–1321 – Sources. 3. Latin
literature, Medieval and modern – History and criticism.
I. Title.
PQ4394.D76   1985   851'.1   85–19464

ISBN 0 521 32152 2

CE

Contents

Preface

My purpose in this study is to sketch and illustrate a range of ways in which medieval Latin traditions can help us to comprehend Dante's *Commedia*. The focus is on a number of poetic techniques, ideas, symbols and myths which Dante came to know through the Latin Middle Ages, but which become alive in new ways in his poem. I have chosen to concentrate on a few problems only, and to link these throughout with attempts at detailed interpretation. But the selection has been planned, it is hoped, along lines that will lead towards fuller understanding of many of Dante's principal strategies, and towards meeting the challenges – even obstacles – that he deliberately sets.

There is a pervasive belief, supported by a consensus that begins with the earliest commentators and still flourishes today, that the most fitting approach to the *Commedia* lies in attempting a predominantly allegorical reading. Many elements of allegorical explanation have become so firmly, almost unanimously, established that it may seem foolhardy even to question them. At all events, to question them on poetic grounds, by suggesting that the conventional allegories proposed do not do justice to the stature of Dante's imagination, will always sound too impressionistic, too subjective, to carry conviction. We may feel that Dante has an 'esemplastic power' – unifying meanings and making language dense with meaning through awareness of an associative kind – that transcends the schemes of allegory; yet it remains difficult, historically, to set the hallowed approach aside in favour of a more unfettered criticism.

The best hope in this dilemma, it seems to me, is to try to show from a group of texts that subtler, more imaginative approaches to poetic meaning were possible in and before Dante's time. Here and there in the Latin Middle Ages I believe we can find certain insights into poetry that would still strike us today as worthy of great poetry. The allegorising methods, such as were used by biblical – and at times classical – commentators, were neither the only nor the most outstanding instruments of interpretation available.

I am also encouraged to question afresh even some of the most deeply rooted assumptions of the commentators because in our century two of the scholars whose work on Dante means most to me have distanced themselves from that exegetic tradition in notable ways – ones, moreover, that they could substantiate on historical grounds. I refer to the writings of Erich Auerbach and Bruno Nardi. By examining the medieval notions of *figura* as something distinct from allegory, Auerbach was able to arrive at a well-founded premise that was adequate to some fundamental aspects of Dante's imaginative richness. It was no longer necessary to follow Guido of Pisa, Jacopo della Lana, or Dante's sons, Jacopo and Pietro, in explaining Vergil and Beatrice as allegories – of Reason and Theology, or similar concepts – or to fear that it would be 'unmedieval' to reject such crude conceptual equations. For, alongside allegory, the equally well-attested medieval concept of *figura* allowed for the simultaneous presentation of vividly individual creations and hidden meanings – meanings that do not conflict with the perception of individuality but are consubstantial with it.

So, too, Nardi was able to argue, on the basis of his incomparable detailed knowledge of medieval thought, that the notion of sustained allegorical, moral and mystical reading of the *Commedia* was *historically* inappropriate, that 'any attempt to extract from Dante's poem the hidden senses which Jewish and Christian theologians were wont to extract from the Bible is simply an attempt at cabbalistics'.[1] And yet – so the objection runs – was it not precisely this kind of reading that Dante himself had espoused, in the letter in which he dedicates the *Paradiso* to his patron Cangrande? Where in 1944 Nardi spoke of a 'grave and justifiable doubt'[2] about whether Dante wrote that exposition, in his later work on the question he concluded, with a wealth of observations, many of which have been neither countered nor superseded, that the expository text which follows the dedication – the seeming foundation-stone for the systematic allegorising of the *Commedia* – could not be attributed to Dante himself.

The present study takes some of Nardi's and of Auerbach's insights as points of departure. It is clear – and both scholars were fully prepared to admit – that moments of allegory do occur in the *Commedia*, that Dante worked with fixed meanings at times, as

well as with open ones. In identifying the moments of true allegory and delimiting their scope, many questions still seem to me
debatable, and in some, on which I touch in the course of the
book, I follow neither of the two great pioneers. Nor would I
quite follow Nardi to the extent of staking so much on the in-
authenticity of the explanation for Cangrande. I have many
reasons – including some unsuspected till now – for thinking
Dante did not write this explanation; these emerge both during
the first chapter and in a separate Excursus. Nonetheless I still
think it just conceivable that on this one occasion Dante should
have resolved to bring to his own otherworld journey an explanatory method similar to that which Bernard Silvestris and others
had thought appropriate to the otherworld journey of Aeneas, or
which the Fathers had imposed on many parts of the Bible. It was
a method that may well have been so deeply assimilated by most
commentators of the time that, inasmuch as they perceived the
Commedia as a text with striking analogies to the *Aeneid* and the
Bible, they automatically began to organise the new text in the
anciently familiar pattern. At least it can be seen that the author of
the Cangrande exposition, though tempted in this direction, did
not persist with it: after a general statement, and an example
drawn from the Bible, he did not go on to apply the method even
to the handful of lines from *Paradiso* that he chose to elucidate.
Still more important is for us to recognise how far the allegorising
method differs, first, from the other Latin discussions of poetic
meaning that Dante could have known (and that, even if he did
not need them for instruction or inspiration, offer at least some
appropriate co-ordinates for his poetic craft); second, from the
brilliant perceptions of the nature of meaning that can be found at
certain moments in the *Commedia* itself. Some of these, too, are
discussed in Chapter 1.

The chapters that follow are in a sense only fragments of what
would be, ideally, a more extended inquiry. I have selected three
principal moments – those of the giants in *Inferno*, of the apocalyptic showings in *Purgatorio*, and of the first circle in the solar
heaven in *Paradiso* – to examine in detail some of the ways in
which these moments rely upon medieval Latin traditions, and in
which Dante's medieval Latin inheritance helps to illuminate his
poetic practice. Many cross-references are made, naturally, to
other parts of the *Commedia* and to Dante's other writings; but I
decided to focus on these parts, rather than others, because taken

together they involve us in a substantial group of complementary problems, and hence can in some measure be regarded as exemplary. Considered in conjunction, these parts can be seen to unite a large range of Dante's modes of generating poetic meaning; they reflect many of the kinds of creativeness that can be encountered in the *Commedia* as a whole; they illustrate many aspects of the medieval Latin imaginative world upon which Dante relied, and can help show how he both used that world and went beyond it.

What kind of imaginative reality do the beings that appear in the *Commedia* have? To perceive and define this, for a range of apparitions as diverse as the giants in hell, the phantasmagoria in the earthly paradise, and the philosophers and theologians in the sphere of the sun, certain Latin evidence is crucial. Thus, for instance, Dante's treatment of the mythological giants and the historical Nimrod would not have been possible without the kinds of euhemerism that the medieval Latin world had developed. Yet no one before Dante had used those euhemeristic techniques so many-sidedly, to achieve such complex effects. It was possible for the Church Fathers to reduce the gods and demigods of the pagans to human, or demonic, status: if Christ is the 'true Apollo', the pagan Apollo can only have been a human king, or else – if he still exists – an evil spirit. Dante's course, however, is not that of opposition but of integration: for him, the fabled giants Ephialtes and Antaeus are real in the same way as the biblical giant Nimrod – they share a human brutishness and wretchedness. But by his language Dante's integration extends far beyond this – into the realms of the comic, the scary, the colloquial. No one had brought such things into the domain of biblical–classical confrontation before. Dante inherits certain conceptions of the literal and the mythical, as well as notions of imaginary languages and of the nature of illusions. What he brings to all these is his own: he makes them serve the purpose of distancing the giants, in the dramatic sense, and demythologising them, in the philosophical, while at the same time through his resources of language he allows the encounters with the giants to become fearsomely real.

The phantasmagoria that are shown to Dante in the earthly paradise exemplify an even wider spectrum of imaginative realities, that extends from emblematic constructs to visions of obsessive vehemence. Controlling all these is the double standpoint which some medieval thinkers – including ones that Dante celebrates later, in his solar heaven – had perceived in the prophetic

books of the Bible, seeing the content of the prophets' visions simultaneously as inner events within a human being and outer ones
that the seer projects upon the world. Yet there was also a corresponding double standpoint known to the finest authors of medieval poetics: the poet in the act of making 'hidden comparisons
(*collationes occultae*)' could, like the prophet, realise something that
was 'both within and without'. Dante's achievement in the last
cantos of *Purgatorio* cannot be accounted for in terms of either the
poet's or the prophet's mode alone; he avails himself of both, sure
that, because his thought is integrated, the two will coalesce.

This approach necessarily calls in question a number of received
allegorical interpretations of images in these enigmatic cantos,
such as those commonly advanced for the tree, the eagle, or the
dragon. With these and the others, my method is to begin from
Dante himself, trying to ascertain what imagery he might, historically, have known, and how he has transformed it; I leave aside
the method that begins from the assumptions of Jacopo della Lana
and the other early commentators. It is still, of course, open to
scholars to claim that these commentators fathomed Dante's
intentions correctly. But I hope to have shown at least that this is
not self-evident: it is a case that would have to be argued anew, on
its own merits.

In the fourth chapter, my principal endeavour is to look at a
group of medieval Latin texts and authors with Dante's eyes, to
see what he might have seen in them. Here I begin with the hypothesis – which, strangely, seems not to have been entertained
before – that the twelve sages in the first circle of the solar heaven
were chosen because Dante was familiar with the work of each one
of them, and had seen in each something that illuminated his
central poetic concerns in the group of cantos (*Paradiso* X–XIV)
that describe this sphere. Testing this hypothesis revealed a far
deeper coherence in Dante's design than anyone who had not followed Dante into the thought of these figures could have surmised. Thus, from attention both to the authors Dante knew and
the poetic context in which he sets them, it becomes possible to
understand more precisely just what each of these thinkers meant
to him.

The book concludes with two Excursus, which give detailed
documentation for some controversial points that arise in the
course of discussion in Chapters 1 and 2. In the first Excursus, I
aim to set out in a more rigorous form than hitherto the technical

difficulties involved in the claim that Dante is the author of the expository part of the *Epistle* to Cangrande. These difficulties concern the patterns of Latin prose rhythm. Since Tore Janson's remarkable study of this topic (1975),[3] the medieval Latin rhythmic cadences have been precisely quantifiable, and intended cadences have become effectively distinguishable from fortuitous ones – a fact that requires the revision of a number of earlier assessments and opinions.

In the second Excursus, my object is to distinguish for the first time, among the medieval Latin texts relating to Nimrod, the details of the legend of Nimrod the astronomer, adducing substantial extracts from the still unpublished early medieval 'Book of Nimrod (*Liber Nemroth*)'. This allows one to differentiate clearly between the Nimrod of the *Liber*, who is a lofty and noble sage, and the debased giant Nimrod – a figure Dante will have known especially through the tradition preserved by 'Pietro Mangiadore', one of the theologians whom he names in the sphere of the sun (*Par.* XII 134).

While so much of the book sets medieval Latin traditions in relation to Dante, I should like to stress here, once and for all, how little, in the last resort, Dante's intellectual and imaginative processes can be accounted for in terms of his learned sources. He leaves nothing in his sources as he finds it. The materials of the world of learning – the medieval Latin world – set him a constant challenge, conscious and unconscious. He was never going to copy simply: all understanding for Dante implied transformation. Almost nothing can be 'traced back' in an uncomplicated fashion. In the study of Dante, *Quellenforschung* must inevitably retain something elusive: his was a mind for which every assimilation was already instinctively the beginning of an alchemy. There is a rare and obstinate independence – which is close to the heart of his creativeness. Thus the traditions here evoked reveal no more than possibilities that lay open to Dante; they take us only to the threshold of the mystery of how he came to surpass what he knew.

This book is addressed in the first place to medievalists and Dante scholars; but I hope it may also be a fresh invitation to non-specialists to the reading, or revisiting, of Dante's *Commedia*. That is why, in the chapters, citations from Italian and Latin are translated throughout. Those from the *Commedia* are rendered line by line: not because I make any claim for the English versions as poetry – they are no more than aids to understanding – but in order to try to convey, at least by approximations, something of the movement as well as of the content of Dante's thoughts.

My debts of thanks must begin with an affectionate remembrance of Bruno Nardi, from whom, at the start of my postgraduate work, I was privileged to learn much about Dante and about medieval philosophy. His intellectual penetration and his generosity are unforgettable. Since 1969 I have been delighted by the warm welcome of the Cambridge Italian Department, who, first under Uberto Limentani and more recently under Patrick Boyde, have invited me regularly to contribute to their series of public lectures, the 'Lectura Dantis Cantabrigiensis'. Preparation for these has helped me incalculably in crystallising the ideas expressed in this book; many of them, indeed, were first risked in the context of a *lectura*. A large part of Chapter 1 was offered as a talk, '¿Interpretación medieval o moderna? El caso de Dante', in a symposium 'Literatura medieval y literatura contemporánea', at the Universidad Internacional Menéndez Pelayo, at the invitation of Francisco Rico; Chapter 2 was given its final shape while preparing an address, 'Die Riesen in der Göttlichen Komödie', for the annual meeting of the Deutsche Dante-Gesellschaft.

I am grateful to Sebastian Brock and Charles Burnett for their advice on diverse aspects of the *Liber Nemroth*, and to Theresia Payr, editor of *Mittellateinisches Wörterbuch*, for expert information on the meaning of certain expressions in medieval Latin. Patrick Boyde, Ursula Dronke, and Jill Mann have most kindly read the complete typescript; I have been helped and heartened by their observations.

Palm Sunday, 1985   P.D.

The *Commedia* and Medieval Modes of Reading

(i) Allegory and Vision

It often looks as though medieval poetic theory is lamentably incapable of characterising, or even of recognising, what it is in medieval poetry that still moves and excites us today. Nowhere has there seemed to be a greater chasm between theory and poetry than with regard to Dante's *Divina Commedia*. Is this because of the poverty and inadequacy of medieval notions of poetic interpretation? Or do we as modern readers fail sufficiently to perceive the 'otherness' of medieval poetry,[1] so that our responses to it are in large measure subjective and anachronistic? Should we, to achieve a more authentic approach, return as far as possible to that of the medieval interpreters, and resign ourselves to their limitations, even if our poetic response is diminished by this?

There is a disconcerting unanimity about those old interpreters of the *Commedia* in some of their basic assumptions.[2] The problem is made more acute by the fact that one of the earliest testimonies to these assumptions purports to be a statement by Dante himself about the lines along which his poem should be interpreted. In six of the nine extant manuscripts, Dante's letter dedicating the *Paradiso* to his patron, Cangrande della Scala, continues with a general introduction to the *Commedia* and an exposition of the opening verses of *Paradiso*.[3] The author of this introduction affirms that the whole *Commedia* has many meanings, and he proceeds to distinguish these as if the poem could be read as the Bible was traditionally read:[4] it has a literal meaning, and another which can be alternately allegorical, moral, or anagogical (leading the mind aloft to contemplate the heavenly). The *Commedia* has a twofold subject (*duplex subiectum*): literally, its subject is 'the condition of souls after death, considered in itself'; allegorically, its subject is 'man, inasmuch as he is exposed to the justice of reward and punishment, through the merit and demerit he has attained by free will'.[5]

I shall say a little more about the vexed question of whether this passage is by Dante presently. For the moment, I hope it is not irreverent to suggest that, if this is indeed the mature Dante's own definition of the subject of his *Commedia*, he has not defined it well. It is true that many poets and artists, even today, can say little that is satisfying about their own work – yet Dante had previously, in his *De vulgari eloquentia*, shown exceptional critical acumen, about his own earlier lyrical poetry as well as that of others. 'The condition of souls after death' might seem superficially to correspond to the literal subject of the *Commedia* – yet it could apply equally to any of the dozens of medieval visions of the otherworld that were set down in literary form; it in no way indicates that Dante's poem is radically different from these.[6] The authors of such visions, who claimed to have been shown diverse conditions of souls in the beyond, never made claims as far-reaching as those that Dante makes within the context of his poem. No medieval author before Dante had measured himself against Aeneas and St Paul,[7] as one impelled by divine grace to undertake an otherworld journey for the sake of mankind, in order to right the world's injustices at a crucial moment of its history.

At the opening of the second canto of *Inferno*, Dante, alone with Vergil, reveals both the height of his conception of his own mission as poet–prophet (*vates*) and his intense fear of embarking on it:

> O muse, o alto ingegno, or m'aiutate;
> o mente che scrivesti ciò ch'io vidi,
> qui si parrà la tua nobilitate.
>   Io cominciai: 'Poeta che mi guidi,
> guarda la mia virtù s'ell' è possente,
> prima ch'a l'alto passo tu mi fidi ...'

> Muses, high imagination, help me now –
> you, memory that have written what I saw,
> here will your worth be seen.
>   I began: 'Poet, you who guide me,
> see if my nature has strength enough
> before you commit me to the vast leap ...'   (7–12)

Aeneas' political mission and Paul's spiritual one were divinely sanctioned, it was not unfitting that they should have journeyed into the beyond –

> 'Ma io, perché venirvi? o chi 'l concede?
> Io non Enëa, io non Paulo sono;
> me degno a ciò né io né altri 'l crede.'

> 'But why should *I* go there? or who allows it?
> I am not Aeneas, I am not Paul –
> neither I nor others think me worthy of that.' (31–3)

And Vergil, though in this very scene he is called both *magnanimo* and *cortese*, answers Dante with a brutal reproach: he accuses him of baseness of spirit (*viltade*), of an ignoble cowardice, because of his hesitation before so great a venture.

For Dante the unswerving truth of his memory is vital, since, however much literary elaboration we may have to reckon with, this begins from the visionary perceptions which had ignited his mind and which it mattered to him intensely to record aright:

> O isplendor di Dio, per cu' io vidi
> l'alto trïunfo del regno verace,
> dammi virtù a dir com' ïo il vidi!

> Oh splendour of God, through which I saw
> the high triumph of the true kingdom,
> give me the power to tell how I saw it! (*Par.* xxx 97–9)

Dante is not embodying familiar ideas about the conditions of souls in hell, purgatory, and heaven in a poetic fiction;[8] he is not 'feigning', in the way he had done, with keen self-consciousness, in his *Convivio*, as he unfolded the tale of his love for the Donna Gentile, Filosofia – the lady whose eyes are her demonstrations and whose smile, her persuasions.[9]

The early commentators on the *Commedia*, however, speak again and again of Dante's feigning – at times probably in order to shield the poet and his poem from accusations of hubris, indeed of blasphemy. Even St Paul had thought it unlawful to utter the words he had heard in the third heaven. At other times the commentators seem to attenuate the reality of Dante's mental experiences because they can hardly conceive that so great a claim as Dante appears to make could have been meant literally. But Dante is uncompromising. He intimates many times throughout the poem that he has had visions in the same sense as Paul and the prophets had, and that his concern is to remember and relate these faithfully.[10] This visionary element tells us little of itself about his poetic and imaginative processes. Dante was clearly an intellectual as well as a seer; his prophetic insights were nourished by, and developed out of, what he had read and thought. Yet his insistence on memory, on the experiential aspect of his work, remains important. It is for this reason that, setting forth on the task of remembering, he prays for aid: the muses and high imagination (*alto ingegno*) are not only the poetic powers within him, they embody his sense that a force greater than himself is at work in him as he writes.

It is a question of striving for absolute fidelity to the inner imaginative process and reality that are his own, but are also beyond him – that are at moments perceived as the god speaking in the vessel he has chosen. These moments of conviction of divine direction also reveal the deepest aspect of the bond between Dante and Vergil, his cherished guide. Vergil, who had imaginatively experienced an unearthly journey, by taking Aeneas through the underworld, is equally the poet in whom an *alto ingegno* had been at work greater than he could consciously express: it was a true prophetic gift that had led Vergil to foretell a divine child in his *Fourth Eclogue*, and to show in the *Aeneid* the divine revelation which led to the founding of Rome, and, through Rome, to what Dante saw as the order that God's providence had established for the world's just government. As poet, Vergil became the prophet of that world-order, Roman flowering into Christian, prophet of 'that Rome of which Christ is a Roman' (*Purg.* XXXII 102).

Through Vergil's answer to the frightened Dante, we learn that Dante's venture – as visionary and as poet – has been granted to him solely because of Beatrice, whom he had loved since boyhood. It is not because Dante is more perfect than other men. On the contrary, as Beatrice tells Vergil –

> ... temo che non sia già sì smarrito,
> ch'io mi sia tardi al soccorso levata,
> per quel ch'i' ho di lui nel cielo udito.

> ... I fear he may already be so far lost
> that I have moved too late to rescue him –
> by what I have heard in heaven about him.   (*Inf.* II 64–6)

No, Dante's special capacity to experience and record the more-than-earthly stems from the fact that the more-than-earthly had been revealed to him in an unparalleled way: through the highest moments of earthly love that he had known. And it is as Dante fully fathoms that the revelation comes through his beloved, who is now in heaven, and realises that if anyone can bring him to heaven's blessedness it is she, that he conquers his doubts and becomes sure that his mission is a true one, not one spurred by some manic delusion of grandeur of his own.

The literal subject of the *Commedia*, then, is the *itinerarium mentis* of Dante Alighieri, the poet guided by Vergil and inspired by a dead Florentine woman, Beatrice. To her he attributes exceptional intellectual powers: indeed she epitomises that conjunction of intellectual and visionary insight which he is trying to communicate in his verse. The *Commedia* tells the inner experience of this poet who saw himself called to the rôle of prophet, in order to fight for peace and justice in the temporal sphere like Aeneas, in the spiritual like Paul. It is a subject of such daring that, if Dante really wrote the exegesis for Cangrande, we should have to say that here for once his courage failed him. Here he drew back from what he had affirmed with passionate earnestness throughout the *Commedia*, and relied instead on a kind of timorous *captatio benevolentiae*, telling his patron reassuringly, 'this is a poem about souls in the otherworld', and thereby assigning it as it were to a familiar genre. Was Dante really beset by such faintheartedness that, having completed the *Commedia*,[11] he no longer dared to avow what mattered to him supremely about its composition?

According to the explanation in the *Epistle*, 'the condition of souls after death', which the poem shows literally, has as its hidden meaning that each of these souls justly receives its reward or punishment after death, in accordance with its free choice of worthy or unworthy deeds on earth.[12] This may be a salutary moral reflection, and one that many of the descriptions of souls in the *Commedia* might stimulate. Yet it is also a perfectly obvious reflection; it has nothing of hidden meaning about it. I cannot see that it belongs with what the author of the *Epistle* himself calls *isti sensus mistici* – the three hidden senses which, he goes on, can all be called, in general terms, allegorical. To say that the destinies of souls in the otherworld match their choices in this life – is that really to reveal the hidden meaning of the *Commedia*?

There are moments in the *Commedia*, to be sure, where the overt sense has a hidden or allegorical meaning. At times Dante explicitly signals the latent presence of such a meaning – as in *Inferno* IX, when he admonishes his readers:

> O voi ch'avete li 'ntelletti sani,
> mirate la dottrina che s'asconde
> sotto 'l velame de li versi strani

> Oh you that have sound understanding,
> note the doctrine that hides
> beneath the veil of the strange verses   (61–3)

– the enigmatic verses, that is, about the Furies and the heavenly messenger. But the very fact that Dante sets certain moments in relief in this way should make us wary of following those early commentators who wished to find allegorical meaning hidden everywhere. It is not enough for them that Dante, at the opening of his journey, evokes swift, violent experiences – of being lost and terrified in a dark forest, his way barred, at the foot of a sunlit hill, by a leopard, a lion, and a she-wolf; that Dante calls out for help to a human apparition he sees, who, to his joy, turns out to be the shade of Vergil. The real meaning, allegedly, is not this at all, but that Dante and, implicitly, all mankind stray in the forest of the sinful life; they cannot ascend the bright hill of virtue; their way is cut off by three bestial vices – lust, pride, and covetousness. In this harsh plight human reason – embodied in Vergil – guides the sinner on his cathartic journey, after explaining that the journey has been sanctioned by theology – which, needless to say, is embodied in Beatrice.[13]

I do not wish to suggest that this venerable tradition of seeking specific allegories at every point is wholly baseless. It represents one way of recognising what every alert reader must recognise: that the forest and beasts, the lostness and the dangers, the guide and the journey mean more than they say – that they are no simple elements of an adventure-story, but evoke complex states of mind and conscience, complex responses to the outer world. Yet, apart from the fact that there have always been disagreements about what particular elements signify, this time-honoured exegetical method cannot easily illuminate the imaginative purpose of the poem. It tries to make the poet's vision into something else. If Dante chose to stimulate his readers' imagination by mystery, what do we gain by reducing this to commonplaces, that take us no trouble to comprehend? It is something undefined and evocative that here challenges understanding, not a tract on sin and repentance. (Those are much easier to understand.)

It looks as if we must rescue Dante the poet from the conceptions of poetic meaning that were current in his time, and perhaps even – if he is the author of the explanatory part of the Cangrande letter – rescue Dante from himself. Yet the picture, if we look more attentively, is not quite so bleak. The range of ways of thinking about poetic meaning in the period up to Dante is greater than most modern scholars have realised.

A notable contribution to showing this was made by Erich Auerbach, in his essay '*Figura*' and a group of related studies.[14] Auerbach suggested that, while allegory undeniably plays an intermittent part in the structure of the *Commedia*, it is far from being the dominant principle of structure. It is much less important for the imaginative workings of the *Commedia* than *figura*, the concept which Auerbach documented systematically, and rightly distinguished from the more familiar modes of allegory, though recognising that often it interacts with these and cannot be wholly separated from them. Historically and critically, however, the distinction remains vital:

> Figural interpretation establishes a relationship between two persons or events ... that are both real and within time ... it is not concerned with concepts or abstractions: these are entirely secondary ... *Figura* is clearly distinguished from most of the allegorical forms known to us from other contexts, by the historical reality of both what signifies and what is signified.[15]

This is evident when the persons and events that are figurally related belong to the Old and New Testaments – when Adam, for instance, is a *figura* of Christ, or Isaac's sacrifice a *figura* of the crucifixion. But it is Auerbach's merit to have seen that this same concept of *figura* can likewise illuminate certain key characters and situations in the *Commedia*. Thus Cato, Vergil, and Beatrice can 'mean more' than themselves precisely because Dante conceives them as fully alive and real, and *not* as allegories. The Cato who guards the shore of *Purgatorio* fulfils the *figura* of the historical Cato; he is 'not an allegory for freedom; rather, he remains Cato of Utica, the unique individual, just as Dante saw him'.[16]

But even if the concept *figura* is fertile for the understanding of Dante's poetic art, it seems to me that a number of other medieval concepts should likewise be considered for what they may be able to contribute to this understanding. In particular, the concepts of image (*imago*) and metaphor (*metaphora* and its synonyms), hidden comparison (*collatio occulta*), symbol (*symbolum*), and mythopoeic fiction (*integumentum*) had all been elaborated in diverse subtle ways by the time that Dante wrote. Given the sheer breadth of his imaginative range, would it not be surprising if some medieval uses of these concepts were not also pertinent to

Dante's artistry and intentions? Figural interpretation can admittedly shed much light, correcting what is simplistic in allegorical interpretation, yet it too can cope with only one aspect of Dante's multifarious ways of generating poetic meaning.

It is true that in the high Middle Ages there was no comprehensive critical vocabulary comparable to that of the present day; yet there are many intimations in medieval Latin texts that critical insight could be acute. In particular, while theologians were still often concerned, as the Church Fathers had been, with fixed allegorical meanings in Scripture, in non-theological writing we can find evidence of an awareness of unfixed, open meanings – meanings such as could be incorporated in a text but could hardly be spelt out. It was possible to think profoundly about the creative aspect of poetic imagination. It was possible, too, to see a poet's imagery not just as a pretext for allegorical meaning, nor again as mere ornament (*ornatus*) – though these were familiar scholastic notions – but as a direct means of cognition: neither hiding meaning nor adorning it, but creating it. This conception clearly has a greater bearing on Dante's art than the more conventional ones. Again, it was possible to think about the art of conveying *hidden* meaning in terms that went beyond allegory, and indeed beyond *figura*, to creative uses of symbol and of myth. I should like to adumbrate one or two of these less familiar ways of thinking about poetic meaning up to Dante's time, indicating how they are germane to Dante's art.

(ii) Alan of Lille: Poetry and Creativity

Let me begin with a major twelfth-century Latin poet who notably influenced Dante,[17] and whose thoughts about poets and poetry present some of the same anomalies as I have already mentioned, but also hint at some different solutions. Alan of Lille, in the prose prologue to his verse epic, *Anticlaudianus*, composed 1182/3, makes large claims for his poem, ones that may well remind us of the letter to Cangrande. The work, Alan affirms, has not merely a literal sense, that will 'caress the hearing' – that is, a sense enjoyable purely as a story – nor only a moral sense, that, like a mirror for princes, will 'instruct a mind growing in insight'. It has a third sense, 'a more acute subtlety of allegory', that will sharpen the intellect as it sets out on its heavenward journey. For in this poem, Alan continues, one can find not only something of all the seven liberal arts but 'an abundance of celestial theophany (*theophanie celestis emblema*)': the poem, that is, can figure and be a manifestation of the divine.[18]

Theophany, the concept at the heart of the thought of the Carolingian Platonist Scotus Eriugena, is here taken over by Alan and combined with another of Eriugena's pivotal words: Alan invites the reader not to rest content with the poem's 'base images', but to rise beyond them 'to the contemplation of *supercelestial* forms (*ad intuitum supercelestium formarum*)'. A theophany, that is, can allow the perception even of forms as they exist in the divine realm. Alan, as we see, believes that his epic can lead to a kind of insight such as poetry seldom attains. Indeed in the poem itself he makes some scathing allusions to the epics of his contemporaries – Joseph of Exeter's on Troy and Walter of Châtillon's on Alexander – for these, he thinks, are mere narratives, they have no hidden meanings, they are not theophanies.

At the midpoint of his poem Alan sets an invocation that I am convinced meant much to Dante, where he makes an even more audacious claim than at the outset:

> Till now my muse has sounded with thin murmur,
> till now my page has played in fragile verse
> to the sound of Phoebus' lyre; but now, leaving such
>   paltriness aside,
> I tune a greater lyre and, casting off the poet's part,
> I lay claim to the new words of the prophet.
> Earthly Apollo shall yield to the heavenly muse,
> the muse to Jove, the words of earth shall yield,
> obedient, to those of heaven – earth shall give place to
>   Olympus.
> I'll be the reed-pen of this song, not its scribe or author ...
> the night irradiated from without, the muddy cup
>   streaming with nectar.
>
> Supreme begetter, God eternal, living power ...
> shine before me with your radiance, bedewing
> my mind more copiously with divine nectar –
> rain upon my spirit, wash its stains away and, tearing the
>   dark open,
> dispel it, make me serene with the splendour of your light.
> Repair my reed-pen, purge my tongue of rust,
> let me, the stammerer, speak your words, give speech to
>   me

who am dumb, give me a fountain in my thirst, a path in
  my lostness,
be my ship's helmsman, in my fear grant me a haven,
billowing my sails with a celestial wind.[19]

I believe Alan's prayer for inspiration as prophet to be pas-
sionately serious, as the exalted language suggests – but what is it
that Alan prophesies? Till now he had depicted how Natura plans
to create a new, perfect human being (the *novus homo*), and how,
to achieve this, Fronesis – the personified human mind, at its
highest or divinest capacity[20] – makes an ascent into the heavens.
After the poet's invocation, Fronesis reaches the presence of God,
implores him to give her the form of the *novus homo*, and, receiving
it, brings it back to earth. Natura and the Virtues welcome the
form and make it into a physical reality. A number of threats and
dangers – from Fortuna and from the Vices – are overcome, the
perfect one survives, uncorrupted, and the poem ends with an
evocation of paradise re-established on earth. Through the *novus
homo*, the world is renewed.

This renewal must be the prophetic vision that meant so much
to Alan. Its details remain mysterious, just as those of Dante's palpably prophetic passages do. Alan's thoughts and hopes may here
be quite close to those of the prophet who was his exact contemporary, Joachim of Fiore.[21] Alan's 'earth made heavenly' could
well be that age of complete justice, brotherly love and free
sharing of all property which Joachim, in the 1180s, believed was
already on the horizon. And yet for Joachim this age also implied
the discarding of all outward authority, both of Church and State,
whereas for Alan, it would seem, even the renewed world will still
need a ruler – blessed and idealistic, but a ruler nonetheless. If for
Joachim the *novus homo* realises the finest potential of monasti-
cism, for Alan he is rather a philosopher–king, graced with intellectual and chivalric virtues, not only with spiritual ones.[22]

It is likely that Dante shared something of Joachim's vision as
well as of Alan's; but the identity and the precise temporal and
spiritual rôle of Dante's saviour of the world – that Veltro whom
Vergil predicts, who is nourished on wisdom, love, and valour,
and who will cause the death of the wolf,[23] that deliverer whom
Beatrice promises, who will slay the harlot and the giant[24] –
remain (perhaps intentionally, perhaps inevitably) enigmatic.

To return to Alan's invocation: it is also one of a series of
moments in his poem in which Alan reflects upon the nature of

poetic creativity. In his poetry, he claims, earth shall give place to Olympus – *tellus ... locum concedet Olimpo*. This key phrase prefigures the close of the poem, where earth is in truth made Olympian – *iam terram vestit Olimpus* (IX 395). But already at the opening Alan had said that in the garden of Natura, the divinely ordained creatrix who holds all the forms that she incarnates in the world, 'earth strives to paint a new heaven (*terra novum contendit pingere caelum*: I 63)'. This same creative striving, to show the heavenly in an earthly mode, is fulfilled by the poet, if he is granted a prophetic gift, and, at the close of the poem, it is he who projects the historical fulfilment of his poetic prophecy on earth.

Throughout the *Anticlaudianus* parallels are established between the cosmic process of creation and the poetic. When Fronesis approves Natura's plan to fashion the *novus homo*, she stresses its creativeness:

> let it go forth
> into the common good: it will be better manifest in light.
> For the good ... shines more if it enjoys the light:
> thus flower will pass into fruit, the stream, flooding,
> into a river, and the rich corn become a harvest. (I 345–50)

The 'common good (*commune bonum*)' is the paradise on earth of the poem's close. But the three kinds of image – light, water, and fertility – are also those that Alan uses for himself as poet at the opening, in a prayer to Apollo, god of poetry and of light:

> Phoebus, perfuse your poet with your fount,
> so that the dry mind, rained on by your stream, may bring
> a bud forth and fulfil that bud in fruit. (*Prol.* 7–9)

Similarly, when Fronesis asks God for the form of the *novus homo*, she speaks in words that tellingly echo Alan's own plea to God to aid him as poet:

> Natura's task would languish ...
> unless your hand would duly sign the work,
> directing her unsteady hand and guiding
> her reed-pen as she writes. (VI 346–50)

The poet's task, that is, reflects Natura's task, which is itself a kind of 'creative writing'. But Alan's insight goes further. Fronesis, dazed in the highest heaven, is guided by a celestial girl (*puella poli*), a goddess (*dea*) who wears a dress that portrays mystic emblems:

> A subtle needle here depicts the mysteries
> of God, the abyss of the divine mind ...
> how God enfolds within himself the names
> of all things – God's nature does not refuse them,
> but conceives them all by way of trope and figure.   (v 114–27)

The divine nature, Alan suggests, is a poetic one: it conceives the world in poetic form, *mediante tropo, dictante figura*. And insofar as we can glimpse the divine, it will also be by way of images, poetically rather than rationally.[25] Hence Alan conceiving his epic and Natura conceiving the *novus homo* are both imitating God conceiving the world.[26] This is the secret behind the loftiness of Alan's – and Dante's – poetic claims, and the reason why the poet's images are a necessity, not simply an adornment.

Nonetheless, Alan also claimed for his poem something very similar to what the Cangrande letter claims for the *Commedia*: that it can reveal moral and allegorical meanings behind the literal, just as the Bible can. With the *Anticlaudianus*, I feel some uneasiness about this claim on closer inspection, as I do with the *Commedia* – though for a slightly different reason. Since nearly all the characters in the plot of the *Anticlaudianus* have allegorical names, it is hard to see any literal sense of the story which is not allegorical from the outset. In this respect the *Anticlaudianus* is wholly different from an epic such as the *Aeneid*, which has living human protagonists and a self-subsistent *historia*. Commentators, especially in the twelfth century, were fond of seeking hidden meanings in the *Aeneid* – interpreting Aeneas, for instance, as the human being growing in wisdom, Dido as his sensual nature, Anchises as his heavenly origin.[27] But what could the characters in the *Anticlaudianus* – Fronesis, Natura, Concordia, Astronomia, Fortuna and the rest – possibly mean, other than themselves? The only exceptions might be Alecto, the Fury who summons the Vices to do battle against the *novus homo*, who could presumably be lent a more abstract significance (though little would be gained thereby); and, more importantly, the 'celestial girl', *puella poli* – the only figure in the epic who is not invested with a specific name or meaning but is left enigmatic. This has not satisfied modern scholars, who have mostly asserted (without argument) that this *puella* stands for Theology[28] – just as so many, modern as well as ancient, have made a similar claim about Dante's Beatrice. Yet if Alan, who loved to make all else very explicit, has left this one figure unexplained, I am sure this was no oversight or carelessness on his part. We can fathom some of the connotations the *puella* had for Alan (and these, in my view, are of a celestial *power*, rather than of a subject, such as Theology) – just as we can, far more fully, discover the connotations that Beatrice had for Dante. But to impose fixed allegorical meanings where the poets have left something open is merely to read without poetic awareness.

Alan, like Dante, laid claim to the rôle of prophet as well as poet; Alan, like the author of the Cangrande *Epistle*, also tried to suggest the further meanings in the poetry by borrowing the terms of biblical allegorêsis (though, unlike him, he made no attempt to encapsulate those meanings in a banal formula). Even though the terms of the exegetes fit the poetry awkwardly, both writers were concerned to stress in this way that the poetry was no mere fiction, but embodied valuable moral and spiritual truths. The Cangrande author even went to the length of explicitly defending the idea that a sinful human being could receive a genuine divine vision.[29] Thus there is no *a priori* reason why Dante himself, though filled with a prophetic conception of his task, might not also – like Alan – have attempted to speak of his poem in the language otherwise used for interpreting the Bible.[30] Dante the prophet could still in principle be responsible for the seemingly inept statements of the allegorist in the letter to Cangrande.

And yet I have another reason for believing this to be highly unlikely. The exegetic part of the letter to Cangrande shows none of Dante's normal habits of Latin prose cadence, habits that Dante touches on in sophisticated, expert fashion in his *De vulgari eloquentia*. In this work (which has not hitherto been analysed for its use of rhythmic prose), a distinctive pattern of cadences can be seen, which is so startlingly different from that of the fitful cadences in the exposition to Cangrande that it is very difficult indeed to imagine that both could stem from the same author (see the detailed discussion below, pp. 103–11). To mention just one illustration here: in the 96 sentences of literary argument in the Cangrande *Epistle*, only 10 end with a 'swift (*velox*)' cadence, according to the criteria that were established by medieval teachers of prose rhythm. In a sample of 96 sentences of literary argument from *De vulgari eloquentia*, by contrast, no fewer than 30 – exactly three times as many – end with this *velox* cadence.

But even if the author of the exegetic fragment in the Cangrande letter was not close to Dante in rhythmic prose,[31] he had some perception of Dante's prophetic claim and also, as I shall now suggest, of Dante's way of using poetic language.

(iii) Image and Metaphor

As modern readers we sense that poetic images, and especially metaphors, were central to Dante's art, and that, even if occasionally he uses images which amplify and adorn but add nothing essential to meaning, for the most part his imagery is consubstantial with meaning. It is used functionally, to clarify rather than to ornament; it is used in order to say things that Dante could not say in other ways. Hence we are disappointed at the many places in ancient and medieval works on rhetoric and poetics that seem to ignore this possibility. In the Latin tradition, it is commonest to discuss concepts such as *imago*, *similitudo*, *metonymia*, *metaphora* (and its cognates *translatio* and *transumptio*) in terms of *ornatus*. And often – though not always – this carried the implication of beautifying expression rather than of illuminating or intensifying meaning: as if there were a choice – 'penny plain, tuppence coloured'; as if poets could make language poetical by applying 'the colours' to it.[32]

Happily the writer to Cangrande was not of this view. Commenting on Dante's words at the opening of *Paradiso*, that in the highest heaven 'I saw things which whoever descends from there neither knows how, nor is able, to tell again (*nè sa nè può ridire*)', he relates the first negative to the failure of memory, but the second to the failure of language:

Indeed we see many things through the intellect for which verbal expressions are lacking: this is something that Plato shows abundantly in his books by his adoption of metaphorical locutions[33] – for he saw many things through intellectual light that he could not express in their own terms.   (*Ep.* XIII 29, 84)

Thus the Cangrande writer perceived that metaphor could be philosophically and poetically necessary, when it is a question of saying what is otherwise unsayable. This sense that metaphor can be a necessity, not merely a pleasant luxury, was shared by a number of writers on the subject from Antiquity onwards, though with varied emphasis. I should like to pause briefly at one or two of the more important testimonies.

It is often maintained that Aristotle in his *Rhetoric* (a work that
the Cangrande writer also cites, in another connection)[34] was one
of the chief promulgators of the 'luxury' view of metaphor. To cite
E. H. Gombrich:

Aristotle ... sees in the metaphor just one of the 'figures of speech' ... To
him words were names either of individuals or of classes of things, and, in
theory at least, all classes had such a name as could be used in non-
metaphorical or 'literal' language. Metaphor, in this view, is only a decor-
ation, an embroidery which is enjoyed ... because it teaches us to see
unexpected similarities, but which can easily be dispensed with.[35]

At the same time, Aristotle speaks not only of the delight that
metaphor affords, of learning new names for things we know
already, but, more strikingly, speaks of learning, 'in an unknown
language, something that we know in our own: metaphor accom-
plishes this most of all'.[36] And while that is still not a matter of
necessity, there is at least a hint of achieving new insight or cognition here. This emerges likewise in another passage where
Aristotle speaks of how to make language adorned (*ornata*): 'for
this purpose it is necessary to use alien expressions – for men
wonder at newcomers, and what is wondrous (*mirabile*) is delec-
table'.[37] Finally, Aristotle adds to the qualities of delight and alien-
ness in metaphor that of *claritas*: metaphor should clarify
meaning; if it is too far-fetched, it obscures (*metafore ... obscure
autem si a longe*).[38] Thus, while he does not wholly exclude a
cognitive aspect from metaphor, it is also clear, as Gombrich
observes, that Aristotle's premises about language prevented him
from arriving at a truly functional conception.

Cicero (whom Gombrich here contrasts with Aristotle) came
much closer to such a functional conception in his *De oratore*. Yet
there too, it must be admitted, Cicero first mentions metaphor in
the context of 'giving lustre and adornment to style (*ad illustran-
dam et exornandam orationem*)'.[39] A moment later, however,
Cicero explains that metaphor was begotten by necessity, and only
afterwards became popular through the delight it brings. So, too,
clothes were first functional (invented to keep out the cold), and
only later became ornamental and delightful. Cicero's implication
is plainly that the non-functional is the intellectually superior, less
primitive stage. He shows how 'even country folk' spontaneously
use metaphorical expressions, when appropriate literal ones for
what they wish to say are lacking.[40] This does not yet take us to

the heights of artistic metaphor; but Cicero admits that there are 'somewhat more daring metaphors, which do not indicate neediness of language but bring a certain splendour to it'. Again his contrast of terms links neediness or poverty (*inopia*) of style with necessary metaphors, *splendor* with the brilliance of ornament. Yet Cicero once more shifts his position slightly as he goes on to say that metaphors should be used (by orator and poet – his example is in fact from poetry) for two purposes: either if they make meaning clearer (*clariorem faciunt rem* – and here *clarior* suggests lucidity rather than rhetorical brilliance), or if by a metaphor the whole meaning of an action or thought is more fully conveyed (*quo significatur magis res tota, sive facti alicuius sive consilii*).[41] Both these notions are fruitful for the study of medieval poetic practice.

In the early years of the thirteenth century two theoreticians brought outstanding new insights to the question of the potentialities of imagery. From Geoffrey of Vinsauf's *Poetria nova* stems the concept of the 'hidden comparison (*collatio occulta*)' – a concept that embraces all imagery other than that of 'open comparing (*collatio aperta*)', as in similes. For the first time a completely functional conception emerges: the image 'assumes its place as surely in the design as if it were born of the theme itself . . . it is a brook in which the source flows purer'. In the 'subtle mode of conjoining' of image and theme, 'they touch as if they were not touching, as continuous as if Natura's hand, not that of art, had joined them'. The source – the poet's theme – can flow more purely in the brook – his image – than it can elsewhere: in the image, the source becomes crystalline. And it is no longer simply a question of making clearer, as for Cicero, but of making new, of creating: the relation of image to theme can become so completely organic that it approaches the perfect conjunction of form and matter which Natura achieves, in her task of living creation.[42]

In Italy, Geoffrey's contemporary Boncompagno, teaching in Bologna, developed in his *Rhetorica novissima*[43] a more comprehensive theory of metaphor than the Middle Ages had previously known. It is original especially in its breadth of conception, ranging from metaphor in solemn metaphysical insights to metaphor in ribaldry, insult, and coarse wit. This many-sidedness makes it particularly apt as a *speculum* for Dante's ways of using metaphor to generate poetic and dramatic meaning.

Boncompagno begins with some abstract distinctions among the possible functions of metaphor, though these give only a faint

foretaste of all he goes on to set before us. At the outset he speaks
of metaphor (*transumptio*) as ornament, or rather as the mother of
all ornaments; next he sees it in terms of the image (*imago*) that
can imply more than it states;[44] then in terms of the metamorpho-
sis of expressions – 'a transmutation that always re-enacts an
imaginative perception (*representat intellectum imaginarium*)'.
Next he speaks of metaphor as the substitution of expressions, in
order to gain an enhanced effect of praise or blame (the second, in
its satiric potential, looms particularly large in Boncompagno's
thoughts). Lastly he defines a use of metaphor that had not to my
knowledge been formulated before in the context of rhetoric:
metaphor can be 'a natural veil, beneath which the secrets of
things are brought forth more hiddenly and more secretly'.[45]
Metaphor, that is, can have a consciously hermetic function, con-
cealing even more than revealing. Dante's prophecy of the Veltro,
who will cause the death of the wolf (*Inf.* I 100 f), would exemplify this function admirably.

Boncompagno then touches upon the uses of metaphor both in
prophetic, apocalyptic visions and in the interpretation of dreams:

Heavenly things and earthly are seen to be used metaphorically for one
another, as we perceive in the visions of the prophets and observe more
fully in the Apocalypse of John. Indeed we know that the earthly Jerusalem is 'transumed' into the heavenly one. The soul also often 'transumes', for it gives those who are asleep premonitions of dangers or
advantages by way of diverse imaginings, as well as of contrary ones.

It is hard to convey the richness of Boncompagno's use of *transumere* in another language. Not only is the earthly Jerusalem used
as a metaphor for the heavenly, it is in a sense transformed into the
heavenly. And when Boncompagno uses *transumere* intransitively,
of the soul's activity in dreaming – 'the soul transumes' – the verb
suggests not only that imaginings are taken over by it (directly or
antithetically) as portents, but that in this taking over the soul is
acting like a poet, creating metaphors, and that it is through these
metaphors that dreams take on their prophetic meaning.

Metaphor, Boncompagno continues, was invented in the
earthly paradise – in two ways, one cosmological and the other
linguistic. God was the creator and primordial user of metaphor,
both when he 'formed man to his image and likeness', and when
he said to man, 'You shall eat of every tree of paradise, but not of
the tree of the knowledge of good and evil.' In the act of creation,

man became as it were a metaphor for God; in God's prohibition, he used 'tree' as a metaphor for 'fruit'. But this second metaphor shows another common feature in metaphorical usage: metaphors can be enigmatic and obscure. Thus there can be diverse interpretations of the nature of that paradisal fruit – the only one that Boncompagno rules out as erroneous is that the forbidden fruit was sexual love.

After this, Boncompagno's exposition of the possibilities of metaphor proceeds in a headlong, helter-skelter fashion: I shall allude to only a few of his illustrations, that will serve to indicate the rich imaginative variety of 'transuming', as he sees it.

Thus animal images, for instance, can extend from exalted uses – for three of the four evangelists – to degrading ones, used in order to epitomise human vices. So, too, 'God is transumed into a lion, and the devil into a lion, on account of diverse effects.' Or again, a metaphor can itself generate new metaphors: 'God is transumed into a lamb, and the lamb into the Paschal feast; prelates are transumed into shepherds, shepherds into preachers, preachers into oxen, and even into hirelings and dogs.'

When Boncompagno speaks of God transuming bread into his body, the sense of transformation, as well as of metaphor, is probably latent. Yet here, he says, the metaphor must depend upon a 'hidden likeness (*occultam similitudinem*)', for 'bread does not seem to have a likeness to flesh, though wine has some likeness to blood'. In the case of alchemists, who 'transume gold into the Sun, silver into the Moon, copper into Venus, quicksilver into Mercury', it is not certain whether Boncompagno means that the alchemists' operations are purely metaphorical – as Jung was to suggest in our century – or whether by these *transumptiones* the diverse metals actually take over the powers of the corresponding planets.

A number of different kinds of metaphors, Boncompagno shows, are employed to speak of sexuality and of bodily functions. There is, first, a 'courtliness of metaphor' (we would call it 'euphemism') – 'gate' for the vulva, or 'staff' for the penis. There is again a wide range of animal metaphorics – husbands as goats, rams, bulls, or stags, and all the derisive language of horns and of cuckoos. In the metaphorics of love, Boncompagno stresses both the idealising and the satiric possibilities: 'A beautiful woman is transumed into a goddess, into Venus, Pallas and Juno, into sun, moon and star . . . into Helen and Yseult', but likewise 'into viper, scorpion, chimera and she-goat ... into Eve and Medea'. He also gives witty examples of the distorting of sacred texts by turning them into erotic metaphors: 'A nun can say to her lover: "Your rod and your staff have comforted me."'[46]

Finally I would mention one other development of Boncompagno's metaphorics: for him, acting and impersonation of every kind is tantamount to using one's self as metaphor. He brings the two contexts into direct conjunction when he writes that in their satiric jests 'jongleurs transume a large nun into a threshing-floor, a small one into a coin', but goes on to say, 'the jongleurs also transume *themselves* into other people, by their voices and ways of speech, their gestures, dress, movements and actions. Similarly, poor people transume their healthy voices, putting on the voices of the infirm.'

From God's creative act to the 'act' involved in begging, from prophets and Apocalypse to amusing and malicious lewdness – Boncompagno grasped the unity and diversity of *transumptio*, and, by relating so many apparently unrelated manifestations of it, showed it as a fundamental human (and even divine) exercise. At times, too, his approach and his examples surmount all the hurdles of 'otherness'. Where much in medieval works on rhetoric speaks to us as from a remote world, with Boncompagno there are moments when we seem to be listening to a subtle, knowing contemporary. His account can still help us in thinking about Dante's art of metaphor.

Even in 'the sacred poem / to which heaven and earth have set their hand' (*Par.* XXV 1–2), the lower as well as the higher ranges of metaphor that were sketched by Boncompagno are present in many episodes. I shall say something about Dante's satiric uses of metaphor when I discuss his treatment of the giants (pp. 32ff). Here let it suffice to recall the ease with which metaphors from the animal world can occur – to express contempt, as when Vergil fends off the violent Filippo Argenti: 'Away there with the other dogs!' (*Inf.* VIII 42), or to convey the macabre, as in the savage sport of the demons skirmishing in boiling pitch: 'Even so the duck, when the falcon nears, dives suddenly down ... the other was a full-grown sparrowhawk to claw him well' (*Inf.* XXII 130ff). Again, Dante does not flinch from expressing the greed of Pope Boniface VIII by sexual metaphors: in the outcry of the earlier simoniac pope, Nicolas III, Boniface is the rapist of the bride of Christ, the Church: 'Are you so soon sated with that possessing, /

in which you did not fear by fraud to seize / the lovely lady, and then to ravage her?' (*Inf.* XIX 56–8).

I should like to consider in more detail, however, some examples from one group of metaphors that is particularly rich in cognitive implications – metaphors that concern the sea. With many of these we may observe how, in Cicero's terms, they 'can convey the whole meaning of an action or thought more fully', and how, as in Boncompagno's analyses, they can compass divine and human associations, positive and negative ones.

Curtius has skilfully adumbrated the long tradition of nautical metaphors for beginning and ending a poem,[47] but he did not try to suggest the gamut of connotations, extraordinary in their variety and intensity, that these metaphors had for Dante. To begin with their metaphysical dimension: all natures in the uni-verse, Beatrice tells Dante in the opening canto of *Paradiso*, receive an inclination that conditions them in a particular way in their course of life:

> onde si muovono a diversi porti
> per lo gran mar de l'essere, e ciascuna
> con istinto a lei dato che la porti ...
> questi ne' cor mortali è permotore;
> questi la terra in sé stringe e aduna.

> Therefore they move to diverse ports
> over the great sea of being, each one
> with an instinct given to it to bear it on ...
> This is the motive force in mortal hearts,
> this binds together and unifies the earth.   (112–17)

Among mankind, this inclination or instinct is the will.

The sea evokes not only the voyage but its goal: not only the unfolding of life but the fulfilment. In the renowned lines spoken by Piccarda in *Paradiso* III, it is the divine will which 'is that sea towards which everything moves, / both what the will creates and what nature brings about':

> ell' è quel mare al qual tutto si move
> ciò ch'ella crïa o che natura face.   (86f)

Dante in this sea-imagery conjures up a world-picture that is Neoplatonic rather than Aristotelian. He will have assimilated it partly with the help of Plato's *Timaeus*, but even more through many later interpretations – from Boethius and the *Liber de causis*

to Avicenna and Albert the Great – which seemed to make the
Neoplatonic cosmos not only compatible with the Christian one
but also its most fitting imaginative extension. The sea, in these
metaphors, suggests the Neoplatonic dialectic of a universe proceeding from God, turning to voyage towards him and returning
into him (*processio, conversio, reditus*). And what is true of the
cosmic process is equally true in the microcosm, of human will. At
the opening of *Purgatorio* Dante, newly emerged from hell, had
declared:

> Per correr miglior acque alza le vele
> omai la navicella del mio ingegno,
> che lascia dietro a sé mar sì crudele ...
>
> To course over better waters, the little
> boat of my imagination now lifts its sails,
> leaving so cruel a sea behind ...   (I 1–3)

And at the beginning of *Paradiso* II he addresses his readers in an
appeal both impassioned and heavy with foreboding:[48] his otherworld journey has become a sea-voyage so prodigious that it may
be too much for them:

> O voi che siete in piccioletta barca,
> desiderosi d'ascoltar, seguiti
> dietro al mio legno che cantando varca,
>   tornate a riveder li vostri liti:
> non vi mettete in pelago, ché forse,
> perdendo me, rimarreste smarriti.
>   L'acqua ch'io prendo già mai non si corse.
>
> You who are in a little boat,
> longing to hear, having followed
> behind my ship that, singing, makes its way –
>   turn back to see your own shores again,
> do not set forth on the high sea, for perhaps,
> losing me, you would be left all dazed.
>   The water I embark on has never yet been crossed.   (II 1–7)

Only a brave few shall follow him: those who hunger and thirst
insatiably to be the Argonauts of the spirit:

> metter potete ben per l'alto sale
> vostro navigio, servando mio solco
> dinanzi a l'acqua che ritorna equale.

> you indeed can bring your vessel
> over the ocean's depths, watching my furrow
> before the water becomes smooth again.   (13–15)

This sea-imagery is transformed in one of the most thrilling moments of the fourth canto of *Paradiso* to tell us something further: it can evoke not only the proceeding and return of all creation, and the daring quest of the human spirit to reach its divine harbour, but also an inner process, that begins in the divine source and fulfils itself in a human being, in the poet: Beatrice's words to Dante are the billowing waves of the holy stream (*l'ondeggiar del santo rio*); they flow out from the source from which all truth flows; they inundate the poet (*m'inonda*), giving him new ardour and fullness of life (IV 115–20). So, too, in the evocation of Dante's passing beyond the human (*trasumanar*) in the first canto: beholding Beatrice, Dante was transmuted like the fisherman Glaucus in the ancient myth – Glaucus who, on tasting a miraculous herb, felt his whole being tremble with longing for a new nature, and cried out 'Earth, farewell!', then plunged into the ocean, where the sea-gods welcomed him into their number and washed away all traces of his mortality.[49]

As Dante in *Paradiso* II embarks on his quest for the highest poetry, on the high sea (*per l'alto sale*), in his ship (*mio legno*), to face the perils of waters never sailed by man, he is fulfilling in the realm of the spirit all that his creation, Ulisse, attempted in his ultimate sea-voyage (*Inf.* XXVI). Dante's personal echoes of Ulisse's narrative are I think unmistakable and moving. They continue in *Paradiso* IV, where the unquenched longing to comprehend the unknown becomes metaphorically a climb: 'our intellect remains forever unsated . . . and it is nature makes us clamber from hill to hill, right to the summit'.[50]

Dante's Ulisse, notwithstanding his political treachery, was fired by this passion to know, which is of the essence of human nobility (*seguir virtute e canoscenza*: *Inf.* XXVI 120). He too had only the fewest faithful companions for his voyage beyond the known world, the voyage at the end of which he caught sight of the mountain-summit in the Antipodes –

> ma misi me per l'alto mare aperto
> sol con un legno e con quella compagna
> picciola da la qual non fui diserto.

> yet I set forth on the open high sea
> with one ship only and that little company
> by whom I had not been abandoned.   (XXVI 100–2)

The identical group of metaphors is used for the two quests.[51]
And yet the final meaning of those quests diverges: Ulisse's
voyage, for all its magnificence, ends in destruction, Dante's in the
vision of God. The ambivalence of the sea – demonic and divine,
and dangerous in both aspects – emerges from Dante's whole
metaphorical usage.

Hell is 'so cruel a sea' (*Purg.* I 3); in Dante's dream in purgatory,
the siren tells how 'I beguile sailors in mid-sea . . . I turned Ulisse,
eager on his journey, / to my song' (*Purg.* XIX 20–3). Again, the sea
suggests the limitless ambition of the diviner, Aruns, peering into
the secrets of fate: from his cavern, 'watching the stars / and the
sea, his view was without bound' (*Inf.* XX 50f). It suggests dangers
for Dante, from the very opening of *Inferno*, when he looks
behind him at the dark forest, from which he has just emerged, 'as
one who, breathing painfully, / having escaped from ocean to
shore, / turns back to the perilous water and gazes' (I 22–4). And
on a larger scale the sea means danger for the Church, the ship of
Peter: a saint like Dominic can keep it 'on the right course on the
high sea' (*Par.* XI 120), yet only for the brief span of his life.

The beautiful and welcoming aspect of the sea, the divine will
towards which all things move, has its dark counterpart in the
terrible aspect of divine justice. Thus Thomas Aquinas in *Paradiso*,
speaking of human destinies, warns Dante how little we know
about the journey's end: 'I have seen a ship, crossing the sea /
straight and swift in the whole of its course, / perish at last on
entering the harbour' (*Par.* XIII 136–8). Similarly the eagle in the
sixth heaven tells Dante that on earth a human gaze can penetrate
eternal justice only as far as the eye penetrates the sea: in mid-
ocean, no eye can see to the bottom, for the depth conceals it (*Par.*
XIX 58–63). In the microcosm, too, the sea can suggest both limitless bounty and perils: Dante perceives in his guide, Vergil, 'the
sea of all wisdom' (*Inf.* VIII 7), and perceives within himself how
he was 'drawn from the sea of twisted love / and set upon the shore
of upright love' (*Par.* XXVI 62f).

Dante's words about the human intellect in *Paradiso* IV continue: 'it remains forever unsated, / if it is not irradiated by that

truth / outside which nothing true can range'. He is speaking to Beatrice, addressing her exultantly ('Oh love of the first lover, oh goddess'), aware of the divine grace that she embodies for him. It is this that distinguishes his blessed sea-voyage from Ulisse's doomed one. Ulisse could not reach his goal alone, without grace; to undertake his final venture at all, he had to reject his home and 'the love which should have given Penelope joy' (*Inf.* XXVI 96). For Dante, the compulsive quest is equally his homeward voyage, his return to Beatrice, who realises all his longings of knowledge and love together. Ulisse was lost irrecoverably, the sea overcame him. Dante at the close of this canto almost loses himself too (*quasi mi perdei*); but what overcomes him is the dazzlement – 'the sparks of love' – of Beatrice's 'divine gaze'.[52]

(iv) Symbol and Myth

Another mode of considering metaphor in Dante takes us in the direction of the concepts 'symbol' and 'myth', that are central to much present-day critical inquiry. In his writings Dante does not employ the principal medieval counterparts to these terms – *symbolum* and *integumentum* (or *involucrum*) – which had loomed large in the writings of the twelfth-century Platonists. Yet he recognises the nature and possibilities of *symbolum* and *integumentum* more splendidly than anyone before him.

The twelfth-century mystic to whom Dante paid special tribute, Richard of St Victor, gave the definition: *Symbolum est collectio formarum visibilium ad invisibilium demonstrationem* – 'a symbol is a gathering of visible forms for showing invisible ones'.[53] Here, that is, Richard takes cognisance of the unpredictable, inexhaustible aspect of symbols, which many scholars have wrongly thought was ignored by the Middle Ages and not emphasised before Goethe. It is of the essence of Richard's *symbolum* (as of Goethe's *Symbol*) that it means more than can be said, that it shows what cannot be said, intimating those invisible realities that elude language's known categories.

Richard's conception is rooted in the Neoplatonism of Dionysius. But in a different way, a concern with what remains mysterious and can never be fully stated through images can also be seen in one of the basic textbooks of the medieval schools. As Goethe was anxious to distinguish allegory from symbol, so Isidore of

Seville, eleven hundred years before him, distinguished allegory from enigma:

> The difference between allegory and enigma lies in this, that the force of allegory is twofold – it indicates something figuratively beneath other things; but an enigma is a dark meaning alone, adumbrated by means of certain images.[54]

As an enigma 'means more' than the images that adumbrate it, so too such 'meaning more' is implied in the twelfth-century Platonists' concept *integumentum*. Literally a covering, *integumentum* is used both for a myth that conceals hidden meanings and for the hidden meanings themselves, that lie covered beneath its narrative surface.[55] In principle there is no limit to the meanings that an *integumentum* can conceal and generate; like a *symbolum*, it can 'show invisible forms', taking the reader to the unfathomable realm of the intelligible and the divine. This holds even if the literal meaning of the myth should be a scandalous account of pagan gods and goddesses – indeed, in the mystical Platonic tradition that Dionysius had transmitted to the medieval West, the unfitting and the monstrous is, by its sheer bafflement of human attempts to imagine the divine, most apt to convey truly how far the divine is beyond all imagining.[56]

Dante in the fourth canto of *Paradiso* hears from Beatrice's lips a profound account of the principles that underlie the use of symbol and myth. At the opening of the canto, he is troubled by two perplexities: since he has just beheld souls in the sphere of the moon, does this mean that the Platonic myth, that each soul returns to a particular star at death, is true? Secondly, these souls, according to Beatrice, have been 'relegated here (in the lunar sphere) for failure to fulfil their vows' (*Par.* III 30). And yet Dante has also learnt that this failure was due to coercion – that Piccarda Donati, for instance, the sister of his Florentine friend Forese, had been snatched away from her convent unwillingly, forced to enter an arranged marriage. How can souls be said to have failed in will – so that, in their lack of steadfastness, they are linked with 'the inconstant moon' – if they were forced? Such a thought seems to undermine the Aristotelian concept of free choice. Both Dante's difficulties conjure up the problem of determinism: Plato's myth of the return of souls at the macrocosmic level, Aristotle's analysis of human will at the microcosmic.

Plato in his *Timaeus* had laid the foundation for that conception of the bonds between the Creator and the created universe which, variously adapted in the medieval Platonic tradition, was still alive in Dante's imagination. For Dante as for Plato, it is by way of the spheres, and the intelligences who govern and animate them, that the divine creative power is transmitted downwards, as far as the sublunary world. Thus in the *Timaeus* the Creator (Demiurgos) addresses the intelligences,[57] saying:

'It is right that you should carry out the rest, so that you wrap the immortal and celestial nature in a mortal fabric, command it to be born, provide it with sustenance and cause it to grow, and that, after its dissolution, when soul secedes from body, you take back your loan.' ... And soon, when the whole mechanism of the universe had been compacted, the Creator chose souls equal in number to the stars, and matched each soul to its own star ... And to those who overcame their passions it would be open to return to the habitation of their consort star and thenceforth live a true and blessed life.

Dante thought particularly keenly about this myth in the form in which it was summarised by Boethius, in a poem set at the centre of his *Consolation of Philosophy*, some lines of which are consciously echoed in the second canto of *Paradiso* and others in the seventh.[58] This poem, *O qui perpetua*, is a hymn invoking the Demiurgos – 'you who by perpetual reason govern the universe'. For Boethius, he is the profound mind that sets the whirling spheres in motion, because lovingly they take the image of that mind; he is devoid of envy, and so communicates beauty spontaneously to the spheres, by diffusing the world-soul through the harmonious limbs of the cosmic body. From the same principles as determined the world-soul, Boethius goes on, 'you fashion souls and lesser lives; setting those souls upon light chariots, you sow them in heaven and on earth; then, by a benign law, you let them turn again, returning to you impelled by the heavenward-guiding fire'.

Dante had to confront the question which was crucial to any medieval Christian who was both a believer and an intellectual: to what extent could Plato's and Boethius' myth of the origin and return of souls be true, or a symbol of something true? How could the divine influences, that Plato and Boethius evoke with such imaginative power, leave room for the Christian conviction that the human will is free?

Beatrice begins by explaining that the appearance of souls in the lunar sphere does not mean that the Platonic myth – that souls return to particular spheres and stars at death – is literally right.

For it is only an appearance: all souls in paradise, from the least to
the most exalted, subsist in the first heaven, the empyrean. This
particular cluster of souls showed itself in the lunar heaven

> not because their lot
> lies in this sphere, but to provide a sign
> of that celestial state which has risen less high.
>   This is how one must speak to your imagination,
> for only from the sensible can it grasp
> what later it makes apt for intellection.
>   Because of this the Scriptures make concession
> to your mode of knowing, and attribute feet and hands
> to God, and yet intend another meaning.
>   So, too, for your sake Holy Church portrays
> Gabriel and Michael with a human semblance,
> and the other who made Tobit whole again.
>   What Timaeus propounds concerning souls
> does not resemble what can be seen here,
> for he seems to apprehend it in the way he says.
>   He says the soul returns to its own star,
> believing it was cut off from that star
> when nature gave the soul as an earthly form.
>   Yet perhaps his theory is of another kind
> than the words proclaim, and may contain
> an attempted meaning that should not be mocked.
>   If he intends to give back to these spheres
> the credit and blame of their influence, perhaps
> his bow does hit the mark of something true.
>   This principle, ill-understood, once led astray
> almost all the world, inducing men to apply
> the names of Jove and Mercury and Mars.   (IV 37–63)

The human mind needs images, for only by way of images can it
begin to understand something superhuman. This principle is
clearly stated in Plato's *Timaeus*, and is explained, with slightly
different emphasis, in Aristotle's *De anima*, where imagination
(*phantasía*) gathers sensory images and enables the intellect to
abstract knowledge from them. Intellection, that is, must have
both a sensory and an imaginative base. Beatrice adds (43ff) that
this is also the principle underlying the anthropomorphic biblical
images of God and angels.[59] But when Timaeus in Plato's dialogue spoke of the souls descending from their stars at birth and
returning to these at death, did he mean it scientifically? Did he
envisage an earthly existence totally determined by those stars, in

which the souls bring down their natures from the planetary spheres, and are jovial or mercurial, martial or venereal in nature just because of this and not because of any choices they can make? That was the problem which had particularly troubled earlier medieval interpreters of this myth: in what sense had Plato meant it? Thus for instance the Chartres Platonist William of Conches, whom I cite here not as the specific source for Dante, but as an illustration – indeed the finest known to me – of the kind of thought about Plato's myth-making which Dante will have encountered in his studies:[60]

When Plato says God chose as many souls as there are stars, and set each soul on its own star, some people, expounding this literally, say that Plato here taught heresy, for Scripture says that God creates new souls each day ...[61] Yet if one comes to know not only Plato's words but his sense and mind, he will find not only no heresy but the most profound philosophy, under the cover of mythopoeic language (*integumentis verborum tectam*), which we who love Plato shall show. When he said that the stars are the vehicles of the soul ... Plato meant that souls are set on stars causally, not spatially: they are the soul's vehicles in that, through the effect of the stars, the body becomes apt for a soul to be created in it ...

One must not think, as some expound, that Plato meant the soul was first among the planets and thence descended to earth: no, he meant that the beginnings of human generation are on earth and in the planets, for without the sustenance and fruits of the earth, and without the warmth of the planets, the body would not be capable of life, and without life there would be no soul ...

But lest anyone think that all things come about for man out of necessity and nothing out of free choice, Plato adds 'all things except ... the adversities, whose source and cause could lie with them' – with men, that is, for on account of our sins, which stem from us, we do suffer certain adversities: so if we did not sin out of free choice, how perfectly we could be ruled by God through the effect of the stars and the administration of their spirits! Or again, the source of ills might lie in the planets: for the planets are the cause of all our evils, of famine, death, and other things: they are the cause through which, not on account of which, the evils happen – for the planets are the ministers of the Creator ...

It was possible, then, to see Plato as using the cover of myth in order to adumbrate insights so profound that they could scarcely be analysed conceptually. Aristotle, on the other hand, distrusted the use of myth in metaphysical inquiry, and this distrust, even disdain, was shared by the medieval Aristotelian tradition. Thus Aquinas went so far as to write that Plato had 'a bad method of teaching ... by way of symbols (*per symbola*), meaning by the words something other than the words themselves proclaim'.[62] The phrase is very close to the one Beatrice uses of Plato, though she does so without any hint of distaste: 'perhaps his theory is of another kind / than the words proclaim' (IV 55f).

Here Dante does not take the part of Aquinas, but is close in outlook to the twelfth-century Platonists, 'we who love Plato'.[63] The reason for this is simple: for Dante as poet, and specifically as poet of the *Paradiso*, the use of an *integumentum* was essential. What we can see in Beatrice's words is not only a possible defence of Plato's myth-making, but the poetic principle underlying the *Paradiso* itself. Had Dante simply set all the paradisal souls in the empyrean, without differentiation, his description of paradise could hardly have been sustained for more than one or two cantos. To give paradise a poetic geography and an imaginative richness matching those of hell and purgatory, Dante had to assume an *integumentum* like the Platonic one, making different souls appear in different spheres. And to give this differentiation a poetic logic and motive, Dante had to go further and assume that the souls in each planetary sphere had been inclined and conditioned by it: that those in the sphere of the Moon would show traces of inconstancy, those in the sphere of Venus, of amorous sensuality; there would be warriors in the sphere of Mars, rulers in that of Jove. The architectonics of Dante's paradise are an *integumentum* in precisely the sense that medieval Platonists understood this of the *Timaeus*.

An *integumentum* is not an arbitrary fiction: it has an *intenzion*, to use Dante's expression – it strives towards an understanding of what cannot be fully known. Dante indeed believed there was some truth in the notion that planets could, for good or ill, determine the inclination of the souls born under them. Thus for instance in *Paradiso* IX, Cunizza, who had been well known for her sensual life on earth, says, 'The light of the star (of Venus) overcame me ... it was the cause of my destiny'; so too, in *Paradiso* XXII, Dante himself invokes the sign of Gemini, under which he was born, 'Oh glorious stars (*O glorïose stelle*)', and recognises all his own genius as deriving from their power (*virtù*). At the same time Beatrice affirms that Dante's disposition was brought about 'not only by the work of the great wheels' – that is, by the planetary spheres – but also 'by largess of divine graces'.[64]

The planets, for Dante as for the twelfth-century Platonists, are ministers of the Christian God; they are not gods. To see them as such was the error that Beatrice referred to (IV 61–3) – when the world applied the names of gods to what were only created forms. The planets do not have the Creator's omnipotence: they can condition human beings and determine their character, but not eliminate the power of free choice.

It has not, I think, been observed by scholars that the macrocosmic, Platonic question raised by Dante in *Paradiso* IV is set by him in precise parallel to the microcosmic, Aristotelian one that follows. The soul descending from its star at birth, and returning to that star as its final goal, is an exemplification of that universal sea-voyage – all creation proceeding from God and returning to God – which the divine will ordained. But the complexities and anguish of the human will, trying, even when oppressed by force, to rejoin the sea of the absolute divine will, are equally an exemplification of that voyage. The relation between the soul and its star is mirrored in the relation between the individual will and the absolute will.

Both Piccarda and Constance, the mother of Frederick II, were violently seized from their cloisters. But does that mean it was wholly against their will? Or was there some element of complicity with their ravishers, some degree of consent, because of fear? Beatrice analyses the question in the language of Aristotle's *Ethics* and of Aquinas' commentary on the *Ethics* (a work that Dante refers to on two occasions in his *Convivio*).[65]

Violence is defined as the situation in which 'the one who suffers / brings nothing (to the deed)': Aristotle's words, *nihil confert . . . patiens*, are rendered literally in Beatrice's *quel che pate / niente conferisce*.[66] And Beatrice explains that the two victims, Piccarda and Constance, were not heroines to that extent: they could have fled back to their convents –

> ché volontà, se non vuol, non s'ammorza,
> ma fa come natura face in foco . . .

> for will, if it's unwilling, is not quenched,
> but it behaves as nature does in fire . . .   (76f)

The inner flame, like the physical one, will always leap upwards again, no matter how often it is forcibly diverted. (Implicit in her image, perhaps, is the cosmological image from Boethius' hymn – the flame that impels each soul heavenwards, back to its star.) To evoke such absolute heroism, Beatrice subjoins two horrifying images of flame: St Laurence refusing to stir from the grid on which he was burnt alive (it was Aquinas who had introduced this *exemplum* when expounding Aristotle's theory of will in the *Ethics*[67]), and the pagan Roman hero Mucius Scaevola, who, as Livy tells, when he was prisoner of the Etruscan king Porsena, cried out, '"Look, that you may grasp how paltry is the body to those whose eyes are set upon great glory!" and thrust his right hand into the fire which had been kindled for a sacrifice, letting it burn there as if he were unconscious of the pain'.[68]

At the close of Beatrice's analysis of the less heroic will, that 'abets force (*segue la forza*)', she distinguishes, again in words that echo the language of Aquinas' commentary:[69]

> Voglia assoluta non consente al danno;
> ma consentevi in tanto in quanto teme,
> se si ritrae, cadere in più affanno.

> Absolute will does not consent to the wrong,
> yet will consents inasmuch as it is afraid,
> if it resists, to sink to greater anguish.   (109–11)

Absolute will is the person's highest or divinest aspiration; it is like Plato's star to which the soul longs to return. But the soul on earth has more of the fallible timebound will, still longing for its star (as Constance, according to Piccarda, continued to love the ideal of the nun's life, even after she had abandoned it); but only the heroic can set their course to that star unswervingly.

Thus Dante makes the Aristotelian account of the will reflect in the microcosm Plato's myth of the soul's cosmic journey, and the related Neoplatonic myth of the return of all beings to God. In Dante's new creation, the Aristotelian concepts parallel the Platonic ones, but also in a sense refine and correct them: they show in detail why the myths of return do not necessarily entail a deterministic image of the universe, but can still leave room for human freedom of choice.

The Platonic myths and the Aristotelian concepts (as well as the Christian and pagan *exempla* – Laurence and Scaevola – that Dante associates with these) qualify and mirror one another *in integumento*. In his use of Plato and Aristotle in *Paradiso* IV, Dante is theoretician as much as creator: here he shows, even more than the twelfth-century Platonists had done, the vast poetic and intellectual potential of which an *integumentum* is capable.

2

The Giants in Hell

(i) *Umbriferi prefazii*

Gianfranco Contini, in a perceptive study of Canto XXX of *Inferno*, has stressed how astonishing are some of Dante's juxtapositions there: of Myrrha, the incestuous heroine of a Greek legend, with the Florentine confidence-trickster Gianni Schicchi; of Potiphar's wife, seductress of the biblical Joseph, with the Trojan traitor Sinon – 'the Greek from Troy'. Sinon punches the hydroptic, drumlike belly of Maestro Adamo, a forger of false coins who was executed by the Florentines when Dante was sixteen. Such a kaleidoscope of characters is matched by Dante's drawing on multifarious resources of language: to cite Contini: 'rooted in his attachment to the encyclopaedia of possibles, Dante wants to give audience to the gossiping of slatterns and carters and at the same time – without in fact renouncing that audience – to proclaim the sublimity of the ivory tower'.[1]

In dramatic terms, we might add, Dante wants the full range of effects both of empathy and of distancing. Near the close of Canto XXX a noisy *tenzone* breaks loose between Sinon and Maestro Adamo: the ancient Trojan and the modern Florentine exchange abuse, they dwell sadistically on each other's guilt and torments, and Dante the character, all agog with listening, is suddenly harshly censured by Vergil for his absorption in such baseness. After six lines (XXX 136–41) that, by tortured reflection on dream and reality, express his paralysed mortification and mute plea for excuse, Dante wins Vergil's forgiveness, though in words that still carry a hint of warning: 'unburden yourself of all sadness, and take note, I am always at your side . . .'

This double moment is recalled at the opening of the next canto – that of the giants – by way of a learned simile:

> Una medesma lingua pria mi morse,
> sì che mi tinse l'una e l'altra guancia,
> e poi la medicina mi riporse;

32

così od' io che solea far la lancia
d'Achille e del suo padre esser cagione
prima di trista e poi di buona mancia.

One and the same tongue first cut me,
so that both my cheeks were suffused,
and then gave me the healing remedy;
    even so, I have heard, the lance
of Achilles and his father would effect
first a dolorous service, then a good.   (XXXI 1–6)

Vergil's tongue, that had cut Dante with rebuke and healed him
again with benign pardon, is like the spear of Achilles and his
father Pelias: Achilles, whose spear had given Telephus, son of
Hercules, a festering wound, was sought out to heal the gash with
the rust of the same spear, after an oracle had declared, 'Only he
who inflicts the wound can cure it.' Dante will have known the
allusion especially through Ovid's *Remedia amoris*: his first three
lines seem to echo Ovid's 'one and the same hand will bring you
wound and remedy (*Una manus vobis vulnus opemque feret*)' – a
paradox that had undergone more serious modulations in medieval Latin love-poetry, when the beloved is seen as the lover's
wounder and healer.[2]

Where in Canto XXX Dante had taken involvement to the
point of fault, now, after Vergil's reproach, comes the distancing:
a canto that is among the most aloof in the whole *Commedia*.
After the bursts of rage, an encounter tinged with dark ironies;
after scenes of horror, an interlude that has touches of *opera
buffa*.

Nonetheless, at least three times in this canto, Dante the protagonist is seized with fear. The first moment is just after he and
Vergil have resumed their journey (the motion of their travelling
is alluded to over and over in the course of the scene, distinguishing the two poets palpably from the giants, who are each
fixed to one spot). It is then that Dante hears

        sonare un alto corno,
tanto ch'avrebbe ogne tuon fatto fioco ...

Dopo la dolorosa rotta, quando
Carlo Magno perdé la santa gesta,
non sonò sì terribilmente Orlando.

        a horn ring out, so loud
it would have made any thunderclap seem feeble ...

> Even after the piteous overthrow, when
> Charlemagne lost his holy warrior-band,
> Roland did not sound so terrible a blast.   (XXXI 12–18)

What was the terror that surrounded Roland's horn? Dante, I believe, expected his readers to bring to this moment the force of the original narrative: for Roland, sounding the horn at Roncevaux had meant the crushing of his own overweening pride, of that mad defiance which had led him to refuse Charlemagne's aid in fighting, and thus cause the massacre of the emperor's finest men. When at last, his spirit broken, Roland blows the horn, 'from his mouth the blood spurted clear, his temples burst near the brain' (1764f).[3] Then, as Roland lies dying, and a Saracen tries to steal his consecrated sword, Durendal, Roland has no weapon left save his horn, which he shatters on the marauder's head. And suddenly he realises:

> Fenduz en est mis olifans el gros,
> Caiuz en est li cristals e li ors.

> Through this the mouth of my horn has cracked,
> its crystal and its gold has fallen.   (2295f)

With the horn, that is, all Roland's bravery and splendour fell. Roland was a giant in his ambition, and in the terrible laying low of that ambition. His horn is symbolically both: it sounds a motif foreshadowing what follows in this canto.

(ii) Illusions

Dante, peering into the distance to descry the source of the sound, thinks that he sees the towers of a city. It is an illusory image. In each of the three *cantiche* of the *Commedia*, I would suggest, Dante places a particularly detailed, analytic evocation of his own visual delusions at the same moment in the dramatic structure: in each case, it is the vision that leads into the climax of the *cantica* which is first seen by Dante defectively, in a delusive apparition that gradually turns into true awareness.

In *Purgatorio* XXIX, at the advent of the heavenly host, and of the chariot with Beatrice at its summit, Dante first experiences a flash of brightness, and asks – was that lightning? Then he seems to recognise something inanimate – seven trees of gold – yet this too is a false visual percept. Dante comes nearer and sees the trees as walking candelabras, harbingers of the holy procession, painting the sky with flame, and hears their melody, which had been indistinct at first, as 'Hosanna', and then as the praise of Beatrice. In *Paradiso* XXX, Dante's sight of the celestial rose, *la rosa sempiterna*, is likewise attained by a process in which delusion is gradually purified. First Dante is blinded as if by a sudden shaft of lightning, that takes his visual powers away; then with new vision (*novella vista*) he sees light in the form of a river fulvid with radiance, from which living sparks rise and settle on flowers all round, like rubies on gold, like topazes, and then whirl back into the river again. Yet these too are mere 'shadowing prefaces (*umbriferi prefazii*)' of the true perception in which, when Dante's eyes have drunk of the stream of light, the flowers and sparks transform themselves into the total vision of the empyrean – the rose, the circular city brimming with luminousness.

Here in *Inferno* it is Dante's illusion of a dark city ringed with towers that is gradually dispelled. The towers – like the gold trees in Purgatory and the gold flowers in Paradise – are alive. Yet here the seemingly inanimate that reveals itself alive is not awe-inspiring but frightening. Vergil, with unexpectedly tender solicitude after his earlier sharp outburst, warns Dante in advance:

> 'Però che tu trascorri
> per le tenebre troppo da la lungi,
> avvien che poi nel maginare aborri.
> Tu vedrai ben, se tu là ti congiungi,
> quanto 'l senso s'inganna di lontano;
> però alquanto più te stesso pungi'.
> Poi caramente mi prese per mano
> e disse: 'Pria che noi siam più avanti,
> acciò che 'l fatto men ti paia strano,
> sappi che non son torri, ma giganti ...'

> 'Because your eyes are skimming
> over the darkness from too far away,
> your visual conception has a flaw.
> You'll see clearly, if you attain that place,
> how far the sense deceives itself with distance;
> so spur yourself a little more'.
> Then, affectionately, he took me by the hand
> and said: 'Before we move farther on,
> so that the fact may seem less outlandish to you,
> know that they are not towers, but giants ...'   (22–31)

As Alessandro Parronchi showed in a remarkable essay,[4] Dante was familiar with the technical discussions of the theory of vision, as expounded in the *Optica* of Alhazen and the *Perspectiva* of Witelo. In a passage such as this, we can perceive the poet's deft allusions to the scientists' modes of explanation. When Witelo, for instance, outlines the reasons why one thing can be mistaken for another, 'in a visual error by way of understanding, through the inappropriate application of a form that is in the mind', he begins with the condition of 'defective light (*defectus lucis*)' and goes on to that of 'excessive distance (*distantia nimia*)'.[5] When he writes of the sensory misjudging of distance, he illustrates with the example of a tower (*turris*) seen through 'murky air (*aer nubilosus*), such as often occurs in twilight'.[6] It is just such conditions of flawed vision that Dante in this canto recreates as an imaginative experience. Already on hearing the horn he had stressed: 'Here it was less than night, and less than day, / so that my view did not reach far beyond me.' Now, after Vergil's warning about the 'towers', he meticulously traces his process of recognition:

> Come quando la nebbia si dissipa,
> lo sguardo a poco a poco raffigura
> ciò che cela 'l vapor che l'aere stipa,
>   così forando l'aura grossa e scura,
> più e più appressando ver' la sponda,
> fuggiemi errore e crescémi paura.

> As, when mist disperses,
> the sight recovers shapes moment by moment,
> which the vapour, thickening the air, conceals –
>   so, piercing the dense and murky atmosphere,
> coming closer and closer to the edge,
> my error fled and my fear grew.   (34–9)

Yet even then the force of his first, delusory image lingers with him: he still perceives the giants *as if* they were towers, and the towers that circle Montereggione, the citadel near Siena, come to his mind. Throughout the passage, Dante's language shows that he takes cognisance of the theoretical accounts of true and false vision, but he is not confined by them: he integrates them with keenly individual analysis and reminiscence.

The towers of Montereggione had been built by the Sienese in the 1260s to resist the Florentines. Later, when Siena and Florence were allied in the Guelf resistance against the emperor, these towers may well in Dante's eyes have come to epitomise rebellion against empire – a modern political counterpart to the giants' rebellion against heaven.[7] At all events the connotations of the towers were not picturesque but sinister: they were essentially engines of military attack and defence. If, like the giants round their pit, they look motionless, lifeless, this makes the sudden movement of a giant – or the sudden animation of the towers during a siege – the more fearsome.

(iii) Demythologisation

Yet even as he stresses the fearfulness – by the forceful coinage *torreggiavan* ('enturreted': 43) and the slow, heavy phrase *li orribili giganti* (44) – Dante adds an aside that suggests a different perspective: 'the horrible giants, whom Jove still threatens / from heaven whenever thunder breaks'. To equate thunder on earth with Jupiter's menacing of the giants in the primordial conflict, *in illo tempore*, is to introduce a touch of that wry euhemerism which was dear to medieval mythographers. Dante has a similar aside in *Paradiso* VIII, about the giant Typhon: while according to ancient myth Typhon's body lies beneath Sicily (Trinacria) and his writhings cause the volcanic eruptions there, Dante says: 'fair Trinacria is darkened ... not by Typhon but by rising sulphur' (67–70). Such swift allusions demythologise – they draw a fabled realm back to naturalism. In *Inferno* XXXI the lines about the thunder are the first hint of an imaginative process that reveals much about the canto.

As Dante begins to distinguish the first of the giants, he reflects with rueful humour on Natura's capacities:

> Natura certo, quando lasciò l'arte
> di sì fatti animali, assai fé bene
> per tòrre tali essecutori a Marte.

> Natura, to be sure, when she dropped the art
> of fashioning creatures so, did well enough,
> depriving Mars of such executives.　　　　　　(49–51)

Natura had, especially in the twelfth-century Latin cosmological epics, come to be personified as the embodiment of God's creative impulse, whether as goddess or theophany or divine agent.[8] In one of these epics, John of Hauvilla's *Architrenius*, which it is at least possible that Dante knew, the magnitude of Natura's power is proclaimed ironically by the fact that she can create not only regular beings but prodigies – monsters, freaks, giants.[9] At the command of Natura the creatrix, the planetary intelligences transmit modes of action to the sublunary world: thus Mars finds 'executives' whom he inclines to warfare, just as Venus inclines others to love. But to fashion *essecutori* who are not only huge and fierce but who can consciously, malevolently cultivate their inclination to Mars – that is too much! What a relief, thinks Dante, that Natura realised this in time, and, while maintaining the production of elephants and whales, discontinued that of giants (52–7).

The giants, first perceived erroneously as towers, are again and again seen in terms of inanimate images. The face of the first (58ff) is like the vast bronze pine-cone, 4 metres high and thickening to about 2 metres near the base, which in Dante's day stood in the porch of St Peter's basilica (and today stands in the Vatican gardens). Later, Ephialtes shaking himself is like a tower struck by an earthquake; Antaeus when he stoops is like Garisenda, the leaning tower in Bologna, and, when he rears himself up again, like the mast of a ship. The lifeless images suggest the giants' subhuman numbness, they distance us from them and make us apprehend them as misbegotten; and yet this apprehension is disrupted by the violent moments – the dread horn-blast, the wild incomprehensible howl, the seismic shudder. I shall suggest a reason for these double effects later (p. 54).

Dante dwells in leisurely, sardonic fashion on the first giant's size, by way of incongruous images – the pine-cone, and three Frisians on end – and by the superbly inept expression *perizoma* (61). While the Frisians were known as 'mighty, tall, forbidding, and ferocious' from encyclopaedias,[10] the rare Graecism *perizoma* was familiar to Dante and his audience from one particular context: in Genesis, it was the word used of the fig-leaves with which Adam and Eve covered their genitals. Isidore of Seville, explaining this, added that even today some barbarian races go about naked except for a *perizoma* over their sex.[11] For the giant, the pit itself served as *perizoma*: only his upper half (some 11 metres, if we follow Dante's calculations) was visible. Suddenly his fierce, unintelligible cry breaks forth. Dante's ironic aside – 'sweeter psalms did not accord with him' (69) – suggests he was astounded by the cry, but not afraid. Vergil reacts by turning upon the giant angrily: don't try to speak, you idiot, the horn is the right outlet for your passions. (Presumably Vergil had not realised what terror the earlier horn-blast had inspired in Dante.) Vergil shows the giant the place of the horn on his chest, speaking as if to a half-wit who has behaved perversely and needs therapy. And at last this giant, who has been observed for thirty lines, is named. He is Nimrod; his garbled language is the lasting testimony of his guilt, an inescapable accusation. Vergil admits he knows that Nimrod understands no language but his own, which itself cannot be understood by others. And yet he had spoken to Nimrod, perhaps hoping – as we might, when speaking to an animal, or a very young child, or an idiot – that something at least would get across.

Vergil's naming of the giant compels us to retrace the scene in a new light. The full significance of Nimrod and his cry will be discussed in the next two sections. For the moment, it is enough to know that the Old Latin (Vetus Latina) translation of Genesis – which was quoted by numerous Church Fathers – repeatedly calls Nimrod not only a mighty hunter but a giant,[12] and to note (though we cannot find even a hint of this in Genesis) that Augustine in *The City of God* shows Nimrod as the giant who instigated the building of the tower of Babel. Augustine stresses that this building was intended not merely to 'touch heaven' (*tangere caelum*, as the Bible has it), but was a conspiracy to usurp heaven, to snatch the rule of heaven away from God.[13] And a passage in Dante's *De vulgari eloquentia* elaborates on God's punishment for this presumptuous venture: the confusion of tongues, by which God countered Nimrod's plot, was arranged in such a way that 'the more excellently the builders worked, the more crudely and barbarically do they speak now'.[14] From this it follows that in Dante's eyes Nimrod, whose language is a bitter howl meaningless to anyone but himself, has suffered the extreme of linguistic punishment, because he was the mastermind among the builders – not only the mover of the conspiracy but its supreme architect. With him, the horn is no longer the shining emblem of Roland – it is the toy of the mighty artist reduced, by his vaulting ambition, to imbecility.

But Dante knew of other giants who had tried to assail heaven with a tower: the Aloides – Ephialtes and Otus – had heaped mountains on top of one another to scale and seize heaven, just like Nimrod.[15] It is remarkable that, in a canto where from begin-

ning to end towers are used as images for the giants, the two
thematically central towers – those raised by Nimrod and by
Ephialtes – are kept implicit, but are never mentioned. Ephialtes,
whose name had in the learned world come to mean 'nightmare'
(as Dante will have known from Macrobius' account of the diverse
kinds of dreams and apparitions),[16] is shackled, his vigour
curbed, subdued in complete immobility. Vergil makes it plain
that Ephialtes' threat against Jove had been as real as that of
Nimrod against Jehovah:

> 'Questo superbo volle esser esperto
> di sua potenza contra 'l sommo Giove',
> disse 'l mio duca, 'ond' elli ha cotal merto.
>   Fialte ha nome, e fece le gran prove
> quando i giganti fer paura a' dèi;
> le braccia ch'el menò, già mai non move'.

> 'This arrogant one wanted to make a trial
> of his might against the highest Jove,'
> said my guide, 'so this is his reward.
>   Ephialtes is his name: he made his great bid
> when the giants filled the gods with fear;
> the arms he exerted then, he never moves'.   (91–6)

The giants' menace had been dire, the outcome of their challenge
was no foregone conclusion.

The next moment in the canto is filled with comedy. Dante the
character has by now lost his fear of giants and regained his in-
satiate curiosity. As a good reader of Vergil's *Aeneid*, he knows of
another giant, who should be far more exciting to glimpse than
the chained Ephialtes: Briareus, whom the *Aeneid* shows as having
fifty heads and fifty chests – all of them belching fire against Jove
during the war in heaven – and also a hundred arms: fifty for
shields and fifty for swords.[17] This is the giant Dante longs to see:
Briareus, who is 'unfathomable (*smisurato*)',[18] not, I suggest,
because Dante supposes him immeasurably larger than the other
giants, but rather because he wonders how anyone can visualise,
or fathom, the description given in the *Aeneid*. And what does the
author of the *Aeneid* answer? – Briareus? He's rather far off, it's
not worth the detour: he looks just like Ephialtes – that is, he has
normal human features, only they're more ferocious.

Dante is playing games with his readers here – but, as I shall
argue, for an unusual purpose. The jest of making Vergil say the

opposite of what he had said in the *Aeneid* is designed to minimise
the magical–monstrous aspect of the giants. With the same intent,
Dante deliberately discards all the fabulous traits by which the
ancient poets had distinguished the other giant-figures. Thus
when Antaeus appears, there is not a word about his mysterious
chthonic power of regaining strength by touching his mother, the
Earth; when Tityus is mentioned, it is only as a possible alternative
means of transport for the two poets. Not a word about the
famous vulture gnawing Tityus' liver, Tityus who, stretched out
over 9 acres, as the *Aeneid* tells,[19] could not – if the myths were
true – have risen even a centimetre to help the two poets in their
journey. The same holds good of Typhon, whom the myths claim
to be spreadeagled under Mount Etna – a claim that, as I indicated, Dante in *Paradiso* explicitly rejects.

The giants, then, are only outsize humans, devoid of mythic
attributes. Yet Ephialtes' shaking himself (106–8) – another
moment of mortal terror for Dante the protagonist – is a warning,
grim and comic, that one can't afford either to regard the giants as
mere spectacle, as if they were circus-freaks. Is Ephialtes' cata-
clysmic shudder a sign of his rage at Vergil's claim that another
giant, Briareus, looks more ferocious than he? Or is it one of his
spasmodic attempts to unshackle himself? These are two ingeni-
ous suggestions that scholars have made. Yet I suspect that his
action may be on a par with Nimrod's horn-blowing – motiveless
rather than malicious gestures, by beings who, like captive beasts,
continue automatically to repeat the now pointless actions of their
former freedom.

The last giant, Antaeus, did not take part in the assault on
heaven, but, after a long reign as a murderous ogre in Libya, was
defeated in combat and killed by Hercules. As the two poets
approach him, Vergil addresses him, beginning in a high-flown
manner that I would see as a parody of the form of prayer to gods
in classical Antiquity. There petitions are mostly preceded by an
'aretalogy (*aretalogia*)', in which, in parallel clauses of the structure
'Oh you who ... You are the one who ...', the high deeds of the
god who is addressed are celebrated. Dante knew such prayers in
their exalted form from Boethius, and was himself to put a
sublime aretalogy of the Boethian kind in the mouth of St
Bernard, in his prayer to the Virgin (*Par.* XXXIII 4ff).[20] Here,
however, the words of the 'prayer' given to Vergil echo passages
from Lucan, with deliberate inappropriateness:

'O tu che ne la fortunata valle
che fece Scipïon di gloria reda,
quand' Anibàl co' suoi diede le spalle,
  recasti già mille leon per preda,
e che, se fossi stato a l'alta guerra
de' tuoi fratelli, ancor par che si creda
  ch'avrebber vinto i figli de la terra:
mettine giù, e non ten vegna schifo,
dove Cocito la freddura serra.
  Non ci fare ire a Tizio né a Tifo:
questi può dar di quel che qui si brama;
però ti china e non torcer lo grifo.
  Ancor ti può nel mondo render fama ...'

'You who, in the valley blessed by fortune
– which made Scipio heir to glory
when Hannibal and his men turned their backs in flight –
  once carried off a thousand lions as prey,
– who, had you been at hand in the high battle
waged by your brothers, some, it seems, still believe
  that the sons of Earth[21] would have been victorious:
bring us down – don't show distaste at that –
to where Cocytus is locked in by cold.
  Don't make us go to Tityus or to Typhon:
this man can offer what is longed for here –
so down you get, don't pull such a grimace:
  he can still confer on you fame in the world ...'   (115–27)

Anteaus' massacring of lions (Vergil, exaggerating Lucan's text, makes it 'a thousand lions') is linked, mock-heroically, with Scipio's feats against Hannibal,[22] and Vergil primes Antaeus by reminding him that some people (again, notably, Lucan) believe that his intervention in the battle of Phlegra would have been decisive in ensuring the giants' victory over the gods.[23] After the aretalogy, as in the ancient prayers, comes the plea: here, to be lifted down into Cocytus. And now, it seems to me, as Vergil notices that his *captatio benevolentiae* has worked, that the giant has laid the flattering unction to his soul, we hear imperatives rather than supplications, and the tone becomes less solemn, more colloquial: '*mettine giù, e non ten vegna schifo ... però ti china e non torcer lo grifo*' (122, 126). The last phrase is one that could as easily be addressed to a moody child: 'Don't pull such a face!' Admittedly, Vergil goes on to promise that Dante will, in reward, give Antaeus new glory on earth, through his poetry – yet Antaeus is in effect being used ingloriously, like an object, a kind of crane to lower his human cargo into the hold, or – in the eyes of the once more affrighted Dante – a leaning tower as seen directly from underneath, when a moving cloud gives the illusion that the tower is falling (137ff). A double irony colours the episode: within the narrative, Vergil is aware of having won the gullible Antaeus' compliance through a rhetorical trick; outside the narrative, Dante the creator knows he is conferring a new immortality on Antaeus through his *Commedia*, making Antaeus' name familiar to generations of vernacular readers who would never have come to know it through the classics.

(iv) Nimrod

These suggestions about aspects of movement, tone and structure in the canto of the giants have not yet touched upon the two principal enigmas that it sets: one, what is the precise significance of Nimrod, and of his garbled attempt at speech? the other, how exactly does Dante conceive of the pagan mythological giants? Does he invest them with the same kind of reality as the biblical – that is, historical – giant, Nimrod? Do the 'true' giant and the fabled ones have the same imaginative and ontological status in the scheme of the poem, and if so, why? To approach these enigmas, I believe it is necessary to take some of the learned traditions about both biblical and classical giants into account. As a cue for this inquiry I can think of no text more apt than one – well known to Dante – from the epic *On the Complaint of Natura* by Alan of Lille. There the heroine, Natura, says:

Sometimes poets combine historical events with fabled phantasies, as it were in a single finely-shaped structure, so that from the harmonious joining of diverse matter a finer narrative picture may result.[24]

St Augustine in *The City of God*, as we noted, saw Nimrod both as a giant and as the planner of 'that famous conspiracy (*illa conspiratio*)', the building of Babel:

Babylon indeed means 'confusion'. From this we infer that the vaunted giant Nimrod was its founder ... Thus with his people he built a tower against God, a tower that signifies impious pride.

Because a ruler's power to dominate lies in his tongue, Augustine continues, it was in the tongue that Nimrod's pride was punished, so that, giving commands, he was no longer understood.[25]

But Nimrod was also known to the Middle Ages through a number of other legends. One of these is found in the 'Book of Nimrod (*Liber Nemroth*)', an unpublished work that survives in Latin, in a small number of manuscripts from the eleventh century onwards. I have discussed and edited some of its key passages concerning Nimrod in Excursus II below. The date and origins of the 'Book of Nimrod' remain problematic. According to a recent scholarly study, it is a western concoction, perhaps of the tenth century.[26] But the character of the Latin, especially in the earliest manuscript, leads me to think rather of a work that was translated, and of a time and place – quite possibly the eighth-century Merovingian world – where classically correct Latin was particularly hard to achieve.

On the basis of the prologue of the *Liber Nemroth*, which had already been printed, Richard Lemay claimed that this work was especially relevant to Dante's conception of the giant. Here, he alleged, Nimrod is presented as an atheist astronomer, who disdainfully ignores God by giving his own materialistic explanation of the heavens.[27] This is how Lemay interpreted the sentences:

... when Nimrod reflected on the form of the firmament, he recognised that it had a creator, not knowing who it might be. He saw the firmament move circularly, not leaving its station, and realised that it had nothing below to impede it, or above to suspend it, and in this he could say nothing except that there is a force that sustains it. He called it the strength which sustains the firmament and itself stands below nothing. So the knowledge of Nimrod is wondrous, in that he measured heaven's form and knew the courses of the stars, and yet did not know that God had created them. Yet this he knew, that there was a mighty ruling creature above, and he called it 'creator' ...

Bruno Nardi, in a rejoinder, rightly saw that nothing in this prologue implies that Nimrod the astronomer was arrogant or rebellious against God.[28] And Nardi's intuition is more than confirmed if one goes on from the prologue to read the work itself. For this shows Nimrod arriving, through cosmology, at an increasingly profound understanding of the creator, whom he comes to call not only 'God' but 'Lord', and whose existence he finally argues to be necessary, in that nothing in the visible universe can exist of itself (*a se*). The author portrays Nimrod as filled with an insatiable thirst for wisdom. Yet it is an unselfish thirst – he imparts all that he learns to his disciple, without thought of reward – and even, we could say, a pious one: Nimrod gives thanks to God for what he has discovered.

The only way that one could make this Nimrod (who, incidentally, is never said to be a giant) into a villain is to claim, as Lemay tries to do, that in Dante's eyes *any* attempt to understand the heavens is presumptuous and therefore punishable by God. But such fundamentalism is wholly alien to Dante: Dante who, in *Paradiso*, places in the heaven of the sun two saints – Albertus Magnus and Thomas Aquinas – who had written at length about Aristotle's treatise on the heavens, *De caelo*, without, as far as one can tell, incurring any guilt or loss of sanctity thereby. Lemay tries to link Nimrod with the scientist–translator Michael Scot, whom Dante places in *Inferno* among the diviners in Canto xx: both, Lemay believes, are condemned by Dante because they studied the heavens in a purely natural way, and, by so doing, flouted God. Yet this is in my view a grave misunderstanding of Dante. Dante is quite specific about why Michael Scot is in hell: not because of his scientific researches, nor even because of his astrology, but because *veramente / delle magiche frode seppe il gioco* (xx 116f) – 'truly he knew how to play the game of magic frauds'. Dante is not condemning the desire for unlimited knowledge; what is at issue in the case of the diviners is the misuse of knowledge for charlatanry and deceit.

The morally admirable astronomer who is the hero of the *Liber Nemroth* is as far as can be from Dante's giant; moreover, there is no evidence for Lemay's claim that Dante was familiar with this relatively rare work. If Dante knew of Nimrod as an astronomer, it will have been through the twelfth-century Bible commentary (*Historia scholastica*) of Peter Comestor – one of the theologians in the second circle of the sun in *Paradiso* (xii 134). In the *Historia scholastica*, which 'became a classic with both clergy and laity',[29] Nimrod is not only astronomer but also giant and ruler of Babylon, and a somewhat sinister figure. Peter's account in the main follows an earlier one, that of pseudo-Methodius, which had been translated into Latin in the eighth century.[30] But in that account there had been no hint of anything dubious about Nimrod's character. Peter's additions to this effect probably derive, directly or indirectly, from Jewish sources.[31]

Whilst, in the *Liber*, Nimrod is an idealistic sage, who teaches a disciple called Ioathon, in Peter's account 'Ionithus' (a son of Noah, of whom the Bible knows nothing) is the teacher, and Nimrod – again a giant – his pupil:

Ionithus received from the Lord the gift of wisdom, and invented astronomy. Nimrod, a giant ten cubits high, coming to him, was educated by him and received advice as to the places in which he might begin to reign … Returning from him, Nimrod, inflamed with the love of ruling, asked Shem for his people, that he might rule over others as if he were the first-born, but they refused; so he then went to Ham, who acquiesced, and he reigned amongst his people in Babylon, and hence was said to be of the sons of Ham.[32]

Here Nimrod's concern is not pure research into the causes of the heavens: it is to gain, through Ionithus, astrological predictions that will let him become a world-conqueror. Ionithus outlines the future empires of the world to Nimrod, and thus the giant, prepared, sets about acquiring kingdoms by trickery. This Nimrod is more readily comparable with a figure such as Dante's Michael Scot. Quite unlike the disinterested seeker of wisdom in the *Liber Nemroth*, he learns about the stars with only one end in view: how much power can this knowledge help him to win?

One other text, of enormous diffusion and almost certainly known to Dante, may have contributed something to his conception of Nimrod. In the Latin translation of Flavius Josephus' *Jewish Antiquities*,

Nimrod persuaded men not to ascribe it to God if happiness came to them, saying that it was given them through their own power (*propria virtute*). He won his kindred to the cause of tyranny, presuming in his own right to call men away from the fear of God and make them set their hopes in their own power.[33]

Such thoughts are not made explicit by Dante when he writes of Nimrod, yet they can illuminate the parallels between Nimrod and the classical giants that underlie the canto. What Vergil says, for instance, of Ephialtes, the giant whom he and Dante encounter next — 'This arrogant one wanted to make a trial / of his might against the highest Jove' — is implicitly true of Nimrod also, as again it is true of the supreme giant, Lucifer, in the last canto of *Inferno*. The biblical Nimrod has been transformed, so that his life is seen in the same pattern as that of the classical giants and of Lucifer: glorying in his own power, challenging the highest God, and then punished by humiliation.

(v) Invented Languages

The presentation of Nimrod as an astronomer in the *Liber Nemroth* prompted Richard Lemay to a further conjecture:

namely that Nimrod's savage cry – *Raphèl maì amècche zabì almi* (67) – is not, as Vergil in the canto affirms, unintelligible (*a nullo è noto*: 81). On the contrary, it is (making a few allowances) a perfectly intelligible phrase of Arabic, in which Nimrod laments the abyss to which his science has brought him.[34] Dante, on Lemay's view, to be able to write such a line, must have been a first-rate Arabist, skilled enough to read in the original not only works of Arabic science but even of Islamic poetry and mysticism.[35] Naturally this line – like that at the opening of *Inferno* VII (*Pape Satàn, pape Satàn aleppe!*) – has always held a fascination for cryptographers, who have revealed the secrets of these words to be Arabic, or Hebrew, or Aramaic, or even (on one occasion) Sardinian.[36] What neither the cryptographers nor the more sober Dante-scholars have done, however, is to look at any parallel evidence for the uses of *imaginary* languages in the Middle Ages. These have not, as far as I know, been systematically studied, but five or six examples will suffice for our purposes.

Thus, for instance, in the twelfth-century Latin Magi-play from Rouen, the dramatist is concerned to differentiate the central king, who greets Herod in Latin, from the other two. One of these speaks an imitation Semitic language –

> Ase ai
> ase elo allo
> abadac crazai
> nubera satai
> loamedech amos ebraisim . . .
> adonay moy –

while the other king's language would appear to be an unknown Hellenic one:

> O some tholica lama ha
> o some tholica lama ma
> chenapi ha thomena.[37]

Already in a second-century A.D. papyrus containing a fragmentary Greek mime-scenario, the scene is set in a country on the Indian Ocean, where a Greek girl is held captive. The king of the country can speak some Greek, but the native women speak an invented Oriental language:

> Kraunou. Lalle. Laitalianta lalle . . .[38]

The device may well have been a stock one that continued in the mime repertoire, even in the centuries from which no evidence survives.

In the twelfth century, again, the poet-scientist Hildegard of Bingen constructed her own *Lingua ignota* – 900 words, with Latin glossary.[39] In her songs she occasionally intersperses the invented words, creating an enigmatic effect:

> O *orzchis* Ecclesia . . .
> tu es *caldemia*
> stigmatum *loifolum* . . .
> et es *chorzta* gemma![40]

'Oh *immense* Ecclesia . . . you are the *fragrance* of the wounds of *peoples* . . . and are a *glittering* bud!'

Many of Hildegard's new words have, not surprisingly, a vaguely Germanic air.

Two of the Latin-trained poet-clerks who made major contributions to medieval French drama, Jean Bodel († 1210) and Rutebeuf (*fl.* 1250–85), use imaginary languages to set certain moments in dramatic relief. In Jean's *Jeu de Saint Nicolas*, the statue of the Saracen idol, about to be destroyed, speaks perfect octosyllabic couplets of unintelligible words, which occasionally sound somewhat Hebraic (*aron, geheamel*).[41] So too in Rutebeuf's play *Le miracle de Théophile*, composed a few years before Dante's birth, the Jewish sorcerer Salatin conjures up the devil in nine verses such as these:

> Lamac lamec bachalyos
> Cabahagi sabalyos . . .
> Harrahya![42]

Here the feigned Hebraic element is more evident, and is meant to create a cabbalistic impression.

Perhaps the most interesting invented language in relation to that of Dante's Nimrod, however, is the one that was used during the *Cornomannia*, the exuberant 'Feast of the Ass' celebrated in Rome on the Saturday after Easter. We have a testimony of it already from the ninth century, and a detailed account from the twelfth.[43] The ceremonies included *laudes* sung for the Pope by the papal *schola cantorum*, whose prior played a buffoon's part on the occasion, horned like Silenus and mounted on an ass. Later, the sacristan, who wore a horned cap and jangled a set of bells, went visiting houses with a priest and two companions. While the priest blessed the houses,

... the sacristan chanted these verses, in barbaric language:

Iaritan, Iaritan, Iarariasti,
Raphayn, Iercoyn, Iarariasti,

and the others that follow.[44]

Unfortunately, we are not told the rest.

These parallels, I believe, can illustrate the artistic purpose behind Nimrod's *Raphèl maì amècche zabì almi!* It is a wild and fearsome shout, and yet, through its outlandishness, it cannot help being also comic. It is an evocation, by a poet with a matchless ear for sounds, of dazed proto-Semitic. From his Latin theological and scientific reading, Dante knew enough Hebrew and Arabic words to be able to construct, not a conundrum to await the advent of twentieth-century cryptographers, but rather, a convincing line of spoken Babelese, in the tradition of invented language that had been used in the Church for performances on Twelfth Night and at Easter.

Dante, as is well known, had begun by believing, with many theologians, that Adam spoke Hebrew, and that the diversification of languages was a divine punishment for the building of the tower;[45] yet he finally arrived, as he wrote *Paradiso*, at a de-mythologised, far more relativist, position. There he makes Adam say: 'The language that I spoke was all spent before Nimrod's race became intent upon their unachievable effort – for no rational construct has ever been free from change: human choice renews itself, with the course of the heavens' (*Par.* XXV 124–9). The treatment of Nimrod in *Inferno* XXXI is a stage on Dante's way towards this insight. The expressions used of the giant in lines 77–8 – *per lo cui mal coto / pur un linguaggio nel mondo non s'usa* ('because of whose wicked thought / one single language is no longer used in the world') – do not necessarily, I believe, imply a sudden, magical, universal confusion of tongues. Rather, God specifically punishes the presumptuous giant–builder, blocking Nimrod's master-plan to conquer heaven, by making him unintelligible to his accomplices. These he scatters all over the world, and this scattering itself ensures the divergence of their ways of speech – ensures it by natural, not magic, means, since language is from the outset subject to change. (This, at least, is the way I would reconstruct the evolution of Dante's thought on the question.)

(vi) The Parity of Biblical and Classical Giants

Nimrod, divinely afflicted by losing the power to communicate and understand, is all too human in his crushed state of alienation. Here the classical giants – whom, as we saw, Dante has wholly stripped of their fabulous qualities – can meet him on common ground. In bringing the biblical giant together with the classical ones, without any disjunction of history from legend, false from true, Dante chose to remain within a particular ancient tradition of *contaminatio* of the two giant-realms. When in one of the earliest extant Sibylline prophecies (second century B.C.) the Sibyl gives an account of the flood and of Babel, and says that, at the time of the tower, Kronos and Titan and Iapetos ruled the earth, it seems that she is transposing these for the three sons of Noah – Shem, Ham and Japhet – probably influenced by the near-homonym Ιαφεθ/Ιαπετός:

> When the threats of the great God were carried out
> with which he menaced mortals when they built the tower
> there in Assyria – they all spoke the same language,
> and wanted to climb up into starry heaven –
> at once the immortal one laid a great compulsion
> upon the breezes, and the winds on high then shattered
> the vast tower and caused strife among mortal men:
> because of this men gave the city the name Babylon.
> But when the tower fell and the tongues of men
> diverged in every way in sounds, and the whole
> earth became filled with mankind, with divided kingdoms,
> it was already the tenth race of human beings
> since the flood befell their forefathers.
> Then Kronos and Titan and Iapetos reigned,
> the bravest sons of Gaia and Uranos:
> men named the parents after earth and heaven,
> because they were the first and foremost among mortal
>   men.[46]

This Sibyl is decidedly a euhemerist: the three rulers, like their parents, she claims, were not gods or titans – as the Greeks might believe – but human beings.

Even earlier, in the Old Testament prophecy of Baruch (3: 24–9), we encounter, in what is ostensibly a reference to the scene of Babel, not the builder Nimrod but a primordial race of giants, who share the dwelling of the God of Israel, yet who, being 'skilled in warfare', plan to take for themselves a divine wisdom that God refused to give them, and who are then destroyed by him. The allusions are difficult to grasp fully, yet they appear to diverge so much from the Genesis account of Babel that an influence from a different range of giant-myths seems almost certain.

St Augustine, in *The City of God*, adduces Vergil, Homer, and Pliny as witnesses to corroborate the historicity of the biblical giants; he spontaneously adds a personal testimony, of finding a giant's tooth once on the beach at Utica.[47] So, too, the author of the *Liber monstrorum*, writing in Anglo-Saxon England around 700, drawing on many sources, including Vergil and Augustine, discusses on the same plane of reality the ancient giants, Tityus, Ephialtes, and Otus (1 47, 55), the immense men, 15 feet high, who 'as fables pretend' are still born in the Orient (1 43), and an early Germanic king, Hyglacus, killed in the year 516, 'whose bones are preserved on an island of the river Rhine, where it flows into the sea, and are shown as a marvel to visitors who come from afar to see them' (1 2).[48] Yet this author's attitude, unlike Augustine's, is essentially sceptical: he inclines to reduce all *mirabilia*, from mythological giants to prodigies reported in his own day, to legend and literary artifice.

In the twelfth century, both poets and theologians tended almost unreflectingly to fuse the two worlds of giant-myth. When Walter of Châtillon, in his vastly influential epic *Alexandreis*, allows Darius, who is Alexander's mightiest opponent, to claim descent from the giants of Babylon, even while his allusions are specifically to the episode in Genesis, the language – speaking of the battles against the gods (*bella deorum*), and of the giants themselves as sons of Earth (*Terrigenae*) – embraces the connotations of the uprising at Phlegra as well as at Babylon:

> 'Who does not know that our race stems
> from the lineage of the Giants? Who does not know the battles
> against the gods, the bricks baked and the tower mortared
> with pitch
> by our ancestors? Who has forgotten the great city
> to which confusion of speech gave an everlasting name?
> So come, my captains, summon up your ancestral
> strength!' ...
> Darius' origins blaze forth, and the profane line
> of the Giant race – they whose Earth-born brothers you
> could see,
> under Nimrod their prince, settled on Sennachar's plain,

> where, as they thought again about the fateful flood,
> the brickwork rose. Language, common to all before,
> was – wondrous to relate – cut into different tongues.[49]

For Walter's contemporary, the biblical exegete Peter Comestor, the Titans, dwelling in Egypt, were refugees from Hebron, descending from a race of giants whom the Israelites had encountered there during the Exodus.[50] Even more remarkable are certain expressions in Peter's commentary on the tower of Babel in Genesis:

Fearing another flood, at the advice of Nimrod, who was eager to rule, they began to build a tower that would reach up to the heavens ... But the gods (*dii*), sending winds, overturned the tower, and allotted to each person his own language. It is this tower that the Sibyl recalls, saying: 'When all mankind had the same language, they began to build a lofty tower, as if to climb into heaven by means of it ...'[51]

The first motive for the building of the tower, to which Walter of Châtillon likewise alludes in the verses cited, is one that is not found in Genesis, but is made explicit in Josephus:[52] the notion that, if a high enough tower could be built, God would be unable to punish rebellious mankind again by a flood. Yet then, in Peter's text, it is as if the pagan myth were being superimposed on the Jewish one: it is the gods – *dii*[53] – who, as agents of the God of Israel, accomplish the destruction of the tower and the division of tongues. And for authority the twelfth-century theologian cites the Sibyl (in his eyes a pagan witness). She, like St Augustine, ascribes to the biblical tower-builders the motive that inspired the Aloides – to construct something high enough for them to be able to climb up into heaven and seize possession of it.

For Dante, then, there was abundant precedent for seeing Nimrod, Ephialtes, Antaeus and the rest as belonging to one and the same imaginative world. But what was the imaginative significance of that world? For many, including Dante's early commentators, it was primarily, if not entirely, allegorical. Just as, in the twelfth century, Bernard Silvestris could interpret the giants in Book VI of the *Aeneid* microcosmically, as the enslaving desires within the human being, that try to overcome the innate divinity, the Jove who is man's soul,[54] so Dante's son Pietro, commenting on this canto, while he concedes that giants really did exist in former times, claims that 'nonetheless, Dante is here speaking of giants allegorically ... to mean affects or impulses of pride'.[55] One

of the earliest commentators, Guido of Pisa, is more of a euhemerist: he stresses that the pagan mythical giants were only human,
and juxtaposes them not merely with Nimrod but with Goliath
and even with St Christopher – 'take note, Lucan', says Guido, 'we
can find no other giant who was holy!'[56] Yet for Guido too the
significance of the giants lies principally in their allegorical and
moral meanings.[57]

These meanings seem to me most pertinent to another moment
in Dante, where he very consciously shows us certain giants as
emblems of pride: on the pavement of the terrace of pride, on the
mountain of purgatory (*Purgatorio* XII), Dante sees carved figures
not only of the giants Briareus and Nimrod, but of Lucifer and of
three of the Olympian gods, followed by classical and biblical
figures, men and women, intermingled. The carvings are indeed
emblematic – yet thereby they contrast with the living encounters
of *Inferno* XXXI. In these, too, we should not rule out the presence
of elements of underlying allegory – the aptness, for instance, of
having giants, whose rebellion was both deceitful and treacherous
towards the highest god, stationed at *Inferno*'s boundary between
the deceivers and the traitors: between Malebolge and Cocytus.[58]
Moreover, Dante establishes what we might call a typological relation between the giants and Lucifer. Lucifer, we learn in Canto
XXXIV, is immersed even deeper in ice than they are in their pit,
and he is a giant on a far larger scale than they:

> Lo 'mperador del doloroso regno
> da mezzo 'l petto uscia fuor de la ghiaccia;
> e più con un gigante io mi convegno,
> che i giganti non fan con le sue braccia.

> The emperor of the dolorous realm
> loomed up out of the ice from mid-chest;
> and I can better match a giant in size
> than the giants can match his arms.   (28–31)

The various giants' insurgences against the divine realm prefigure,
on a smaller scale, Lucifer's supreme insurgence. For Lucifer, too,
the reckless moment of rebellion results in a perpetual, immobile
rootedness. Though he can still torment his victims, for the two
poets he is reduced, like Antaeus, to an object: where Antaeus'
body becomes the crane that lifts them and sets them down in the
ninth circle, that of Lucifer becomes the ladder by which they
climb to the southern hemisphere.

Nonetheless, the allegoric aptness of the giants' location, and their figural links with Lucifer, are subsidiary to the unusual imaginative experience that Dante creates. His synthesis is not only of the biblical and classical giant-realms, but of high language and imagery with the colloquial and the grotesque; he evokes moments of terror (with sudden, frightening involvement) and moments of black farce (with a sardonic distancing). Such a double range of effects was familiar in medieval religious drama in the presentation especially of one character – Herod. Herod's rôle in the medieval plays has been finely characterised by Robert Weimann as a 'fearsome–comic' one (*die furchtbare Komik des Herodes*). He is seen as the contemporary tyrant: 'Naturally Herod is sinister *and* vainglorious, fearsome *and* comic; but the dramatic force of the role lies precisely in the conjunction of these features and the tension between them'.[59]

Dante's giants, I suggest, may be seen as the failed tyrants – like the Herod who, on the twelfth-century stage, was shown meeting his end devoured by worms: *Herodes corrodatur a vermibus*, as the stage-direction says in the *Carmina Burana* Christmas play.[60] This spectacle must have been both horrific and burlesque – the worms being played doubtless by very small boys (the youngest *clericuli*) enveloped in worm-costumes.

Inferno XXXI is dominated by a series of inanimate images – the various shapes of towers, the pine-cone, the ship's mast – that prevent empathy with the giants, that serve to deaden any outgoing human response to them. At the same time, Dante has deliberately left the giants human – or, we might say, has shown them to us as humans dehumanised. This dramatically realised perception integrates the allegoric possibilities of meaning, such as the commentators love to tease out – but also, in a sense, it makes them superfluous. What we experience is the *furchtbare Komik*. Dante has guided our reactions: his giants, brutish and gullible, are beings for whom it is easier to feel contempt or occasional fear than pity; on the obverse of the fear is a grim laughter. These are no legendary beings – no gods or demigods, monsters or demons. Every magical and supernatural attribute has been carefully taken away. They are, on a monumental scale, humans – frustrated, helpless, absurd; forever trapped in their pit.

3
The Phantasmagoria in the Earthly Paradise

(i) Hidden Comparisons

The apocalyptic visions that are shown to Dante in the earthly paradise, after he has beheld the heavenly procession and been reunited with Beatrice, include some of the most enigmatic moments in the entire *Commedia*. Dante is well aware of their obscurity, and he stresses it – fictively for his own benefit, in truth for ours – many times in the concluding canto of *Purgatorio*. There Beatrice challenges Dante to question her about the showings, and, noticing that he is 'too reverent', faltering in her presence, she commands him to 'cast off fear and shame'. She then begins to expound to him, yet her exposition itself becomes – as, in deliberately difficult, allusive language, she concedes – an oracular, and for the moment impenetrable, statement:

> E forse che la mia narrazion buia,
> qual Temi e Sfinge, men ti persuade,
> perch' a lor modo lo 'ntelletto attuia;
>   ma tosto fier li fatti le Naiade,
> che solveranno questo enigma forte
> sanza danno di pecore o di biade.

> And perhaps my dark utterance,
> like Themis and the Sphinx, persuades you less,
> because, in their manner, it numbs the mind;
>   but soon the deeds will be the Naiads
> that will resolve this arduous enigma
> without loss of sheep or corn.   (XXXIII 46–51)[1]

Her explanations grow so hermetic in expression that Dante is at last moved to complain: 'But why do your longed-for words / fly so far above my sight, / which loses them the more, the more it seeks them?' And Beatrice's reply is an accusation: she speaks in this sibylline way so as to bring Dante to realise his great distance, intellectually and morally, from herself and from the divine realm.[2]

Why is the meaning of what Dante had seen in *Purgatorio* XXXII hard to grasp? Is it, as a standard translator of the *Commedia* suggests, because of 'Dante's allegorising ingenuity', which here comes to seem particularly overburdened – 'laboured and unimaginative and lacking even in the superficial qualities of consistency and lucidity'?[3] Certainly the early commentators found no difficulty in proposing specific allegorical meanings for most of the details in the visionary episodes. Yet was it not perhaps this very readiness with identifications – equating the gryphon with Christ, or the chariot with the Church, or the giant with the king of France – that tended to turn the poetry into something 'laboured and unimaginative', and to clothe it with 'superficial qualities' which were not of Dante's making? If it were simply a matter of finding appropriate historical correspondences for all the elements of Dante's apocalypse, it would hardly be a problem of poetic interpretation, merely one of cryptography.

The complexity of the visions, and of their later exposition by Beatrice, seems to me to be of the same order as that of the procession which precedes them, which I have tried to analyse on another occasion.[4] It lies in the interplay between inner and outer meaning. What is revealed is in the first place microcosmic: it is aspects of Dante's own consciousness that are crystallised in the apocalyptic images; but when crystallised in this way they also acquire macrocosmic connotations. The images both objectify inner experiences of Dante's and provide 'hidden comparisons' for his perceptions, hopes and forebodings in the outer world. If the inner and outer force of the images synchronised perfectly, there would be no problem: what we should have would be a mechanical operation, a poetry which could be read on two distinct levels and which would, precisely because of that, be imaginatively poor. The richness of hidden comparisons, as Geoffrey of Vinsauf noted, lies in the fact that they are not like this: they 'fluctuate within and without, here and there, far and near, distant and present'.[5] Solving the 'arduous enigmas' depends upon perceiving these fluctuations in all their detail, perceiving the blend of subjective and objective reference at each moment of the visions.

To attempt this, even in some small measure, is daunting

because of all that was latent in Dante's imagination. Each of the images in *Purgatorio* XXXII, from the despoiled tree onwards, is related first of all to the whole pattern of images that pervades the scenes in the earthly paradise, in seven cantos (XXVII–XXXIII) that are particularly fecund in poetic cross-reference. Again, the apocalyptic images seem to relate closely to some found in the biblical texts in this genre – Ezekiel, Daniel, and the Revelation of John. It is easy to see that Dante was deeply familiar with these texts, and I would add that he was familiar with certain kinds of exegesis of them (though we cannot be wholly sure of the specific commentaries he had read).[6] Yet even if many of the apocalyptic elements in Dante's visions seem recognisable, this is always in some degree illusory, since neither separately nor together do those elements work in the same way in the *Commedia* as they do in the Bible. Even, for instance, when Dante's chariot turns into a monster with seven heads and ten horns, Dante tells us, not I think ironically but almost defiantly: 'never yet was such a monster seen' (XXXII 147). That is, although there are three seven-headed ten-horned monsters in St John's Apocalypse (12: 3; 13: 1; 17: 3), and we might imagine that by recognising this fact we have come close to Dante's intention, Dante warns us to observe the specific differences as well as the resemblance: for him it is not an animal, but the inanimate chariot, 'the holy structure', that sprouts these heads and horns. No element in Dante's individual visions can be reduced to its biblical or exegetic point of departure; nothing can be taken simply or taken straight.

The showings begin when Beatrice descends from the chariot drawn by a gryphon, on which she had arrived in the earthly paradise. Dante is walking with his beautiful guide, Matelda, and with the poet Statius, following the chariot and the 'glorious host'[7] – the twenty-four elders, the four living creatures described by Ezekiel and John, and the seven nymphs who attend upon Beatrice. 'All that soldiery of the heavenly kingdom' turn eastwards, they face the sun and the seven vast candelabras painting the sky with flames, that had been the first harbingers of Beatrice. As she descended,

> Io senti' mormorare a tutti 'Adamo';
> poi cerchiaro una pianta dispogliata
> di foglie e d'altra fronda in ciascun ramo.
> La coma sua, che tanto si dilata

più quanto più è sù, fora da l'Indi
ne' boschi lor per altezza ammirata.
　'Beato se', grifon, che non discindi
col becco d'esto legno dolce al gusto,
poscia che mal si torce il ventre quindi.'
　Così dintorno a l'albero robusto
gridaron li altri; e l'animal binato:
'Sì si conserva il seme d'ogne giusto.'
　E vòlto al temo ch'elli avea tirato,
trasselo al piè de la vedova frasca,
e quel di lei a lei lasciò legato.
　Come le nostre piante, quando casca
giù la gran luce mischiata con quella
che raggia dietro a la celeste lasca,
　turgide fansi, e poi si rinovella
di suo color ciascuna, pria che 'l sole
giunga li suoi corsier sotto altra stella;
　men che di rose e più che di vïole
colore aprendo, s'innovò la pianta,
che prima avea le ramora sì sole.

I heard 'Adam' murmured by everyone;
then they encircled a tree despoiled
of flowers and other fronds on every bough.
　Its shoots, which are the more widespread
the higher they reach, would be marvelled at
by the Indians in their forests, for their height.
　'You are blessed, gryphon, you who do not tear
with your beak at this wood sweet to the taste,
for the belly writhes in pain from tasting it.'
　Thus, around the robust tree,
the others cried; and the twice-born animal:
'In this way is the seed of all that's just preserved.'
　And, turning to the shaft that he had pulled,
he drew it to the foot of the widowed trunk
and left it tied there by a branch of it.
　As our plants – when the great light showers
down upon them, mingled with the light
that shines after the heavenly [sign of the] Fish –
　dilate in growing, and each is then renewed
in its own colour, before the sun
yokes his steeds beneath another star –
　so, revealing less of rose and more of violet
colour, the tree renewed itself,
though its branches were so desolate before.   (XXXII 37–60)

(ii) Dante's Tree

The complexity of the description of the tree's renewal matches the complex symbolism concentrated in the tree itself. It is evidently the tree whose fruit Adam tasted in the earthly paradise, the tree of the knowledge of good and evil; it was Adam who, by eating that forbidden fruit, despoiled the tree. Later, Beatrice tells Dante that the tree has a further meaning: in the moral sense (*moralmente*), it was the justice of God that revealed itself in the command concerning the paradisal tree.[8] Yet this by no means exhausts the connotations. Two others, to begin with, are, I suggest, signalled unmistakably through Dante's choice of language. In the words *legno dolce* ('sweet wood'), Dante, by echoing the opening of the refrain of Fortunatus' renowned hymn in veneration of the cross (*Dulce lignum* . . .),[9] pays homage to the legend that the tree of the Fall is also the wood from which Christ's cross was made. And this suggests a double force of inner meaning: any human offence against God is a re-enactment of Adam's offence, a new snatching of fruit from the tree, and equally it is a violent complicity in the crucifying of Christ, it tears the sweet wood yet again.

Similarly, I believe, the words *albero robusto* are lent further significance by their original context: the 'robust tree' is the tree (*arbor robusta*) seen by King Nebuchadnezzar in the dream that was expounded to him by Daniel.[10] That most beautiful, fruit-laden tree at the centre of the earth, reaching up to heaven, giving shelter and nourishment to all creation – 'that tree is yourself, oh king' (Dan. 4: 19). The primary meaning of the *arbor robusta* is microcosmic, and yet, as with the tree-images in Ezekiel and Isaiah,[11] it carries implications for a whole kingdom. An angel (*vigil*, literally a watcher) descends from heaven and commands that the tree be stripped of branches, leaves, and fruit – in Daniel's interpretation, that Nebuchadnezzar be exiled from human society and live bereft of reason until he acknowledges the sovereignty of God. Only after this is he restored to the glory of his kingdom and to greater magnificence than before.

Thus it is possible to see implicit in the renewal of Dante's tree the redemption wrought by Christ (the flowers that are more violet than rose may evoke Christ's blood),[12] but also – and I think predominantly – Dante's own interior drama. The connotations of the redemption must not be allowed to take precedence, for this tree, having been renewed, is soon afterwards savagely stripped again by an eagle, who has a rôle comparable to that of the angel in Nebuchadnezzar's dream:

> Non scese mai con sì veloce moto
> foco di spessa nube, quando piove
> da quel confine che più va remoto,
>   com' io vidi calar l'uccel di Giove
> per l'alber giù, rompendo de la scorza,
> non che d'i fiori e de le foglie nove . . .

> Never did lightning with so swift a motion
> descend from a dense cloud, when it dashes
> down from the confines that are most remote,
>   as I saw the bird of Jove come down
> through the tree, shattering the bark
> as well as the flowers and the new leaves . . .   (109–14)

This new despoiling clearly cannot mean that Christ's redemption was nullified: the reference must be to an inner destruction, within Dante ('that tree is yourself . . .'), though it can also provide a 'hidden comparison' for destruction in the political world that Dante confronts.

It is not certain that Dante read the moral interpretation of Nebuchadnezzar's dream by Richard of St Victor, the mystic to whom he pays tribute in the sphere of the sun.[13] Yet the guiding notion in Richard's interpretation is of particular interest in relation to the dialectic within Dante himself in the last cantos of *Purgatorio*:

The prophet seems here to show, on the basis of a mystic vision, how it happens that men of virtues ebb gradually, and by certain degrees of detriments fall to the depths, and, through visiting grace, sometimes rise again to their former state of spirit, or rather to a greater one . . . For what is it that Nebuchadnezzar received mystic vision, lost it, and afterwards knew it again more fully . . . except that the grace of contemplation is for a time divinely given, for a time withdrawn, and at last restored in more multiple form?[14]

Dante had been 'crowned and mitred' by Vergil at the moment he had reached the earthly paradise: it was as if he had become a sacerdotal king over himself and thereby entitled to enter and delight in the blissful place.[15] Yet then he is humiliated by Beatrice, who harshly shows him the extent he had fallen from blessedness. But Beatrice is also the 'visiting grace' that enables him to be renewed and to mount higher. Dante, at the close of

Purgatorio, emerges renewed like a tree, with new fronds (*novella fronda*: XXXIII 143f) – realising in himself what he had seen in exemplary fashion in the twenty-four elders, 'each of them garlanded with a green frond' (XXIX 93 – a detail not to be found in Dante's sources, Ezekiel and John), and again in his beloved, 'circled by the fronds of Minerva' (XXX 68).

As with the tree, I am convinced that the primary range of association of both the gryphon and the chariot is likewise microcosmic. Both these dense symbols relate in the first place to Dante himself, and it is from their stratum of personal meaning that their larger connotations arise. As I attempted to show in detail in my study of the procession, the question 'What do the gryphon and the chariot mean?' cannot be resolved by naively equating the gryphon with Christ or the chariot with the Church, as commentators from Jacopo della Lana onwards tried to do. Such equations can only be upheld insofar as the commentators evade precise comment on any of the passages where applying the equations strictly would lead to absurdity.[16]

The chariot, I suggested, must first and foremost be linked with the image that was dear to Dante from Boethius' hymn *O qui perpetua*, where the Creator sets souls upon light chariots, sows them in heaven and on earth, and lets them turn and make their way back to the divine.[17] The chariot that is here tied to the tree by the gryphon is the vehicle of Dante's soul, a vehicle that, in the procession, fittingly came bearing Beatrice. The chariot also has connotations – at different moments, as poetically appropriate – of Dante's ideals, regarding both imperial Rome and the Christian Church; in its degradation, the chariot can suggest the degradation of those ideals. The gryphon that draws the chariot of Dante's soul, we might say Dante's *daimôn*, reflects aspects of his nature, that has metaphorically, like the gryphon, something of both the eagle and the lion; but the individual *daimôn* also reflects the spark of divinity within the human being – hence the divine and Christlike associations of the gryphon at certain moments. That it is 'twice-born' can allude to its origination in eagle and lion, but also to an origin that is simultaneously divine and earthly.

The tree in the earthly paradise, though despoiled of its flowers and other fronds, still has shoots,[18] that give promise of renewal, and these become more abundant the closer the tree approaches heaven. (Metaphorically this holds likewise for the human tree.)

The blessed assembly praise the gryphon for not tearing at the tree
– for not repeating Adam's offence, not perverting divine justice,
not savaging the *dulce lignum* of the cross – and, we might also
say, it is a moment in which Dante's *daimôn* is recognised as
having been purified of sin in the poet's path through purgatory:
the seven marks of sin that the angel had branded on Dante's brow
have been effaced; he has passed through the wall of flame. So,
too, the gryphon can recognise how the tree, by epitomising the
demand of divine justice, preserves the seed of all that is just, how
it allows justice to grow on the earth.[19]

Between the first and second visionary showings come Dante's
elaborate evocation of his sleeping and waking again, a brief scene
with Matelda, and another with Beatrice. Dante falls asleep while
hearing an unearthly melody, as the tree renews itself:

> S'io potessi ritrar come assonnaro
> li occhi spietati udendo di Siringa,
> li occhi a cui pur vegghiar costò sì caro;
>   come pintor che con essempro pinga,
> disegnerei com' io m'addormentai;
> ma qual vuol sia che l'assonnar ben finga.
>   Però trascorro a quando mi svegliai,
> e dico ch'un splendor mi squarciò 'l velo
> del sonno, e un chiamar: 'Surgi: che fai?'

> If I could retrace how were closed in sleep
> the pitiless eyes, on hearing of Syrinx,
> the eyes whose constant watching cost them so dear –
>   like a painter painting from a model
> I would depict how I fell asleep;
> but let whoever wishes represent sleep's onset.
>   So I pass to when I awoke,
> and tell that a radiance tore away my veil
> of sleep, and a shout: 'Rise: what are you doing?'   (64–72)

In the procession, the four living creatures that surrounded the
chariot each had six wings full of eyes, 'and the eyes of Argus, /
had they been alive, would have been such as these' (XXIX 95f). Yet
Argus, ever-watchful with his hundred eyes, had been not only
put to sleep but put to death by Mercury, who lulled him to his
end with the tale of Syrinx, the nymph pursued by Pan and meta-
morphosed into the Arcadian shepherds' pipe.[20] For Argus, to
close all his eyes in sleep meant to die, and the mythological allusions in both moments in Dante stress the likeness between sleep

and death. There is a macabre aspect to this sleep (pointed by the strange synaesthetic image, the pitiless *eyes hearing*); the sudden brightness and the shout '*Surgi*' that awakens Dante – we may surmise that it is Matelda's radiant presence and voice, though the poet leaves it open[21] – make the waking seem like a resurgence out of death. At the same time, as Syrinx, in dying, becomes the poet's instrument, Dante the deathlike sleeper rises to become once more Dante the visionary – and the two rôles, as he notes in a witty throw-away line (69), are in a strict sense incompatible.

Dante invests his waking with still greater symbolic richness:

> Quali a veder de' fioretti del melo
> che del suo pome li angeli fa ghiotti
> e perpetüe nozze fa nel cielo,
> Pietro e Giovanni e Iacopo condotti
> e vinti, ritornaro a la parola
> da la qual furon maggior sonni rotti,
> e videro scemata loro scuola
> così di Moisè come d'Elia,
> e al maestro suo cangiata stola;
> tal torna' io, e vidi quella pia
> sovra me starsi che conducitrice
> fu de' miei passi lungo 'l fiume pria.
> E tutto in dubbio dissi: 'Ov' è Beatrice?'

> As to see blossoms of the apple-tree
> – whose fruit makes the angels avid
> and makes perpetual nuptials in heaven –
> Peter and John and James were led,
> and, overcome, were restored at the word
> by which greater slumbers were broken,
> and saw their school diminished
> by Moses, as well as by Elias,
> and their master's garments changed –
> so I returned to myself, and saw that compassionate one
> standing above me who had been the guide
> of my steps along the stream before.
> And all full of doubt I said: 'Where is Beatrice?'   (73–85)

The basic movement of the comparison is clear: Dante returns to himself, after the vision of the tree's renewal and the sleep-instilling music, as the apostles returned to waking reality after Christ's transfiguration. Of the three Gospel accounts,[22] only Luke mentions that they had been 'weighed down by sleep', only

Matthew that Christ helped them out of their dread, at hearing the divine voice in the cloud, by the words, 'Rise, and do not be afraid.' Yet within Dante's extended comparison subtler elements emerge. For him the apostles' vision of Christ in glory becomes seeing the blossoms of the apple-tree. The metaphor is from the Song of Songs, where the divine lover, unique in beauty, is 'as the apple-tree among the forest trees'; but here the allusion lends new depth to the earlier images of the reflowering of Adam's apple-tree in the earthly paradise: Christ is a celestial counterpart of that tree, an apple-tree of which the angels and redeemed mankind can taste greedily and joyfully and without guilt in the mystical love-union. Christ is also the one who on earth can wake human beings out of the 'greater slumber' of death by a single word. Nonetheless, in its specific aspects Dante's experience diverges from that of the transfiguration. For him the word 'Rise' is not the beginning of dispelling his anxiety but of arousing it. Where the apostles, calmed, at once saw their master again in familiar garb, Dante has a pang of fear that he has been left: 'Where is Beatrice?'

Matelda's reply sets the scene for the second showing: the gryphon goes heavenward with the blessed company and its heavenly music, but Beatrice sits on the bare earth, at the root of the tree, guarding the chariot.[23] Dante's *daimôn*, the divinest aspect of his being, belongs with that music and with the heavenly ones. As Beatrice now promises him: 'endlessly you'll be with me a citizen / of that Rome of which Christ is a Roman' (101–2). But that does not mean that his present ordeals are over. In the previous line Beatrice had said 'Here for a little while you'll be a woodlander'; and while this might seem a reassuring word – 'here' meaning 'the earthly paradise' – the 'little while' foreshadows the phrase of Christ that Beatrice will adopt at the opening of the next canto: 'In a little while you will no longer see me.' Instead, what Dante will see now in vision are violent, sordid, monstrous things; yet, just as the angel in John's Apocalypse repeatedly urges the apostle to set all he sees down aright, so Dante is urged by Beatrice to record truthfully all that he will now behold – even the terrifying showings that signify the absence, or the powerlessness, of Beatrice herself. Can she guard and protect the tree which is Dante, and the chariot that conveys Dante's soul? And – in the macrocosm – can Dante, strengthened by the grace and revelation that Beatrice embodies for him, guard the tree of justice and the chariot that conveys power in the Christian world? The answers suggested by the vision seem deeply negative.

(iii) Eagle and Chariot

The eagle swoops down and shatters both the tree and the chariot. With the eagle Dante has again chosen a symbol replete with microcosmic and macrocosmic meaning. I shall signal only a few of the most relevant contexts for each. The eagle can suggest to Dante a poet of surpassing genius: Homer is 'that lord of the highest song / who flies above the others like an eagle' (*Inf.* IV 95f).[24] In *De vulgari eloquentia* (II iv, 10f), the poets 'who are loved by God and raised by ardent virtue to the aether are those whom Vergil calls the sons of the gods', whereas inadequately endowed poets 'are like geese trying to imitate the eagle'. The gryphon, be it recalled, has eagle's wings. The final cantos of *Purgatorio* are pervaded by personal images of flight. Just as the gryphon flies upwards (*suso*) with the blessed company (XXXII 89), so Beatrice, rebuking Dante, charges that he has neglected his capacity for flying: he should have mounted upwards (*Ben ti dovevi ... levar suso*: XXXI 55f), his wings should not have been weighed down by other delights (*Non ti dovea gravar le penne in giuso . . .*: 58). The allusions to Dante's power of flight must also, I believe, contain an implicit play upon his name: Dante is one of the *aligeri*, literally 'the winged'; for him in a special sense to be true to his name is to be true to his nature. As a mature man, Beatrice tells him, he should have been a full-fledged bird, one of the *pennuti*, who are not easily ensnared (XXXI 61f).[25] This image, biblical in origin (*Prov.* I: 17), is equally applied by Dante in the public sphere, when the 'most accursed Florentines' are seen as captive birds, unwilling to join the 'winged ones' (*pennati*) and be delivered by Henry VII (*Ep.* VI I, 21).

With Henry we reach the macrocosmic eagle-images. The eagle of the Roman banners, emblem of Rome's imperial power, 'the sign that made the Romans awe-inspiring to the world' (*Par.* XIX 101f), is alluded to many times in the *Commedia*. In Dante's political letters, Henry VII's advance upon Lombardy is heralded as that of 'the sublime eagle descending like lightning' (*Ep.* V II); when, 'as successor of Caesar and Augustus', Henry crossed the Apennines,[26] he brought back the *veneranda signa Tarpeia* (*Ep.*

VII 5) – the standards of the Roman eagle, 'the bird of God' (*Par.* VI 4).

Yet the eagle can also carry associations of political might in its destructive aspect. In Ezekiel, whom Dante had mentioned as a source for his image of the living creatures in the procession (*Purg.* XXIX 99ff), an allegory of a tree, a vine, that was planted by an eagle (Babylon), concludes with the threat of another eagle – Egypt – shattering this plantation: 'Will not the eagle break its roots and snap up the fruit, so that all the new leaves will wither when they shoot?' (17: 9). In this allegory itself Rabanus Maurus – one of the theologians of Dante's second circle in the sphere of the sun (*Par.* XII 139) – sees not only a political meaning, 'concerning princes and a royal line', but also a microcosmic one and a divine one. To support the personal meaning he cites Isaiah (40: 31): 'those who hope in the Lord will renew their strength, they will put out wings like eagles'; but then Rabanus goes on: 'He who says "I shall shatter cities ..." [Is. 10: 13] is now described in the persona of the eagle.'[27] Thus Ezekiel's allegory, especially in the light of Rabanus' comments, may illuminate the complexities latent at the beginning of Dante's second showing, when 'the bird of Jove' lacerates the bark, flowers and leaves of the tree (XXXII 109–14, cited above). The eagle goes on to attack Dante's chariot:

> e ferì 'l carro di tutta sua forza;
> ond' el piegò come nave in fortuna,
> vinta da l'onda, or da poggia, or da orza.
>   Poscia vidi avventarsi ne la cuna
> del triunfal veiculo una volpe
> che d'ogne pasto buon parea digiuna;
>   ma, riprendendo lei di laide colpe,
> la donna mia la volse in tanta futa
> quanto sofferser l'ossa sanza polpe.
>   Poscia per indi ond' era pria venuta,
> l'aguglia vidi scender giù ne l'arca
> del carro e lasciar lei di sé pennuta;
>   e qual esce di cuor che si rammarca,
> tal voce uscì del cielo e cotal disse:
> 'O navicella mia, com' mal se' carca!'

> and it struck the chariot with all its force,
> so that it reeled like a ship in a tempest,
> overcome now from leeward, now from windward, by the
>   waves.

> Then I saw swoop down upon the cradle
> of the triumphal chariot a fox
> that appeared starved of all good food;
>   but, reproaching it for dirty crimes,
> my lady put it to such flight
> as its fleshless bones allowed.
>   Then, from the place from where it had come before,
> I saw the eagle descend into the ark
> of the chariot and leave it covered with its feathers;
>   and, as if coming from a sorrowing heart,
> I heard a voice emerge from heaven and say
> 'Oh my little ship, how evilly you are laden!'   (115–29)

In Canto XXIX, the macrocosmic connotations of the chariot had been those of secular Roman power, together with the premonition of the chariot's doom:

> Non che Roma di carro così bello
> rallegrasse Affricano, o vero Augusto,
> ma quel del Sol saria pover con ello;
>   quel del Sol che, svïando, fu combusto
> per l'orazion de la Terra devota,
> quando fu Giove arcanamente giusto.

> Rome indeed could not have gladdened Scipio
> or even Augustus with so fair a chariot;
> that of the Sun himself would be poor beside it,
>   that of the Sun which, straying, was burnt up
> because of the devout prayers of the Earth,
> when, in mysterious fashion, Jove was just.   (115–20)

Phaethon burning up the earth, in his reckless driving of the chariot of his father the Sun-god, epitomises the overweening misuse of power, which provokes a divine nemesis. But it is of just such a misuse of power that Dante accused the Italian cardinals (*Ep.* XI 6), who in their steering of 'the chariot of the Bride (*currus Sponse*)' are 'no other than the false charioteer Phaethon'. In this letter the chariot is an allegory for the Church.[28] This meaning is particularly important too in the context of Dante's present vision: it is reinforced by the superimposed image of the tempest-tossed ship, which – because of the storm described in Luke 8 – had been, traditionally, the ship Ecclesia.

Yet the 'little ship' (as we have seen, pp. 21–4) is also, metaphorically, Dante's poetic imagination or genius – *la navicella del mio ingegno*. Hence in this showing the inner and outer meanings interpenetrate. What Dante sees is, in the first instance, a visionary counterpart to the reproaches Beatrice had levelled against him: he has not flown heavenwards, he has squandered his poetic gifts, he himself has both impaired the chariot of his soul and sullied it by shedding the feathers that should have helped him fly aloft, feathers that instead now weigh the 'light chariot' badly down. At the same time, this image gives rise to further associations – of a perversion of powers in the outer world, one that to Dante appeared historically specific and crucial. When Dante says that the eagle's plumage was 'offered perhaps with healthy and benign intent' (XXXII 137f), the words significantly parallel those used in both *Monarchia* and *Paradiso* about the Donation of Constantine.[29] Emperor Constantine, the Roman eagle, 'made himself Greek': he betrayed his mission of government, when (as the text of the Donation, forged probably towards 800, claimed) he made over to Pope Silvester I the temporal sovereignty of the western empire. Thereby Constantine 'yielded to the Shepherd' of the Church an *imperium* that the Church should never possess, 'beneath a good intention that produced bad fruit' (*Par.* XX 56f). The second book of the *Monarchia* ends with an impassioned outcry against that wrecking of order: 'Oh happy world, oh glorious Rome, if that enfeebler of your imperial power had never been born, or if his pious intent had never deceived him!' Thus the surreal image of the chariot covered with feathers suggests Dante's recognition of an inner degradation, and at the same time the degradation of the Church, through assuming an earthly might that was the negation of her spiritual destiny.

The fox that tries to fling itself on the chariot is not perhaps susceptible of an equally precise inner and outer interpretation, but the connotations – of enmity and cunning, and rapacity born of desperation – are clear. In the Song of Songs (2:15), the Bride implores: 'Catch the foxes for us, the little foxes that make havoc of the vineyards, for our vineyards are in flower.' On the traditional inner interpretation, where the Bride is Anima, the foxes signify 'perverse powers and the wickedness of demons', that 'make havoc of the flower of virtues and the fruit of faith within the soul'; on the outer, where she is Ecclesia, 'we can understand the foxes as the perverse teachers of heretical dogmas, who ... destroy the vineyard of the Lord'. Thus Origen,[30] who, by offering an inner and outer reading in conjunction, laid down some of

the main lines of interpretation for the Middle Ages. But on two
occasions the primary associations of the fox for Dante lay with his
native region: in his letter to Henry VII, Florence is a stinking
little fox (*vulpecula fetoris istius*), and in the invective of the judge
Guido del Duca (*Purg.* XIV), the river Arno 'finds foxes so full of
deceit, they do not fear that any device (*ingegno*) can catch them'.
It is possible that the word *ingegno* – here used concretely for a
cunning trap – carries reverberations of another sense: the poetic
ingegno with which Dante catches at injustice and deceit. At all
events Beatrice, guarding the chariot, is able to ward off the
dangers of the fox: it is not a hostile attack from without, but the
greater danger of the seemingly benign feathering, that leaves her
helpless.

Both eagle and fox penetrate as far as the inner part of the
chariot: literally the fox swoops down upon the chariot's cradle
(*cuna*), the eagle descends into its ark (*arca*). Are these words
used, as commentators affirm, simply as synonyms for 'interior', or
is there further poetic design? To me the first expression suggests
that the chariot cradles the newborn – or newly reborn – soul, the
second that it carries something holy, a divine image, as the ark of
God, with which the destiny of Israel was linked, was borne and
protected by a *carro*.[31]

(iv) Dragon, Giant, and Prostitute

As the vision continues, some moments come very near to apocalyptic descriptions in John; towards the close, however, the details
are again very much Dante's own. –

> Then it seemed to me that the earth opened
> between the two wheels, and I saw emerge from it a dragon
> that thrust its tail up through the chariot,
>   and, like a wasp that withdraws its sting,
> drawing the malignant tail back to itself,
> it dragged some of the chariot's base away, and made off,
>   slinking.
>   What remained was covered, as fertile earth
> is covered by weeds, by the [eagle's] plumage, offered
> perhaps with healthy and benign intent,
>   and covered over by it were
> the one wheel and the other, and the shaft, in less
> time than a sigh holds the lips apart.

> Transformed in this way, the holy structure
> put forth heads upon its parts,
> three on the shaft and one at each corner.
>   The first three were horned like oxen,
> but the four had each a single horn on the forehead:
> never yet was such a monster seen.
>   Secure as a fortress on a high mountain,
> sitting upon it, a loosely-dressed prostitute
> appeared to me, her eyebrows signalling readiness;
>   and, as if to prevent her being taken from him,
> I saw a giant right at her side,
> and they kissed each other many a time.
>   But because she turned her lustful roving eye
> towards me, that ferocious lover
> whipped her from head to foot;
>   then, full of suspicion and cruel in his anger,
> he loosed the monster and dragged it through the wood,
> so far that he made the wood itself bar from my sight
>   the prostitute and the strange prodigy.   (130–60)

In John's Apocalypse the dragon, which is explicitly identified with the devil (12: 9), itself has seven heads and ten horns. 'Its tail dragged a third part of the stars from the sky' (12: 4). This phrase clearly lies behind Dante's evocation of the dragon thrusting its tail through the chariot and dragging away a part of its base. Two of the mystic theologians celebrated in the sphere of the sun, who wrote commentaries on the Apocalypse, may illuminate the connotations of Dante's image. For Joachim of Fiore, the body of the devil or dragon 'is nothing other than the multitude of wicked human beings';[32] Richard of St Victor, interpreting the dragging away of the stars, comes even closer to a microcosmic interpretation:

Its tail takes a third of the stars away: the devil seduces the condemned part even of those souls who remain aloft in their way of life like the stars of heaven, and who are seen to shed light on others through good works. When it cannot do so by open savageness, it does so by hidden fraudulence, which is figured in the tail.[33]

These comments encourage us to look in Dante's image not for an external aggressor, such as Mahomet or Antichrist, as many commentators have proposed, but more pertinently for the enemy within, who can at times seduce even a shining soul. Dante's comparison of the dragon withdrawing its tail to a wasp retracting its sting intimates that it is in a 'little world' that such events may take place. It is Dante's chariot that grows monstrous through the poet's misuse of his eagle wings, even if by implication this also reflects a vision of the larger chariot, that conveys all the souls of Christendom, becoming monstrous through having been decked with alien plumage.

John in his vision saw three distinct monsters with seven heads and ten horns – first the dragon, than a beast ascending from the sea (13: 1ff), and finally (17: 3ff) the scarlet beast ridden by the prostitute, Babylon. This last image is plainly dominant in Dante's mind as he describes a prostitute seated on the chariot-turned-monster. But the idea that it is a chariot which suddenly becomes alive, growing heads and horns, is entirely his own.

In Dante's outburst against simoniac popes in *Inferno* XIX, it was they, he said, who were figured in the prostitute of St John's vision, the woman seen whoring with kings. This has led many commentators to see the prostitute on the chariot as the papacy, or as a particular pope, such as Boniface VIII. The giant – of whom there is no trace in John's Apocalypse – is then often identified with the king of France, Philip the Fair. Yet such historical identifications here lead to implausibilities, not to say absurdities. Even if Philip's legates imprisoned Pope Boniface at Anagni, it is wildly improbable that Dante should have allegorised this by the image of a giant whipping his beloved whore from head to foot. Moreover, the reason for the whipping, in the vision, is that the giant is jealous of Dante, at whom the woman gazes lustfully. The notion that Philip the Fair should have been jealous of Dante seems wholly far-fetched. To overcome this difficulty, commentators have resorted to an equally far-fetched explanation: Dante, whom the prostitute tries to seduce by her ogling, does not mean Dante the poet or the character, but (to cite Bosco–Reggio) 'other sovereigns, like Emperor Albert of Austria or Frederick, King of Sicily; others think that Dante symbolises the Christian populace, and in particular the Italian'.[34] No evidence is given as to how or why Dante should here stand for any of these; it is the last infirmity of an allegorical reading that simply cannot match the poetry.

Even if the prostitute may still, in this vision, carry connotations – from *Inferno* XIX – of popes who have prostituted themselves to kings out of avarice, and even if the giant might conjure up a king who can treat the pope as his whore, it seems to me most unlikely that Dante's scene can be interpreted as a veiled account of a specific historical situation. Once more we must return to what is central, the personal meaning, which, while it can at moments suggest hidden comparisons of a political nature, cannot be forced systematically into a mould of political allegory. Dante's departure from St John's imagery in these final moments itself indicates that we should reckon with a change of poetic focus: we are back with the inner drama, which here (as C. G. Hardie was the first to claim) must assuredly relate to the fantasy at the climax of Dante's canzone *Così nel mio parlar*. If the 'fair stone' (*bella petra*) who torments Dante by her hardness and indifference, who seems to use her power deliberately to make him suffer, could feel the painful longing that Dante feels for her 'in the hot abyss (*nel caldo borro*)' —

> . . . tosto griderei: 'Io vi soccorro';
> e fare'l volentier, sí come quelli
> che ne' biondi capelli
> ch'Amor per consumarmi increspa e dora
> metterei mano, e piacere'le allora.
>
> S'io avessi le belle trecce prese,
> che fatte son per me scudiscio e ferza,
> pigliandole anzi terza,
> con esse passerei vespero e squille:
> e non sarei pietoso né cortese,
> anzi farei com'orso quando scherza;
> e se Amor me ne sferza,
> io mi vendicherei di piú di mille.
> Ancor ne li occhi, ond'escon le faville
> che m'infiammano il cor, ch'io porto anciso,
> guarderei presso e fiso,
> per vendicar lo fuggir che mi face;
> e poi le renderei con amor pace.
>
> . . . I would soon cry out 'I'll comfort you';
> I'd do it willingly, and thus, into
> the golden hair
> that Love has waved and gilded to consume me
> I'd plunge my hand, and then please her at last.
>
> Once I had taken hold of those fair tresses
> that have become a whip and lash for me,
> I'd catch them as day breaks and spend
> vespers and compline in their company.
> And I'd not show pity or courtesy,
> no, I would play in jest as a bear does;
> and if Love takes those locks to whip me,

I'd avenge myself with more than a thousand blows.
What's more, I'd gaze into her eyes
that unleash sparks that make my dead heart blaze,
with close, fixed gaze,
to take revenge on her elusiveness;
and then with making love I'd grant her peace.[35]

The relation between the two contexts seems to me profound in its differences as in its similarities. In the song, Dante is in imagination a ferocious lover, yet the whole scene is one of violent love-making, that brings the seemingly cruel woman, as well as himself, sexual release and fulfilment. In the vision in *Purgatorio*, the giant, possessive and brutish, punishes the prostitute for looking at another man – Dante – and drags her out of his sight. There is no suggestion that the prostitute finds sexual satisfaction in her whipping. In a word, what Dante had imagined as sensually exciting, with himself as protagonist, he now sees in another perspective, distanced and ugly. The erotic dream of the canzone here becomes a nightmare, the unyielding *petra* becomes the prostitute who yields to anyone, the lover whose chastising was playful and voluptuous becomes a monstrously large, sordid bully. The chariot of Dante's soul had entered the earthly paradise crowned by the radiance of Beatrice; here suddenly, having become battered and grotesque, the chariot is crowned, not by the relentless, tantalising *bella petra*, but by a woman who is first brazen and then pathetic. It is hard to see this conclusion of the showings as anything but a mirror held up to Dante's nature, revealing the desires in which he had been disloyal to Beatrice's memory in a light very different from that in which they had previously appeared to him.

(v) *Modicum, et vos videbitis me*

The final canto of *Purgatorio* traces a movement from sorrow to joy that reflects in little the movement of the whole *Commedia*. At first the seven maidens, the attendants of Beatrice – who have been shown to us, iridescently, as virtues, nymphs, and stars (in the microcosm we might link them with the potentialities for virtue within Dante's soul) – lament the debasement and ruin of the chariot, in the words of the Psalm that bewails the pollution of the Temple and the sacking of Jerusalem.[36] They chant the Latin verses of this Psalm antiphonally – their threnody takes on a ritual quality. Beatrice's sorrow over the chariot's fate is evoked even more intensely: it is almost the tragic transformation of Mary at the foot of the cross.

Then, in one of the most daring of the many symbolic links that Dante forges between Beatrice and Christ, she addresses the maidens in the words of Christ to his disciples before the passion (the retention of the Latin text unchanged emphasising its hieratic, divine aspect to the full): 'In a little while you will no longer see me, and then a little while later you will see me again.' The whole of the context in John's Gospel (16: 16ff) bears upon Dante's intentions here and helps to structure the remainder of the canto. Like Dante, Christ's disciples ponder these phrases, yet do not dare to ask their meaning. Beatrice tells Dante that she sees the unvoiced questions in his mind, just as Christ tells this to his disciples. And neither Beatrice nor Christ, though perceiving their listeners' bewilderment, meets it with a direct explanation: both speak oracularly, and are aware of doing so. And as Christ at last promises to relent:

> I have been telling you all this in metaphors;
> the hour is coming
> when I shall no longer speak to you in metaphors
> but tell you about the Father in plain words   (16: 25) –

so too Beatrice:

> Veramente oramai saranno nude
> le mie parole, quanto converrassi
> quelle scovrire a la tua vista rude.

> But truly, from now on my words
> will be naked, as far as shall befit
> uncovering them to your untutored sight.   (XXXIII 100–2)

Beatrice symbolically assumes Christ's part in her own bringing of revelation and redemption to Dante. Essentially it is Dante (or the virtues latent in him) whom she addresses with Christ's words. She will remain in heaven and he must return to earth, remembering and recording her revealed words: in that 'little while' which Dante has left to live, he will not see her, but then – as she has promised – he will see her again and be with her endlessly (XXXII 101–2). In just this way Christ, in the episode in John, promises the disciples a time of weeping followed by a time when 'I shall see you again, and your hearts will be full of joy, and that joy no one shall take from you' (16: 22).

But first, as Beatrice tells Dante (XXXIII 31ff), he must cast off
fear and shame: it is these that impair his clarity of vision and make
him speak like a dreamer. And she continues:

> Sappi che 'l vaso che 'l serpente ruppe,
> fu e non è.

> Know that the vessel which the serpent broke
> was and now is not.

These apocalyptic words link in the first place with the thought
that preceded: the vessel – the chariot ravaged by the dragon – *was*
something Dante had cause to be afraid and ashamed of, while it
was there. The lines, that is, bear out the interior range of reference of the episode. At the same time, Beatrice's choice of the
actual words that occur three times in Apocalypse 17, used of the
beast the prostitute rides, allow us both to specify further and to
retrace the macrocosmic associations that these words might have
carried for Dante. The angel tells John: 'The beast you have seen
was (*fuit*) and now is not; he is destined to rise from the abyss and
will go (*ibit*) into destruction; and those who inhabit the earth will
marvel . . . seeing the beast that was (*erat*) and now is not . . . And
the beast that was (*erat*) and now is not . . . is going (*vadit*) into
destruction.' The tenses indicate not instantaneous death but a
process extending over a course of time, and indeed the angel
expounds the heads and horns in terms not only of the hills of
Rome but of a succession of Roman emperors with their satellite
kings.[37] Similarly, we may surmise that Dante, even while using
the more decisive 'was' (*fu*, not *era*), thought in terms of a destructive process, a succession of events rather than a single event, in
which the monstrous heads of 'the chariot of the Bride' call forth
an unsparing divine vengeance.[38]

The form this vengeance will take is evoked in the renowned
and much-debated prophecy of Beatrice that follows:

> Non sarà tutto tempo sanza reda
> l'aguglia che lasciò le penne al carro,
> per che divenne mostro e poscia preda;
>   ch'io veggio certamente, e però il narro,
> a darne tempo già stelle propinque,
> secure d'ogn' intoppo e d'ogne sbarro,
>   nel quale un cinquecento e diece e cinque,
> messo di Dio, anciderà la fuia
> con quel gigante che con lei delinque.

> Not for all time shall be without an heir
> the eagle which left its feathers on the chariot,
> through which that became monster and then prey;
>   for I see with certainty, and therefore tell it,
> stars are already near to giving us a time –
> stars safe from every hitch and every hindrance –
>   in which a five hundred, ten and five,
> messenger of God, will kill the thievish woman
> together with the giant who sins with her.   (37–45)

To consider the outward meaning briefly first. I have no new suggestions about either the numerical conundrum or the identity of the promised deliverer. Dante clearly knows that his readers will be tempted to speculate, that they may even feel convinced he is inviting them to speculate; nonetheless, he has with great art seen to it that the hidden meaning should remain, in substance, hidden.

Commentators have not, perhaps, been aware of the logical implications of attaching specific historical meanings to the prostitute and the giant in the previous canto. If one assumes that these represent a particular pope (such as Boniface VIII, or Clement V) and a particular ruler (such as Philip the Fair), this has drastic consequences for the meaning of Beatrice's prophecy. She must then be saying that a future emperor (an heir to the Roman eagle – Constantine – who by his Donation feathered the chariot of the Church) will murder both that pope and that ruler. If the prostitute, as others have claimed, represented the whole Roman Curia, this emperor–saviour would here be imagined as indulging in a mass-murder, a veritable bloodbath. If, on the other hand, notwithstanding the violent, dramatic expressions in the prophecy ('will kill the thievish woman / together with the giant who sins with her'), we assume this to refer in a more general way to the deliverer's extirpating what is evil in ecclesiastical and secular government – and this seems *prima facie* more reasonable than the murderous reading – it has the important poetic consequence that the prostitute and giant cannot after all be identified with specific persons or groups of persons. It would be impossible to accept such an identification in Canto XXXII and then simply reject what it entails in Canto XXXIII.

Dante believed ardently in the coming of an imperial saviour, and continued to hope for one even after the death of Henry VII (1313) had dashed his earlier hopes. To attempt to make the external prophecy here more specific (whether by referring it to

Henry VII himself or by proposing another candidate) is to pass unverifiably beyond Dante's text, supplying details that the poet has chosen not to supply.

Yet something more can be said about the inner associations that this prophecy holds for Dante. If, as I argued, the eagle leaving its feathers in the chariot evokes a transgression – a failure to fly aloft – on Dante's part, then Beatrice can well say, with certainty, that Dante's own destined redemption is now at hand. For she herself is that messenger of God who is bringing about Dante's salvation, and who can dispel the demonic phantasms – giant and prostitute – that had grown out of Dante's earlier sensual reverie, in *Così nel mio parlar*.

This brings us to the question – as difficult and as often disputed as the prophecy – of the precise nature of the guilt of which Dante, through Beatrice's accusations, accuses himself. When Beatrice tells Dante that the tree in the earthly paradise 'has now been twice robbed', it is probable that she is conjoining Dante's guilt (the eagle savaging the tree instead of winging heavenward) with the primordial guilt of Adam.[39] But her words become increasingly dark, her language almost a parody of the 'closed' style of the troubadours (*trobar clus*):

> 'And if the vain thoughts surrounding your mind
> had not been water of Elsa,
> and the delight in them a Pyramus to the mulberry,
>   by such great attributes alone
> you'd recognise from the tree and the prohibition,
> in the moral sense, the justice of God.
>   But since I see you in your intellect
> fashioned of stone and, thus petrified, darkened,
> so that the light of my words dazzles you,
>   I want you still to bear them away within you,
> if not in writing, then at least in image,
> just as the staff decked with palm is carried home.'
>   And I said: 'Even as wax, pressed by a seal,
> does not change the imprinted form,
> so my brain is now sealed by you.
>   But why do your longed-for words
> fly so far above my sight,
> which loses them the more, the more it seeks them?'
>   'So that you may recognise that school,' she said,
> 'which you followed, and may see how its teaching
> can follow my words,

and may see that your way is as far
from the divine way as the heaven which races
highest is discordant with the earth.'   (67–90)

Beatrice speaks arcanely in order to startle Dante into recognising the inadequacy of his previous *via*, and its remoteness from
God. Her riddling words pungently bring home to Dante a failure
on his path of intellectual insight, and, implicitly, on that of conscience. If vain thoughts had not encrusted his mind (the waters of
the stream Elsa were noted for their lime-deposits), and if delight
in such thoughts had not stained his mind (as the dying Pyramus'
blood, in the legend, stained the mulberry that had been white
before – the image brings out the fatefulness of such staining),[40]
then the attributes of the tree would have revealed the moral
meaning to him: from its stature, and its growing more abundantly as it nears heaven, Dante could have recognised in the tree a
figure of divine justice. Instead, his understanding is stony, petri-
fied, and hence unable to comprehend what Beatrice says. It is not
her utterance but his mind that is dark – her words merely seem
dark to him because they daze him with a brightness that he
cannot face. It seems to me difficult to interpret Beatrice's allusions to Dante's 'petrifaction' as anything but caustic reminders of
his attachment to the *bella petra*, the woman who had inspired *Così
nel mio parlar* and the other 'stony lyrics (*rime petrose*)'.[41] It is as if
Beatrice were saying, Dante had come to belong so much to that
petra that he is no longer open to herself. At most, she continues,
he can bring back to earth with him some vestiges of what she now
tells him, a reminder only of the full reality, as a palmer returns
with his staff to remind him of his pilgrimage.

From *Purgatorio* XXX onwards Dante had introduced numerous
hints of how his way had gone 'far from the divine way', and hence
far from Beatrice. In her reproaches, for instance, she says: 'he
took himself away from me and gave himself to another ... following false images of good ... He fell so low that all means for
his salvation were already useless, save to show him the people
who are lost' (XXX 126ff). Equally, Dante accuses himself: 'Present
things with their false pleasure turned my steps, as soon as your
face was hidden' (XXXI 34ff), and she, returning to the attack,
telling Dante how he should have mounted higher, adds: 'No
young girl (*pargoletta*) or other novelty with such brief use should
have weighed down your wings' (XXXI 58ff). I would follow the
scholars who see in the choice of the word *pargoletta* an allusion by

Beatrice to Dante's *pargoletta* group of love-songs,[42] and hence a reproach that by composing these he showed himself unfaithful to her memory.

However, even if the passages concerning Dante's guilt and remorse were adduced in full and analysed meticulously, there still remains something – I believe deliberately – secret and elusive about them that does not endure our question. As with the prophecy, it is as if Dante were challenging us to conjecture beyond the data he has given us, yet also tantalising us by providing so many hints and so few fixities. Within certain limits, we are free to interpret.[43] We might suppose, for instance, that Dante's remorse dwelt principally on the fervid fantasy enjoyed – at least in thought – with his *bella petra*, or again, on his having been tempted to see a *pargoletta* in the same angelic, celestial light as Beatrice. Similarly, Beatrice's references to 'that school … which you followed', a school that cannot follow her heavenly teaching, could lead us to infer Dante's remorse for some of the more worldly philosophical elements in his *Convivio*, or perhaps for a certain disingenuousness concealed in that work, in the sleight-of-hand by which the gentle Florentine lady who consoled him after Beatrice's death was transformed into Filosofia. Yet we should be clear, with these or any other attempts to detail Dante's estrangement from Beatrice and the reasons of his repentance, that we are to some extent stepping beyond the premises the poet has supplied us; that, however hard it may be to resist stepping beyond in this way, it also, inevitably, becomes a matter of colouring our own Dante-portrait – and the colours we bring to it are primarily our own intellectual and moral preconceptions.

The allusions to Dante's guilt do not cease in the remainder of Canto XXXIII, yet the tone alters. There is no longer a trace of grief, bitterness, or tormentedness. With Dante's answer to Beatrice,

> 'Non mi ricorda
> ch'i' stranïasse me già mai da voi,
> né honne coscienza che rimorda'

> 'I don't remember
> that I ever estranged myself from you –
> I am aware of nothing that stirs remorse'   (91–3)

the atmosphere lightens. The change can perhaps be best evoked in musical terms – as if from a movement *andante con moto* we passed to an *allegro*, in which the tempo gradually quickens, till at last,

with Dante's exhilarated address to the reader (136ff), it becomes
molto vivace.

Beatrice's answer (beginning with the colloquial *E* – 'And if you
can't remember...') reminds Dante that he has drunk of the
stream Lethe: his oblivion itself betrays 'a fault in your will, intent
elsewhere'. Yet now she delivers her rebuke smiling (95). Dante
goes on to invent a whole minor scene of gentle, lighthearted
by-play: when he asks the source of the streams in the earthly paradise, Beatrice directs him to Matelda, who answers that she has
told Dante these things already – 'and I am sure the water of Lethe
has not hidden them from him'. And there is a touch of humour as
well as of compassion in Beatrice's reply:

> 'Forse maggior cura,
> che spesse volte la memoria priva,
> fatt' ha la mente sua ne li occhi oscura.'

> 'Perhaps a greater care,
> which many a time bereaves the memory,
> has made his mind dark in the eyes' beholding.'   (124–6)

The action of the canto ends with Matelda guiding Dante – and
afterwards the still-attendant Statius – to the stream Eunoe, to
'revive his stunned power to recall'.[44] But the canto itself continues with a buoyant rhetorical flourish. Dante the poet, the now
wholly confident craftsman, bids farewell in a knowing, mis-
chievous use of aposiopesis: he would sing far more about the
draught of Eunoe,

> ma perché piene son tutte le carte
> ordite a questa cantica seconda,
> non mi lascia più ir lo fren de l'arte.

> but since all the sheets are full
> that are destined for this second *cantica*,
> the curb of art does not let me go further.   (139–41)

Yet he still has space for four more lines – simple and lucent – that
gather up implications of two central images from the visions that
had preceded and infuse further meaning:

> Io ritornai da la santissima onda
> rifatto sì come piante novelle
> rinovellate di novella fronda,
>   puro e disposto a salire a le stelle.

> I returned from the most holy wave
> remade, as new plants are

renewed with new fronds,
  pure and disposed to mount up to the stars.

The keynote is the regeneration expressed in the triple
wordplay: *novelle, rinovellate, novella*. Dante, we could say, has
become the renewed tree; and behind his new readiness to mount
to the stars we can still discern a last trace of the chariot-image –
though with a difference: the only 'vehicle' Dante now needs for
his heavenly ascent is the guiding presence of Beatrice. So too,
since he has drunk of the stream Eunoe, Dante's memory is again
unerring. The phantasmagoria seen in the earthly paradise are not
forgotten, but they have lost their terror. The tree is no longer
ravaged by the eagle, the chariot no longer helpless and bestial.
They are made new, as Dante is made new.

Even if particular aspects of the interpretation here proposed
are open to question and prompt different readings, what is
central to my argument is that, for the closing cantos of *Purgatorio*, the concept of the sustained hidden comparison – Geoffrey of
Vinsauf's *collatio occulta* – is critically illuminating and historically
appropriate as a guiding principle. Insofar as they are approached
as *collatio occulta*, these cantos reveal themselves as among the most
poetically fertile in the *Commedia*. If their basic structure were that
of straightforward allegory – if, as is generally supposed, Dante
were here dressing some of his known thoughts about the history
of the Church, and the role of secular and religious power, in allegorical garb – we should be right to see in his 'apocalypse' an
oddity unworthy of his finest poetic powers. We should be right
to feel that it was pointless for Dante to repeat things, which he
tells us lucidly elsewhere, in the form of elaborate, intellectually
unnecessary enigmas. But if, applying Geoffrey of Vinsauf's conception, we see the fluctuations of inner and outer meaning as
essential, then the enigmas appear in a new light. Far from being
strained variations on ideas that could also be expressed 'straight',
they can be seen as nodal points in the poem – knots of concentra-
tion where inner and outer significance are tied together. Tree and
chariot and eagle, dragon and giant and prostitute, not only
gather up inherited meanings: they generate a fuller meaning that
embraces 'within and without, here and there' – the subjective and
the universal. Because in Dante these images are authentically subjective, they can evoke the universal with an awesome power that
writers of treatises cannot match. Imaginatively and intellectually,
the phantasmagoria are a triumph.

4
The First Circle in the Solar Heaven

(i) Knowledge and Love

The tenth canto of *Paradiso* is the first of five in which Dante and Beatrice move in the sphere of the sun. They rise into it early in this canto, and only in the later part of XIV do they find themselves in the next heaven, that of Mars. As the physical sun is the source of light and warmth in the cosmos, so the divine, intelligible sun, the sun of the angels, diffuses the light of knowledge and the warmth of love. The relations between knowledge and love are made manifest in *Paradiso* X: they are exemplified within the godhead, in the ordering of the heavens, in Dante and Beatrice, in a host of images drawn from earthly phenomena, and – most comprehensively – in a circle of twelve lights: twelve radiant, fiery souls that show their power to know and love inseparably.

The activities of knowing and loving come together in contemplation. In medieval Aristotelian terms, the knower becomes one with what he knows, even as the lover becomes one with what he loves. The canto reveals this in every aspect of existence. We can see it, for a start, by observing how certain key expressions – words at the heart of the canto's meaning – create this possibility.

The opening word, *guardando*, is the first of nearly a score that evoke gazing, beholding, contemplating. The Might of God the Father gazes into his Son; the reader is asked to let his own gaze follow Dante's; the divine craftsman never takes his eyes away from his art. Dante is brought to new heights of seeing, encountering light more intense than the sun's; Beatrice's eyes, filled with laughter, recall Dante from total immersion in that light. Later, Dante's sight accompanies the words of his mentor in this heaven, Thomas Aquinas; two lights in Thomas' circle are celebrated explicitly for their power of seeing; and Dante follows with 'the eye of the mind', at last perceiving fully the harmony of that 'glorious wheel'.

But the divine gaze at the opening of the canto is an expression of love, a breathing of love: the Holy Spirit is literally the loving breath the Father breathes into the Son, which the Son inhales and breathes again into the Father. This divine exemplar of reciprocity leaves its trace in the many words of loving and of breathing in the canto. The beautiful word *vagheggiare* – to gaze amorously – which unites seeing and loving, occurs twice: the reader is bidden (10) to look lovingly at the divine artificer's work, just as (92) the crown of twelve lights look lovingly at her whom they encircle, Beatrice. Dante's surge of love in his first moment of cognition (59) momentarily eclipses even his beloved. The twelve luminaries are 'ardent suns (*ardenti soli*)' (76), their breath is an 'ardent breath (*l'ardente spiro*)' (130). Thomas, who commends Dante for the growing splendour of love that multiplies in him, imparts knowledge to Dante, but by an imparting that is itself a loving act. In the last ten lines of the canto – where the harmony of the glorious wheel is seen in the perfectly accorded motions and sounds of a clock – the keynote once more is love.

Love expresses itself in the two gestures, breathing and circling. The one metaphor is ultimately Platonic, the other Aristotelian, in inspiration. An erotic epigram ascribed to Plato, of which a Latin version was current in the medieval West, evokes a kiss as a trans-fusion of breaths and thereby of souls: 'as I guide the sweet flower of the breath (*florem spiritus*) upon its course, my soul ... races to my lips, and into the soft open lips of my beloved, striving to leap across'.[1] The circling motion is a more serene one – it is, in terms of Aristotelian metaphysics, the most harmonious and perfect, the aptest physical approximation to the divine.[2]

The loving exchange of breath between Father and Son in the trinity is shown as heavenly reward to the family of spirits in this sphere (49–51); the most beautiful flame within it, Solomon, 'breathes with such love (*spira di tale amor*)' (110), and three other flames, too, are noted for the glow that their breathing kindles. To these I shall return. For the moment I shall add only a speculation: does perhaps the course of the physical sun, which 'was revolving through spirals (*si girava per le spire*)' (32), evoke not only the astronomical motion that Ptolemy ascribed to it, but also, by a word-play – *spira/spirare* – a movement that is the visible counter-part to the breathing love in the divine sunlight?

With the concept of revolving (*si girava*) we are already with the cyclic motions that express love in yet another way. The divine

Might, we learn at the opening, orders whatever revolves (*si gira*) through mind and place – that is, in both the intellectual and the visible realm. The tenth canto is filled with circular imagery: the wheels of the spheres, the oblique circle (*l'oblico cerchio*) of the zodiac, the girdle or halo that surrounds the moon. The luminous saints form a crown (*corona*), a round dance, a garland (*ghirlanda*, *serto*), and finally a wheel (*gloriosa rota*).[3] Dante revolves over the garland with his gaze (*girando su per lo beato serto*: 102), thereby participating in the circling; indeed he and Beatrice are made the centre of that live *corona*.

Thus all the language of gazing, loving, breathing, and circling – the language that demonstrates the unity of knowledge and ardour, the sun's power of giving light and warmth – is already compressed in the first lines of the canto, where it is affirmed of God:

> Guardando nel suo Figlio con l'Amore
> che l'uno e l'altro etternalmente spira,
> lo primo e ineffabile Valore
>   quanto per mente e per loco si gira
> con tant' ordine fé, ch'esser non puote
> sanza gustar di lui chi ciò rimira.
>
> Gazing into his Son with the Love
> that they, the one and other, eternally breathe,
> the first-existing and unutterable Might
>   made whatever revolves through mind and place
> with such order that any who looks on it
> cannot exist without a taste of him.   (1–6)

Guardando, *Amore*, *spira*, *si gira* ... Other expressions too within these lines, though they reverberate less often in the rest of the canto, match these principal ones. So for instance *l'uno e l'altro* (2) is, I suggest, no merely pedantic way of saying 'both', but conveys further the idea of reciprocity. Hence it is echoed in the physical world, in the intersecting of 'the one motion and the other' at the equinox (9), as well as at the close of the canto (142), where it is loving mutuality that relates 'the one part and the other' of the celestial clock, which itself by its chime awakens love.[4]

Clearly it would be possible to isolate other gravitational fields of language also – those of song, of radiance, of exultation and laughter. One group of images, relating to taste and food, provides, as we shall see, a further element of poetic cohesion. Yet it is the expressions of gazing, loving, breathing, and circling which I believe form the tenth canto's distinctive co-ordinates.

In the opening 'movement' of the canto (1–27) Dante likewise includes a double apostrophe to the reader. The second of his addresses takes up the metaphor of tasting (*gustar*) from the last verse cited:

> Or ti riman, lettor, sovra 'l tuo banco,
> dietro pensando a ciò che si preliba,
> s'esser vuoi lieto assai prima che stanco.
>   Messo t'ho innanzi: omai per te ti ciba;
> ché a sé torce tutta la mia cura
> quella materia ond' io son fatto scriba.

> Now, reader, stay at your bench,
> pondering what has been given in foretaste,
> if you want to have great joy before you're weary.
>   I've set you the table – now it's for you to feast,
> since the matter I have been made the scribe of
> wrests all my study to itself.   (22–7)

Dante's addresses to the reader – an individual feature of his artistry[5] – are more frequent, but briefer, in *Inferno* and *Purgatorio*. In *Paradiso* there are, in the strict sense of direct appeals, only four. The most solemn and ominous comes at the opening of *Paradiso* II, where Dante warns the readers who have followed him thus far of the greater perils that lie ahead.[6] Only those who have long sought 'the bread of the angels', divine Wisdom,[7] and hunger for it still, shall dare to accompany him now. *Paradiso* demands a supreme effort from the reader as from the poet – this is the bond Dante creates with him. In *Paradiso* V, by contrast, Dante's words to the reader are deliberately teasing and tantalising, though once more they play upon, and strengthen, that bond between teller and listener:

> Pensa, lettor, se quel che qui s'inizia
> non procedesse, come tu avresti
> di più savere angosciosa carizia;
>   e per te vederai come da questi
> m'era in disio d'udir lor condizioni ...

> Think, reader, if what is begun here
> did not go on, how you would have
> an anguished craving to know more –
>   then you'll see for yourself how much
> I longed to know from them of their conditions ...   (V 109–13)

The immediate reference is to a relatively minor matter: the state of souls in the heaven of Mercury. But Dante's feigning of such consummate assurance that he holds his reader spellbound, agog to find out all, is what provides him with an image of his own never sated pursuit, as visionary and as artist.

The double address in Canto x, I would argue, brings together the solemnity from Canto II (as well as its motif of intellectual food) and the tantalising element from Canto v. The thought at the opening – that reciprocal contemplation and love within the godhead effected a cosmic order so perfect that human contemplation of it brings a taste of divinity – leads to the first, exalted summoning of the reader:

> Leva dunque, lettore, a l'alte rote
> meco la vista . . .
>
> So, reader, raise your sight to the high wheels
> together with me . . .   (7f)

By joining Dante in this contemplative gaze, he too can 'taste God' (*gustar di lui*). In the tradition of interpreting the Song of Songs mystically, *gustare* and its cognates had all the connotations of erotic tasting – the bride and bridegroom taste each other's fruits – and of divine cognition.[8] Here in the canto, the world below is greedy (*gola*) to learn the love that inspired Solomon (III); the family of this fourth sphere are forever sated by the high Father (*sempre la sazia*: 50); and (in the one verse that foreshadows the fierce attack on unworthy Dominicans in Canto XI), we are told that on St Dominic's path there is rich pasturage (*ben s'impingua*), if this sustenance is not disprized (96).

Dante then invites his reader, somewhat hermetically, to consider how the divine artist has ordered the sun's annual path (the ecliptic), so that its journey through the zodiac, along with the other planets, lies aslant the equator.[9] It is the particular angle, divinely ordained, of zodiac to equator, that determines the conditions of life on earth: if it were otherwise, the planets would not exercise measured and beneficent influences on the sublunary world. If the ecliptic and the equator coincided, there could be no alternation of seasons, only a changeless climate, that would make plant life – and hence human life – impossible. So, too, if the angle of the one circle to the other were greater or less than it is, the resulting heat or cold on earth would be too extreme for men to bear.

It is after alluding to these signs of providential craftsmanship that Dante suddenly says he will leave his reader to his own devices. Let him ponder the implications of this heavenly ordering, let him remain at his bench. Is it a school-bench that Dante has in mind, or (as some have supposed) a banqueting one? The metaphors here – as in Dante's *Convivio* – suggest to me it must be both. Dante meanwhile turns singlemindedly back to his task, of recalling the next stage of his vision, the marvels of the new heaven to which he rises. Yet here lurks the paradoxical quality of Dante's renewed address to the reader: for, if his mind can follow Dante in his ascent, he will in fact be continuing the banquet at his bench, seeing more and more fully into the wonders of the celestial handiwork. In particular, he will see how the astronomic allusions, here given as foretaste, are transformed into an imaginary *human* astronomy in Canto XIII; how the relation between two real (though invisible) circles in the heavens leads forward to that between two metaphoric circles – who are saints as well as suns – in Dante's solar heaven. By threatening to leave his readers alone, Dante is in effect taking them with him.

The sun in his path has now reached the point of crossing the equator: this is the spring equinox, the time of the year in which 'he shows himself earlier each day' (33). Dante ascends into the solar heaven imperceptibly: here as always in *Paradiso*, his rising is something he perceives only in and through Beatrice, who, in miraculous, timeless moments, leads him from height to greater height. Dante not only tries to intimate the new solar luminousness, inhabited by still more luminous suns, but harnesses a particular solar imagery that makes the visible sun the excelling figuration of God, Sol Intelligibilis. Two of the sun-spirits in the dazzling crown, whom Dante will soon meet, had given memorable expression to such symbolism, and this part of the canto could be seen as Dante's variation on their thoughts. For Dionysius, there was continuity between the palpable sun and the sun of the angels:

This manifest image of divine bounty ... moves the generation of bodies to life, nourishes them and makes them grow, perfects and purifies and renews them ... and its light is the measure of all time for us ...

All things are turned towards it and desire it – the intelligible by their intellect, the sensory by their senses, those devoid of sense by an inborn motion of vital longing ... All are utterly contained by that desire for light.[10]

Boethius, on the other hand, stresses the contrast between the two suns as much as the figural likeness:

> All-surveying and all-hearing
> Apollo, radiant with pure light,
> is sung by Homer's sweetly-streaming lips;
> and yet, with the weak gleam of his rays,
> he cannot pierce the inmost viscera
> of earth or ocean.
> Not so the founder of the great orb,
> watching all things from his height –
> no part of the earth resists him,
> nor night with her black clouds . . .
> Since he beholds all – he alone –
> you can call him the true sun.[11]

The epiphany of the true sun in the new sphere for a moment absorbs Dante's outgoing thoughts of love totally. The dialectic here is strange. Beatrice excitedly urges Dante to thanksgiving:

> 'Ringrazia,
> ringrazia il Sol de li angeli, ch'a questo
> sensibil t'ha levato per sua grazia'.
>   Cor di mortal non fu mai sì digesto
> a divozione e a rendersi a Dio
> con tutto 'l suo gradir cotanto presto,
>   come a quelle parole mi fec' io;
> e sì tutto 'l mio amore in lui si mise,
> che Bëatrice eclissò ne l'oblio.
>   Non le dispiacque, ma sì se ne rise,
> che lo splendor de li occhi suoi ridenti
> mia mente unita in più cose divise.

> 'Give thanks,
> give thanks to the sun of the angels, who has raised you
> up to this palpable sun by means of his grace!'
>   No mortal heart was ever so disposed
> to devotion and surrendering to God,
> so ready with the whole of its delight,
>   as I grew at those words;
> and all my love so fixed itself in him
> that it eclipsed Beatrice in oblivion.
>   It did not vex her, but she laughed at it,
> so that the splendour of her laughing eyes
> diffracted my mind's oneness to diverse things.   (52–63)

Dante obeys Beatrice to the extent of forgetting her: briefly she becomes like a moon eclipsed by the greater sun. Yet then the radiance of her eyes, filled with laughter, is even more brilliant – so that it overcomes the supernatural light that had engulfed him: it enables Dante to see not only Beatrice again, but with her the dancing, blazing garland of spirits, whose song is of a beauty irrecoverable in an earthly mode. She is eclipsed in his instant of leaping heavenward; *and* her resplendent eyes, laughing him out of his engrossment, empower him to see more heavenly things. What is the secret of this antinomy?

Some of the most startling moments in the whole of the *Commedia* are those in which Dante plays upon the potential for conflict between his two heavenly loves – Beatrice and God. The sense that these motions of love *could* conflict is never more than momentary, yet one has the feeling in such moments that Dante is setting at stake his poetry, his visions, implicitly the whole of his life. The first – uniquely moving and exultant at the same time – occurs at the transition from *Purgatorio* XXXI to XXXII. For the first time in the otherworld Beatrice smiles at Dante. The effect upon the poet – who sees that smile as 'the splendour of living light' incarnate – is as overwhelming as the soaring invocation and question, with which Canto XXXI closes, are upon the reader. Then, as the next canto opens and Dante slakes his thirst for that holy smile (*santo riso*), he hears the voice of the three goddesses (*dee*) beside Beatrice saying, it would seem rebukingly: '*Troppo fiso!*' – 'Too engrossed!' (XXXII 9).

In *Paradiso* X, and again at the close of XIV, Dante's instant of *raptus* shuts out Beatrice; later, in *Paradiso* XVIII and XXIII, it is conversely the delight in her that shuts out all else:

> Vincendo me col lume d'un sorriso,
> ella mi disse: 'Volgiti e ascolta;
> ché non pur ne' miei occhi è paradiso'.

> Vanquishing me with the light of a smile,
> she said to me: 'Turn and listen –
> for paradise is not just in my eyes!' (XVIII 19–21)

Or again:

> 'Perché la faccia mia sì t'innamora,
> che tu non ti rivolgi al bel giardino
> che sotto i raggi di Cristo s'infiora?'

> 'Why does my face enamour you so much
> that you don't turn to the lovely garden
> which enflowers beneath the rays of Christ?'   (XXIII 70–2)

Each time Dante the artist challenges us to think anew about his central myth. Is his beloved she who médiates the divine to Dante, or she in whom he perceives the divine? The oscillation between these ways of looking is bound up with all the mystery, the dramatic tensions and exhilarations at the close of *Purgatorio* and in *Paradiso*.

(ii) *Quelli ardenti soli*

Now let us turn to the crown or garland of twelve lights that circles Beatrice in this heaven of the sun. What do they mean to Dante, and why has he chosen them? It would ill accord with Dante's art to suppose he compiled a series of names arbitrarily, nor again do I think, as Curtius thought, that they are a largely private, and hence inexplicable, canon.[12] To give at least some tentative indications, I would suggest that Dante sees the twelve lights here as outstanding celebrants of those harmonies on which he dwells throughout the canto. For one or two, this is easy to see at once. Dante's conception of the force of love that moves the heavens, affirmed in the *Commedia* from the first canto to the closing line – *l'amor che move il sole e l'altre stelle* – owes much to Boethius' hymn that reflects on 'the love by which heaven is ruled (*amor quo caelum regitur*)'.[13] Just as Dante invites, 'So, reader, raise your sight to the high wheels', Boethius, in another poem where he evokes cosmic harmony, is addressed by his guide, Philosophia:

> If you want to gaze at the sublime Thunderer's throne
> skilfully, with pure mind,
> look up at the pinnacles of highest heaven …

In this poem too, as in the first part of *Paradiso* x, we are shown how the disordering alternatives have been excluded:

> The sun, roused by his red-glinting fire,
> does not impede the orbit of the moon,
> nor does the Bear, in rapid course
> near the world's upper pole,
> ever plunge into the western sea …
> Thus a reciprocating love refreshes

the eternal coursings, thus love exiles discord
from the star-bearing shores.[14]

Dionysius also, among those in Dante's blissful garland, had given a renowned definition of cosmic love,[15] in a work on which both Thomas Aquinas and Albert of Cologne wrote elaborate commentaries. Albert, like Thomas, returns to Dionysius' words as he writes his philosophical commentary on Aristotle's *Metaphysics*. This love, he says, 'moves the [planetary] gods and the divine intelligences ... who bring the spheres to coherence by the harmonised melody of love (*concentu amoris*)'.[16] And Thomas affirms: 'that love unites [all] things is clear from this – that love itself is a kind of union of the lover and what is loved, since the lover regards the beloved as himself'.[17]

Yet the precise reasons for Dante's choice of Thomas Aquinas as the presenter of the other lights in the crown, and as speaker both here and in Cantos XI and XIII, are not so easy to state. We can no longer follow the earlier generations of scholars who naïvely held Dante to be a disciple of Thomas' ideas, a 'Thomist'. To cite the admirable recent statement of Kenelm Foster, at the close of his essay *Dante e San Tommaso* – in Dante's attitude

... there was such a contrast: on the one hand, an intense admiration for Friar Thomas as a model of holy understanding; on the other, divergence, on so many fundamental points, from Thomist teaching.[18]

Dante, in his *Convivio* and *Monarchia*, cites two works by Thomas: the commentary on Aristotle's *Ethics*, and the *Summa contra Gentiles*. Most revealing are the Aristotelian allusions: Dante had clearly read the *Ethics* closely, with Thomas' commentary to hand.[19] He singles out Thomas' notions that 'ethics orders us towards the other forms of knowledge',[20] and that 'to know the order of one thing in relation to another is the specific act of reason'.[21] Thus we can say at least that Dante prized in Thomas' thought a certain sense and view of ordering; and I think that, if we try to look at Thomas' commentary on the *Ethics* with Dante's eyes, one feature stands out in which Thomas time and again goes beyond Aristotle's text. For when he treats of ordering, he lends the concept a further dimension – that of the Christian God. Both knowledge and love are ordered towards him:

It pertains to the love which should exist among mankind, that a person will uphold what is good even for one person only. But it is far better and more divine that this goodness should be shown to a whole people and to cities. And if at times it is lovable to show goodness towards one city only, it is far more divine for it to be shown to a nation containing many cities. It is said to be more divine in that it pertains more to the likeness of God, the ultimate cause of all good things.[22]

Again, commenting on Aristotle's brief aside, that truth should be honoured even more than friends, Thomas writes:

Truth is a friend so surpassingly excellent, that to her the reverence of honour is due: indeed truth is something divine, found first and archetypally in God.[23]

It is in moments such as these that Dante will have found reflected some of his own principal concerns in *Paradiso* x.

Nonetheless, in certain fundamental aspects of his thought Dante was close not to Thomas but to two of the other luminaries in the garland – Albert and Siger. It is the lasting merit of Bruno Nardi, in a lifetime's work on Dante and medieval philosophy, to have made this clear, differentiating the thought of Thomas from that of his teacher Albert, and establishing the ways in which the thought of Siger (who had likewise studied with Albert) relates to Albert's speculations, and to Dante's, even where those speculations were ones vigorously combated by Thomas. This Nardi showed, in particular, of Dante's profound reflection, in *Purgatorio* xxv, on the origins of the human soul: there Dante comes close both to Albert's thought and to the last phase of Siger's.[24] So, too, Dante sided with Albert and Siger against Thomas in another question, one that was of vital importance to him as poet. Can a human being, in this life, know anything of forms in the celestial world?[25] Thomas denied that this was possible: for him the human mind, united to a body, can know only forms abstracted from sensory images. Albert and Siger, by contrast, take a position which is far closer to that of Aristotle's great Arab commentator, Averroes. For them, the human soul has a capacity of intellection with which a higher, light-giving intellect at times unites:

... and what is compounded thus is called by the Peripatetics the acquired intellect and the divine one ... This condition of the acquired intellect is wondrous and the best of all: for thus, by way of it, man becomes in a sense like God, in that he can thereby bring forth divine things, and lavish divine intellections on himself and others, and in a sense receive all intellections.[26]

It is this optimistic theory of Albert's and Siger's, setting so high the utmost mark of human knowledge, that provided a philosophical basis for Dante's whole claim to have had true insights into the heavenly realm.[27]

Similarly I believe that the spirits next mentioned, after Albert, must relate to specific concerns of Dante's as poet in this canto. Gratian of Bologna, compiler of the collection of decrees that became the basis of canon law, 'helped the one forum and the other' (104). With Gmelin and Foster,[28] I take this phrase to mean the inner forum of conscience, and the outer, of the ecclesiastical court. It is perhaps near the beginning of the *Decretum*, as Gratian distinguishes the laws of custom and constitution from natural law (*ius naturae*), that we can glimpse the ideal harmony which will have captivated Dante:

> For by the law of nature all things are common to all human beings. This is upheld not only among those of whom it is written [Acts 4: 32]: 'in the multitude of believers there was one heart and one soul' – it is also found transmitted by the philosophers of the previous age: thus according to Plato that city is said to be most justly ordered, in which no one is aware of aspirations for himself alone.[29]

The quotation from the Acts of the Apostles shows this blessed state as having existed among the first Christians; yet by adding the allusion to Plato, Gratian affirms it as not just a Christian but a universal human ideal.

A comparable thought, with a more overtly theological emphasis, is stated with great audacity by Peter Lombard, when he claims that human love for fellow human beings is itself the divine Holy Spirit:

> The Holy Spirit is the love of Father and Son, whereby they love each other and love us. Moreover, the Spirit itself is the love or charity (*amor sive caritas*) by which we love God and our neighbour ... And any who loves the love by which one loves a neighbour, in that very act loves God, for that same love *is* God – that is, the Holy Spirit.[30]

Yet Dante also, in his verses on Peter Lombard (106–8), carries a deliberate echo of the theologian's opening words in the prologue to his major work, the *Sententiae*: Dante's expression 'with the poor little woman (*con la poverella*)' renders Peter's *cum paupercula*: both are alluding to Christ's parable of the widow who offered her farthing to the Temple, since it was all she had. Peter's lines read:

Longing, in my penury and neediness, to go with the poor little woman to put something into the treasury of the Lord, I have dared to mount high, to undertake a task beyond my powers...[31]

The awestruck sense of lowliness, inseparable from that of daring greatly, will assuredly have found deep resonance in Dante.

Dante's fifth light is, in theological terms, wholly unexpected – since Solomon belonged to the world preceding Christ's redemption. In terms of Dante's preoccupation in this setting, however, we can see Solomon as the peerless embodiment of the unity of love and knowledge. The love he breathes, 'for which the world is greedy', is manifest in the Song of Songs; the unique depth of his wisdom, in the books of Wisdom and Proverbs, whose highest points are the celebration of a personified Sapientia, a divine emanation of whom Solomon is enamoured:

> I have loved her and sought her since my youth,
> I longed to make her my bride,
> I fell in love with her beauty ...
> Going into my house, I shall lie with her,
> for her companionship has no bitterness,
> living with her has no weariness ...
> for in knowing Sapientia there is immortality.   (Wisdom 8: 2ff)

No one in Dante's day doubted that King Solomon was author both of the love-song and the 'Sapiential' works. His, then, was the supreme experience of love as well as wisdom – hence, in the words of Thomas here, he is 'the fairest in our company'. In Canto XIII (46ff) Thomas turns again to speak of Solomon, to explain his own remarkable phrase 'no second rose to see so much' (*a veder tanto non surse il secondo*: X 114). There (XIII 103–8) the reference is to Solomon as the incomparably perfect embodiment of the philosopher–king. But here it is his conjunction of loving and knowing that must be stressed.

The sixth light, Dionysius – who in fact was an early sixth-century Christian Platonist, but was still thought in Dante's time to be a sage of the Apostolic period, who was converted by St Paul – is recalled for his treatise on angels, *The Celestial Hierarchy*.[32] This laid the foundations not only for the belief in nine orders of angels – who become movers of the nine material heavens in Dante's cosmos – but also for the conception of this cosmos as 'sacramental', in that the angels lovingly mediate the divine to the visible world, and thereby allow the visible to move towards its fulfilment in the divine.

Scholars have proposed several possible candidates for the seventh apparition:

> Ne l'altra piccioletta luce ride
> quello avvocato de' tempi cristiani
> del cui latino Augustin si provide.

> In the next little light there exults
> the advocate of the Christian ages,
> whose narrative Augustine put to use. (118–20)

The widely held view that these verses designate Orosius seems to me the best. His gloomy panorama, or narrative (this was one common meaning of the word *latino* in 120), of world history – *Historiae adversus paganos* – was both stimulated by St Augustine and dedicated to him in the years when Augustine was completing his own *City of God*.[33] Orosius fits well because he was 'the advocate of the Christian ages' in a special sense, one not applicable to the other early Fathers whose writings Augustine knew. Orosius' particular advocacy was of the utmost importance for Dante. He formulated what became a crucial point in Dante's *Monarchia*: the providential historic accord between the rule of Rome and that of Christ. It was at the moment when Caesar Augustus had established universal peace, Orosius argues, that Christ chose to be born: he chose to submit to Augustus' census of the world. Orosius continues:

This is the first and most illustrious avowal that designated Caesar as universal ruler and the Romans as masters of all things . . . by an acknowledgment in which he who made mankind wished to be enrolled among mankind . . . He agreed to let this city grow and to defend it, advancing it to such a summit that he most wanted to belong to it when he came. Indeed by the declaration of the Roman census Christ had to be called Roman citizen.[34]

This vision of a 'pre-established harmony' between the perfect human dispensation and that of Christ, which was to be so deeply thought through by Dante, will, I believe, have been what impelled him to include Orosius in his solar harmony. The objection some scholars make – that Dante would hardly have called Orosius a 'little light' (118) – would be valid only if 'little' implied belittling. But may it not, just as readily, imply affection?

Before turning to Boethius, let us look briefly at the three figures who follow him:

Vedi oltre fiammeggiar l'ardente spiro
d'Isidoro, di Beda e di Riccardo,
che a considerar fu più che viro.

See flaming farther on the ardent breath
of Isidore, of Bede, and of Richard,
who was more than man in contemplation.   (130–2)

With the expression *ardente spiro* Dante forges a link between
Richard of St Victor and Solomon, who 'breathes with such love'.
Richard was indeed one of the finest teachers of mystic, Solom-
onic love in the century preceding Dante's. In the tribute to him
that is here put in Thomas' mouth, Dante is in my view echoing
some words of Richard himself, near the opening of his treatise on
the Song of Songs, where he explains how men may become 'more
than man':

[Christ] set a certain distance between human beings and his own disciples, namely in that, by instilling things divine in them, he made them
more than men (*supra homines*). And we know that, in our resurrection,
body will be bound to spirit in such a way that all which had belonged to
passion is gathered up in the power of spirit.[35]

What of Isidore and Bede – why are they here linked with
Richard? Today we may think of Isidore first and foremost as
compiler of the *Etymologies*, and of Bede as author of the *History of
the English Church*. Thus for instance the most recent commentators on *Paradiso*, Bosco and Reggio, claim, with special reference
to these two, that 'Dante has placed several personages here only
for their importance in the diffusion of culture'.[36] I believe, on the
contrary, that we should understand Dante's selection in terms of
his central thought in this canto, the unity of knowledge and love.
What Isidore, Bede, and Richard have in common is, in Dante's
words, an 'ardent breath'. Is it not significant, then, that Isidore
and Bede were also renowned in Dante's day for having written
expositions of the Song of Songs?[37] This, surely, is their bond
with Richard, and with Solomon.

(iii) Boethius and Siger

It has not, I think, been noticed that the way Dante introduces
Boethius is precisely similar to his way with Peter Lombard and
Richard of St Victor. In each instance he deliberately echoes a

memorable expression from the author. Just as *con la poverella* was Peter Lombard's phrase, and *più che viro* was Richard's, so the eye of the mind – *l'occhio della mente* (121) – is a key concept of Boethius near the close of his *Consolation of Philosophy*. There Boethius, distinguishing the human powers of sense-perception, imagination and reason from a quasi-divine intuitive intellection, says: 'the eye of intellection (*intellegentiae oculus*) is higher ... it gazes on the simple form with the pure eyebeam of the mind (*mentis acie*)'.[38] It is this insight that leads Boethius to his individual solution of the last and greatest problem in his work – the relation of eternity, divine providence, and human freedom.

The *Consolation*, Dante tells us in the *Convivio*, was one of the two books that initiated him into philosophy, after the death of Beatrice. But here it is the personal, rather than the philosophical, part of Boethius' book that specially concerns him. Boethius, imprisoned and awaiting death, had exposed the world's mutability through telling his own wretchedness. Since Boethius was executed by the Arian ruler Theodoric, medieval tradition tended to present him as a martyr in the religious sense.[39] Yet some of the earliest testimonies,[40] and the autobiographic part of the *Consolation* itself, show him rather as a martyr for his belief in the Roman *imperium*: it was Boethius' attempt – as idealistic as it was imprudent – to uphold the integrity of the Roman Senate at whatever cost that led Theodoric to brand him as a traitor. At all events, no one in the Middle Ages doubted that Boethius had suffered an unjust imprisonment and death. And this, I am convinced, was the parallel Dante perceived and wanted to imply between Boethius and Siger of Brabant:

> Questi onde a me ritorna il tuo riguardo,
> è 'l lume d'uno spirto che 'n pensieri
> gravi a morir li parve venir tardo:
>   essa è la luce etterna di Sigieri,
> che, leggendo nel Vico de li Strami,
> silogizzò invidïosi veri.

> This one, from whom your gaze returns to me,
> is the light of a spirit who, amid his grave
> reflections, thought death slow to come:
>   this is the eternal light of Siger,
> who, lecturing in the Street of Straw,
> by syllogism proved ill-received truths.   (133–8)

The melancholy words Dante uses of Siger — 'amid his grave reflections, he thought death slow to come' — have a close counterpart in Boethius' elegy at the opening of his *Consolation*, where, longing for a swift death, now that all is lost, he laments that death turns a deaf ear when she is most desired.[41] Dante sees the sixth-century victim of injustice, like the victim from the time of his own boyhood, as a man who, having given all in the service of truth, was then left isolated and helpless. It is the condition that Blake was to evoke:

> wisdom . . . is bought with the price
> Of all that a man hath, his house, his wife, his children.
> Wisdom is sold in the desolate market where none comes
>   to buy,
> And in the wither'd field where the farmer plows for bread
>   in vain.[42]

A few details about Siger's life and death may help to illuminate the full bearing of Dante's tribute. He taught philosophy — in particular that of Aristotle — in Paris in the 1260s, in the Arts Faculty on Straw Street (still known today as Rue Paillet); there the poet Jean de Meun will have been one of his colleagues. A document of 1265 shows that Siger was involved in some university riots that year. These riots had a nationalist rather than ideological basis — a hostility that opposed the French members of the university to the English and Normans, and to the Picards, with whom Siger was affiliated. After arbitration by the king had failed, the papal legate restored peace. In 1270 the bishop of Paris condemned a number of radical Aristotelian, or Averroist,[43] teachings, and Siger was hit by this condemnation. At the same time Thomas Aquinas, who had been called back to Paris the previous year, published two polemical treatises, one of which was directed especially against Siger. To Thomas, both the notion of a single, common human capacity of intellection, and that of the eternity of the world, appeared incompatible with Christian teachings.[44] In 1276 Siger was summoned to appear before the French Inquisitor. He fled to Italy, to the papal court, in order to appeal and try to clear his name. But the pope who might have heard him sympathetically, the distinguished philosopher Peter of Spain, died in 1277. So Siger in Italy was, if not imprisoned like Boethius, at least placed under some kind of house-arrest.[45] In 1281, the papal legate who had intervened in Paris in 1265 was crowned Pope Martin IV. He may well have been less than favourably disposed to the scholar whom he recalled for his part in the Parisian troubles. Siger had by then waited at least five years for an outcome to his appeal. He waited in vain to the end, for in Orvieto, where the papal court was staying between 1281 and 1284, Siger was murdered.

The two texts that bear witness to this murder must be looked at carefully. One is by an anonymous Latin chronicler of the time:

Siger, a Brabançon by nation, unable to remain in Paris because he had held certain opinions against the Faith, appealed to the Roman Curia, and there, after a little while, he died, stabbed by his own clerk, who was as if demented (*a clerico suo quasi dementi perfossus periit*).[46]

The other occurs in the Italian adaptation of the *Roman de la Rose*, *Il Fiore*, which many scholars, including most persuasively Contini, believe to be a youthful work of Dante himself.[47] The passage has no counterpart in the French of Jean de Meun. Here Jean's figure False-Semblance (*Fausemblant*, Italian *Falsembiante*) boasts that it is he who had Siger put to death:

> A ghiado il fe' morire a gran dolore
> Nella corte di Roma, ad Orbivieto.
>
> I made him die by dagger, with great suffering,
> in the Roman court, at Orvieto.   (XCII)

The two testimonies, I would argue, complement and support each other in a remarkable way. First, 'by dagger (*a ghiado*)' in the Italian text is confirmed by 'stabbed (*perfossus*)' in the Latin – so it cannot be taken merely figuratively, as some scholars have tried to maintain.[48] But also, no one has discussed the force of *quasi dementi* – '*as if* demented'. Did the Latin chronicler suspect that Siger's murderer had not really been demented – that this had been a way of dissembling villainy? It is a suspicion that grows when one sees the author of the *Fiore* claiming that Siger's murder had been arranged by False-Semblance. Mandonnet, the author of the first major study of Siger, wrote: 'there is no reason to doubt ... that Siger died by accident'.[49] Close attention to *quasi dementi* and to *Falsembiante*, on the other hand, suggests to me a very different inference: Siger's death was made to *look* like an accident; it was given out as 'death by misadventure'.

In any event, whether or not the young Dante was the author of *Il Fiore*, we know that the mature Dante felt that – if not on earth, then at least in his *Paradiso* – there was a wrong to be righted.

The way Dante chose to right that wrong is so astounding that it has engaged the attention of countless scholars.[50] Thomas Aquinas concludes his presentation of the blissful garland of souls by paying tribute to the greatness – the eternal light – of the colleague whom he had opposed on earth. The celestial Thomas, whom Dante creates, recognises the sufferings that Siger – like Boethius before him – underwent for his convictions; above all, he admits that what his opponent taught, and suffered for teaching, was ill-received, but true: *invidïosi veri*. Dante sets the eternal light of Siger at Thomas' side. It has often been remarked that, in just this way in Canto XII, Dante makes Bonaventure conclude *his* round of the blessed, showing at his own side 'the abbot from Calabria, Joachim, endowed with the spirit of prophecy' (140f) – Bonaventure, who on earth had attacked Joachim of Fiore bitterly as a pseudo-prophet. In Dante's eyes the Franciscan Doctor of the Church, like the Dominican one, had an injustice to make good. In his heaven of imagination, the two established teachers become more magnanimous than they had been in life. One might almost say they enact a public penance – acknowledging that they had been at fault in their hostility towards the true philosopher Siger, the true prophet Joachim, and atoning for this fault – this lack of charity and wisdom – in Dante's paradisal court.[51]

Dante's treatment of Siger and Joachim is generally held to be a problem and an enigma. Daring it certainly is, and yet, if viewed in the light of the principal themes of this canto, these moments should not, after all, seem surprising. In terms of Dante's particular conception of knowledge and love (and given his extraordinary penetration of the philosophical–theological issues of his time), I would see the tributes to Siger and Joachim as necessary and inevitable. When Dante imagines Thomas' compassionate recognition of Siger, or Bonaventure's affirmation of Joachim – is this not to imagine the loving gestures of true understanding, copying that eternal breath of reciprocal love in the godhead with which Canto X began? Is it not this that allows the Dominican's and the Franciscan's light of knowledge and love to flow at last without impediment? How could the partial knowledge, which expressed itself in polemic on earth, *not* transform into a greater knowledge, which in heaven expresses itself as love?

The canto ends by gathering and lifting up this theme in a metaphor that is both complex and thrilling:

> Indi, come orologio che ne chiami
> ne l'ora che la sposa di Dio surge

a mattinar lo sposo perché l'ami,
  che l'una parte e l'altra tira e urge,
tin tin sonando con sì dolce nota,
che 'l ben disposto spirto d'amor turge;
  così vid' ïo la gloriosa rota
muoversi e render voce a voce in tempra
e in dolcezza ch'esser non pò nota
  se non colà dove gioir s'insempra.

Then, like a clock that calls us
at the hour when the bride of God arises
to sing an *alba* to the bridegroom, that he may love her,
  – a clock where one part and the other pulls and thrusts,
sounding 'ting, ting' with so sweet a note
that the well-inclined spirit swells with love –
  even so I saw the glorious wheel
move and match voice with voice in harmony,
in a sweetness that cannot be known
  save there where having joy untimes itself.   (139–48)

Poetically it is important to leave the metaphoric force intact. Thus for instance to say, as most commentators do, that in 140 *la sposa di Dio* means 'the Church', is not in itself wrong; and yet what Dante intends here is no mere circumlocution for 'the Church' but all the connotations of Solomon's love. Dante was well aware that the dawn-motifs in the Song of Songs had echoed in the *albas* of troubadours;[52] he was equally aware of the beautiful way Richard of St Victor had developed the same motifs mystically:

[The bride] clings on to her lover, though it is dawn ... She has struggled with him all night, while she lay sleeping; but her heart was wakeful ... and strained to seek the beloved. Even though, through the night, she has arrived at dawn, she does not cease from her struggle ... so that she may pass from power to power, and see the God of gods in Sion ...[53]

In such a dawn Dante perceives the glorious wheel – the round of lights who are twelve sages ablaze with divine love – like a clock that expresses harmony in diverse ways: in the reciprocal actions of its parts, in the music of its chimes (a love-song, like that of the bride), and in the circular dance of souls, as if they were the figures, ordered in movement, of the clock sounding the hour. It is possible, as Gmelin noted, that Dante could have seen a clock that chimed the hours: the earliest attested in Italy was built in Milan in 1306, and Dante might have observed it at the coronation of

Henry VII.[54] Yet the 'heavenly clockwork' Dante imagines here outdoes anything that could have been built in his day. This is a harmony that goes beyond human craft and human time, transmuting time into 'always'. Dante's coinage *s'insempra* (148), given special weight through being set at the close of the canto, is one of several such formations in *Paradiso*, where *in*, together with a pronoun or adverb, is made into a new verb, expressing and depicting transformation.[55] The clock of this metaphor is a summit of symbolic intellection, uniting the transformed celestial construct and the earthly image that gives rise to it. It manifests the loving harmony of the solar heaven, and still it measures time for us – like the sun.

Excursus I
The *Epistle* to Cangrande and Latin prose rhythm

In Dante's chapter on construction in *De vulgari eloquentia* (*DVE* II vi), he gives a number of Latin examples before he proceeds to vernacular ones. To show that a *constructio* is 'a regulated structure of expressions', he first adduces a one-clause sentence, 'Aristoteles phylosophatus est *témpore Alexándri*', which ends in what medieval theorists of prose rhythm, or *cursus*, defined as a 'swift (*velox*)' cadence. Then, as he turns to the 'degrees of construction (*gradus constructionum*)', Dante begins with 'the insipid, which is that of novices (*rudium*)', and illustrates this by another one-clause sentence, that ends in a cadence (*dóminam Bértam*) which the theorists did not admit as correctly built. Dante's next three examples all consist of sentences with more than one clause, each clause ending with a cadence of a kind that was allowed by the canons of prose rhythm. In the first two sentences, a *velox* clause (*exílio tabescéntes*, or *magnificéntia preparáta*) is inserted between two 'simple (*planus*)' ones (*pietáte maiórem* and *sompniándo revísunt* in the first example, *marchiónis Esténsis* and *ésse diléctum* in the second); in the third, Dante's example of 'the most excellent degree of construction', a 'slow (*tardus*)' cadence (*túo, Floréntia*) is set against another *planus* (*secúndus adívit*).

It is clear that the rhythmic cadences with which these clauses end constitute only one aspect of the structural finesses that Dante illustrates and evaluates. The special excellence of his third example lies in combining a whole range of subtle rhetorical effects, not simply in using *tardus* and *planus* correctly. At the same time, this passage in Dante's treatise testifies to his effortless familiarity with the medieval theory and practice of Latin prose rhythm. Yet while Dante's use of rhythmic prose has been much discussed since the early years of this century, it was not till 1963 that a serious statistical analysis began to be made, by Gudrun

Lindholm,[1] and not till 1975, with Tore Janson's book *Prose Rhythm in Medieval Latin*,[2] that a method was evolved which was precise enough to distinguish deliberately sought rhythms from those that could be due to chance. Janson's method, though it has meanwhile been valuably discussed in Italy by Giovanni Orlandi,[3] has not yet, to my knowledge, been applied to any of Dante's Latin writings.

Janson adopted a notation similar to that which Dag Norberg had introduced for medieval Latin verse rhythms, in which a figure, giving the number of syllables in a word, can be combined with an indication of its principal stress: paroxytone (*p*) or proparoxytone (*pp*). Thus in the strict form of *velox* (*témpore Alexándri*, or *magnificéntia preparáta*) a word (of three or more syllables) with proparoxytone stress (*pp*) is followed by a four-syllabled word with paroxytone stress (*4p*). Hence *velox* cadences are noted as *pp 4p*. Similarly a strict *planus*, where a paroxytone word (*p*) is followed by a trisyllabic paroxytone (*3p*) – *pietáte maiórem*, or *ésse diléctam* – is noted as *p 3p*, and a strict *tardus* (*túo, Floréntia*), paroxytone followed by four-syllabled proparoxytone, as *p 4pp*. Though Dante's 'insipid' *dóminam Bértam* has superficially the same rhythm as his *planus* cadences, neither he nor the medieval theorists seem to have admitted a proparoxytone followed by a disyllabic word (*pp 2*, in Janson's notation) as a permissible variant of *planus* (though it was in fact used in earlier periods).

From these preliminaries let us turn to the points that raise problems. In all his *Epistles* (*Epp.* I–XII in the recent edition of *Opere minori* II),[4] Dante uses at the great majority of his sentence-endings[5] a *velox*, *tardus* or *planus* cadence. These three cadences are found similarly often in the dedicatory part of the *Epistle* to Cangrande, namely in its salutation and first four sections (*Ep.* XIII I [1]–4[13]). On the other hand, these cadences are scarce among the sentence-endings in the longer, expository part of the *Epistle* (XIII 5 [14]–33 [90]).

It might seem possible to rejoin, as older scholars and more recently Lindholm did, that one should not expect a similar concern with rhythmic artistry and cadences in Dante's expository prose. In the *De vulgari eloquentia* and *Monarchia*, in Lindholm's words,

... the strict observance of *cursus* is confined to the introductory chapters, whilst in the discursive parts no regular use of *cursus* can be found, since technical expressions occur that cannot be fitted into a rhythmic system. This is also the case ... in the letter to Cangrande ... Only in the first four sections, which constitute the actual letter, is *cursus* regularly observed.[6]

This apparently simple distinction, however, does not stand up to closer analysis. For Dante's habits of rhythmic cadence, and particularly his strong preference for *cursus velox*,[7] can be observed very precisely also *throughout* the *De vulgari eloquentia* and *Monarchia*, not just in their openings. Even if Dante's use of *velox*, *tardus*, and *planus* in the sentence-endings in these two works is less regular than in his *Epistles*, it can still be shown, with the help of Janson's notation and testing method, that the cadences are deliberate and not fortuitous. This differentiates Dante's expository prose notably from that of the doctrinal sections (5–33) of the Cangrande *Epistle*, where the *velox*, *tardus*, and *planus* cadences that do occur at sentence-endings are too few and too irregular to be susceptible of any proof that they are more than fortuitous.

Sections 5–33 of the *Epistle* contain 96 sentences that do not end with quoted words. In Table 1, I give in the left-hand column a complete picture of the distribution and frequency of all the rhythms found at the endings of these 96 sentences, following the format of Janson's tables. An appropriate sample to compare with this seems to me to be the first 96 sentences of *De vulgari eloquentia*, beginning, in view of Lindholm's warning, after the more obviously rhetorical introductory chapter (of 6 sentences), and again excluding all sentences that end with quoted words. The sample then extends from *DVE* I ii, 1 (*Hec est nostra vera prima locutio*) to I x, 4 (*Dicimus ergo primo Latinum bipartitum esse in dextrum et sinistrum*). As this part of *DVE*, like the exegetic part of the Cangrande *Epistle* (*Ep.* XIII), consists largely of literary discussion, one would, if it were by the same author, expect a somewhat comparable distribution and frequency of the rhythms at the ends of sentences. The figures for *DVE*, however, which are given in the right-hand column of Table 1, show on the contrary how widely the types of rhythm used diverge in the two works.

Table 1

	Ep. XIII	*DVE*
6p	1	0
6pp	1	0
1 5p	2	0

Table 1 (*cont.*)

	Ep. XIII	*DVE*
p 5p	5	2
pp 5p	2	2
1 5pp	o	o
p 5pp	1	o
pp 5pp	1	o
1 4p	3	o
p 4p	3	o
pp 4p	7	21
1 4pp	1	1
p 4pp	8	9
pp 4pp	3	1
pp 1 3p	1	4
other 1 3p	1	4
p 3p	11	25
pp 3p	1	1
p 1 3pp	2	5
other 1 3pp	4	o
p 3pp	6	2
pp 3pp	2	3
pp 1 1 2	o	1
p 1 2	5	2
other 1 2	3	o
pp 2 2	2	4
other p 2	10	6
pp 2	3	1
1	7	2
Total	96	96

A first point of comparison that emerges is a straightforward quantitative one:

Table 2

	Ep. XIII	*DVE*
velox (pp 4p)	7	21
tardus (p 4pp)	8	9
planus (p 3p)	11	25

Most striking is the difference in the use of *velox* cadences: Dante in *DVE* shows a strong preference for *velox* over *tardus*, whereas the author of the Cangrande exposition appears – if indeed his cadences were deliberately chosen – to slightly prefer *tardus* to *velox*. The difference between the two texts in the use of *planus* endings is also notable, though, as *planus* is in fact one of the commoner 'natural' cadences in Latin, I would attach less importance to this divergence than to that in the use of *velox*.

Dante's use of both *velox* and *tardus* cadences, but with a marked preference for *velox*, can be observed likewise in the philosophical–political writing in the *Monarchia*. If again we leave the more rhetorical opening chapter of this work out of account, and consider the cadences at the ends of 96 sentences beginning with *Monarchia* I ii, omitting sentences that end with quoted words, we have a sample that reaches as far as the third sentence of I xii (*Propter quod ... in intellectu vero pauci*). In this sample I note 15 *velox* cadences (I ii *témpore mensurántur, inférius assumúntur,* iii *naturáliter principári, iv beatitúdinem ordinántur, subsequéntium supponátur, manifestíssimam veritátem,* v *rátio inductíva,* ix *mótibus regulétur, 'Impérium' appellátur,* xi *aúrea nuncupábant, contráriis admiscétur, iúdici relinquántur, hóminum detorquéntis, máxime diligátur,* xii *páteat libertátis*); and 7 *tardus* (I iii *humanitátis appáreat,* v *tóta destrúitur, síve Impérium,* vi *síve Monárchiam,* x *ésse iudícium,* xi *síve Impérium, átque dilúcidat*). I have not included I v *'súis Políticis'* in my sentence-count, reckoning *Políticis* as a quoted word. While the number of *velox* cadences here is smaller than in the *DVE* sample, it is still more than twice that in the Cangrande exposition, and the proportion of *velox* to *tardus* closely resembles that in *DVE*.

To return to the rhythmically fully analysed sentence-endings of the texts in Table 1: it is likewise possible, as Janson showed, to apply a statistical χ^2 test to these. (Both the details and the significance of this method of testing are explained more fully in Orlandi's discussion.) If we compare the χ^2 values, with reference to the cadences *velox, tardus* and *planus,* for *Epistle* XIII and the sample from *DVE*, the difference is decisive (see Table 3).

In *De vulgari eloquentia*, as the sum of the χ^2 values (shown in the right-hand column) indicates, the three principal cadences have been deliberately favoured, whereas the sum of the χ^2 values for the Cangrande *Epistle* (sections 5–33) is too low to establish firmly that the author favoured these cadences, as against using them fortuitously. (The figure 5.42 is barely significant at 5 percent level of accuracy, for which the χ^2 value is 5.991.)

Table 3

	Observed frequency	Expected frequency	$\dfrac{(O-E)^2}{E}$
Ep. XIII			
tardus (p 4pp)	8	6	0.67
planus (p 3p)	11	6	4.17
velox (pp 4p)	7 }	3 }	
others	70 }	81* }	0.58
Total	96	96	5.42
DVE			
tardus (p 4pp)	9	5	3.20
planus (p 3p)	25	16	5.06
velox (pp 4p)	21	6	37.50
others	41	69	11.36
Total	96	96	57.12

*Janson (*Prose Rhythm*, p. 22) points out that the χ^2 test 'will not give reliable results if the expected frequency is less than 5 in any one comparison'. That is why, e.g. in his Table T4 (p. 23), for Cola di Rienzo, Janson must group *tardus* (*p 4pp*), of which the expected frequency is only 4, with 'others', and why this must be done likewise for *velox* (*pp 4p*) in the case of *Ep.* XIII.

A further striking comparison between the two texts suggests itself. As Janson (*Prose Rhythm*, pp. 28f), explaining the concept *consillabicatio*, states:

Medieval theorists of *cursus* ... have given by-forms for the three main forms [*velox, tardus, planus*], in which a proclitic syllable is substituted for the first syllable of the last word of the cadence. Thus they give:

    pp 1 3p sufficiant ad volátum as equal to *pp 4p hóminem recepístis*

    p 1 3pp óvis ad víctimam as equal to *p 4pp íre tentáverit*

    p 1 2 violári non pótest as equal to *p 3p íllum dedúxit.*

Furthermore, they give examples in which the *4p* word in the *velox* has been substituted by two or three graphical words, viz.

    pp 2 2 ágere nimis dúre or

    pp 1 1 2 petítio si est iústa for *pp 4p hóminem recepístis.*

These types of cadences are found regularly in some of the rhythmical authors, and we shall have to take them into account.

This (as will appear from the forms listed in Table 1) gives us the following comparative table for all admitted instances of *velox, tardus* and *planus*:

Table 4

	Ep. XIII	*DVE*
velox (pp 4p, pp 1 3p, pp 2 2, pp 1 1 2)	10	30
tardus (p 4pp, p 1 3pp)	10	14
planus (p 3p, p 1 2)	16	27
Total	36	71

That is, in our sample from *De vulgari eloquentia*, a sample consisting entirely of expository, not epistolary, prose, 71 out of 96 sentence-endings comply with the medieval theorists' prescriptions for the correct formation of *velox*, *tardus* and *planus* cadences; in the Cangrande *Epistle*, only 36 out of 96 comply. This once more brings out dramatically the difference in rhythmic habits between the two texts. In *De vulgari eloquentia*, Dante favours *velox* cadences most of all – slightly more than *planus* and far more than *tardus*; the author of the *Epistle* (who cannot be proved to have positively favoured these cadences), uses *planus* relatively often, *velox* and *tardus* equally seldom.

Finally, it may be helpful to compare the dedicatory part of the Cangrande *Epistle* (sections 1–4) with a sample from another, undisputed *Epistle* of Dante's. In *Ep.* XIII, the salutation and dedicatory sections comprise 18 sentences (if we omit the citation of the Book of Wisdom at 1 2 [6] and the last sentence in 1 4 [13], which introduces the expository sections). Of these 18 sentences, admitting 'consillabicated' cadences, 6 end with a *velox* (*perpétuuɱ increméntum, deíciat in terrórem, devotíssimus et amícus, amicítie sacraménto, pótius dirigántur, dénique recomméndo*); 4 with a *tardus* (*aliquándo supérfluum, credulitáte decípitur, serváre desídero, urgébit ultérius*); 7 with a *planus* (*excessíva cognóvi, coniugári persónas, fuísse constábit, impediátur excéssu, obviáre tenémur, ésse presúmptum, vóbis inquírens*); and 1 (*quod de propósito*), finally, is by the canons of the medieval theorists not strictly rhythmical. If we compare the first 18 sentences, say, in Dante's *Ep.* VI, we find that 8 end with a *velox* cadence (*civíliter degerétur, lácrimis mentiúntur, ália sit Romána, naufrágio properánte, cupídine obcecáto, Hespérie domitórem, ergástula concidétis, nésciens atque nólens*); 5 with a *tardus* (*Florentínis intrínsecis, maluísti insúrgere, főre obnóxia, geminétur et Délius, defensióni confíditis*); 4 with a *planus* (*pallóre noténtur, abhorrérȩt adsénsus, oblítus est déi, ígne cremári*); and again one (*vóbis ablátum est*) is not strictly rhythmical. To summarise:

Table 5

	Ep. XIII 1 [1]–4 [13]	*Ep.* VI 1 [1]–4 [15]
velox	6	8
tardus	4	5
planus	7	4
others	1	1
Total	18	18

This comparison admittedly does not afford a large enough sample of cadences for a decisive judgment on grounds of *cursus* to be possible. But it is safe to say (and indeed confirms the intuitions of earlier scholars) that the habits of *cursus* revealed in the Cangrande dedication, and in particular the preference of *velox* to *tardus*, are *compatible* with the habits we perceive in Dante's undisputed *Epistles*.

The choices of rhythmic cadence give us no grounds for doubting the authenticity of the Cangrande dedication. It is when we turn to the much longer exposition to Cangrande that follows, which does afford an adequately large sample of cadences to compare with those in Dante's known expository prose, that the evidence adduced in the previous pages seriously affects the question of authenticity. The Cangrande expositor shows rhythmic habits significantly different from those of Dante the expositor in the Latin didactic prose that is undoubtedly his. It is very difficult to imagine how Dante might have changed his own steady rhythmic habits so much that he could also plausibly have written the exposition for Cangrande.

On the codicological problem concerning the relation between the dedicatory and expository parts of *Epistle* XIII, I can make no contribution based on firsthand study of the manuscripts. The evidence set out by Brugnoli (*Opere minori* II 52ff) shows that the older family of three manuscripts (α) preserves the dedication only, while the younger, of six manuscripts (β), preserves the exposition as well. But it is important to remember that, in Nardi's words (*Il punto sull'Epistola* (cit. ch. 1, n. 3), p. 17, n. 2),

... the known manuscripts of the Epistle are all relatively late and unreliable, as is shown by the fact that all of them have the blunder *respicientis* at paragraph 20 (56) [where the sense demands a word such as *reddentis*], and that even the three which contain only the dedicatory part have, in the sentence '*Itaque, formula consumata epistole . . .*', the indispensable link for joining to the dedication the doctrinal part, which had circulated anonymously for several decades.

Both families of manuscripts, that is, derive from an exemplar that contained the link-sentence, in which the letter-writer promises, now that his task is done, to embark upon an introduction to the work, taking up the office of a *lector*. If the dedication is genuinely by Dante, was the writing of this link-sentence an act of deliberate deception, aimed at passing off the introduction as a work of Dante's own? Perhaps so. Yet it seems to me at least possible that the writer of that sentence was making what he thought to be a necessary 'editorial bridge': if he believed that the dedication and the fragment of commentary – which he may well have come across copied side by side – actually belonged together, he might have honourably supposed that he was merely filling in a lacuna, rather than doing anything more fateful – that he was clarifying, rather than causing confusion.

Excursus II
Nimrod: his character, ambitions, and thoughts about God
The evidence of the *Liber Nemroth*

The *Liber Nemroth* remains unpublished, except for the brief passages printed by Haskins in his pioneer study,[1] and some lines – chiefly chapter-headings, incipits, and explicits – cited in the recent account of the work by Livesey and Rouse.[2] The extracts discussed and edited below are intended to give a representative selection of the non-scientific material in the book: I have chosen moments, especially of dialogue, that reveal the characters of Nimrod and his interlocutor, as this author sees them, and the nature of their quest for knowledge.

From these passages it becomes clear, first, that the figure of Nimrod the astronomer, as presented in the *Liber*, is entirely distinct from Nimrod the giant, the presumptuous builder of the tower of Babel. Nimrod the astronomer is (*pace* Richard Lemay)[3] a noble and reverent figure; he is neither an atheist nor a scorner of God. While he begins with an imperfect notion of the creator, in the course of the work he arrives at an ever deeper understanding of the nature of the divine orderer. Nimrod is presented as a virtuous sage, inspired by a never-sated thirst to understand, prepared to live ascetically in order not to be deflected from his goal. Nowhere in the work is his Faustlike craving for knowledge disprized: on the contrary, it is what, in the author's view, leads Nimrod to the highest insights that are possible for a human being without the aid of the Christian revelation.

It is not very likely that Dante should have known and used the *Liber Nemroth* (though Lemay has no doubts on this score).[4] Only three manuscripts and two fragments of the book survive today, and even if one of the manuscripts (and perhaps its lost exemplar) stems from northern Italy, the chances that Dante came across the text in his years of exile are not great. Paradoxically, if Dante did see the *Liber Nemroth*, what might have kindled his imagination there is not the portrayal of the astronomer – which is a world away from that of Dante's giant – but rather the author's celebrations of the unquenchable human longing to penetrate what is hidden, a longing that is likewise celebrated in the *Commedia*, at times by way of images akin to those in the *Liber*.

To turn to the extracts in detail. Only the first of the thirteen printed here has previously been known to scholars, since it was cited by Haskins, and only this one could – on an over-hasty reading – give the impression that Nimrod was culpably godless, that (as Lemay argued) 'for the advantage of his disciples, he reduced everything to principles of calculation, dispensing him from having recourse to a Creator', or even that Nimrod 'never experienced the need to refer to the idea of a Creator'.[5]

This second assertion indeed goes against the wording even of extract (1): from the form of the firmament, Nimrod 'recognised that it had a creator', but he did not – or better, not yet – perceive the creator's nature. His knowledge even at this stage, according to the author, was 'wondrous (*ammiranda*)'; yet from observing the heavens and the stars he could only infer 'a mighty ruling creature', which he (mistakenly) called 'creator', not realising that the cosmic creator must in truth be uncreated and divine. He depicted and wrote all his cosmology 'according to his image' of that creative force – that is, giving a naturalistic rather than theistic account of the cosmos. Thus, even if his insight at this point was limited, it was remarkable within those limits – 'he told things hidden in the calculation of astronomy'.[6] Nor is it Nimrod's fault if, awed by his knowledge, 'those who lived at the time wanted to have him as their god': we are not told that he encouraged them.

In (2), not only does Nimrod 'marvel at the power of the creator', when he sees the form and motion of the firmament, but he goes on to discover the forces that hold the firmament in place, 'not like columns, but like a bond (*ligamentum*)'. And here Nimrod speaks of these powers (*virtutes*), or winds (*venti*), as sustaining the heaven 'through the ordering of the creator (*per ordinationem creatoris*)': that is, he is already moving away from his first, materialistic notion of creation towards the concept of an orderer.

In (3) Nimrod sees the two *virtutes* that order the rising and setting of the firmament as placed above it by God: as he tells Ioathon, 'My disciple, know that God (*deus*) placed two creatures, most steady powers, above the firmament'. Nimrod, it seems, has reached the point of distinguishing between cosmic forces, which are *creaturae*, and a creator who is *deus*. He has reached it by a further and deeper inquiry into the heavens. 'Do not marvel at the firmament's turning', he goes on, 'but marvel at the great wonders that stem from the power of the creator, because through his power he commanded the firmament that it should be turned, and so it was done, and he rested and reigned over it.' (The language begins to carry a hint of the first chapter of Genesis.)

Passage (4), which occurs soon afterwards in the text, is philologically the most problematic of those given here. In the first sentence, though both the manuscripts that contain it have *disposuit* and *expositione*, I assume that the prefixes have become confused, and would reverse them so as to construe: 'Thus Nimrod explained (ex*posuit*) the celestial axis, and that the knowledge of God and his might are present in its disposition (dis*positione*)'. The sentence continues (in both manuscripts): *et obcecatum est cor illius non cognoscens deum* ('and the heart of that man is blinded that does not recognise God'). It would be tempting to emend *est* to *esse* here, in order to construe this phrase too as part of Nimrod's exposition. It would also be possible to take the phrase, without emending, as an authorial intervention, contrasting the heart of a man who does not recognise God with Nimrod's heart. It seems very unlikely that the author was trying to say that Nimrod's own heart was blinded: both because, if that were the case, one would expect *cor eius* or *cor suum*, and even more because this interpretation would be at loggerheads with the earlier part of the sentence, where it seems clear that Nimrod perceives the knowledge and might of God in the ordering of the celestial axis. Only on this – the least plausible – interpretation would we have to concede that Nimrod, on his way towards God through cosmology, here had a momentary lapse. Yet this is belied by all else that we hear of his thoughts about God in the rest of the work.

Thus in (5), when Ioathon questions him about the relations between the months and the signs of the zodiac, Nimrod declares that 'on March 22 the Lord created every creature, and on March 26 he created sun and moon and stars'. Nimrod has moved from the term *creator* to *deus* to *dominus* – his perception of divinity is no longer that of an abstract moving force but of the Lord of the universe.

In (6) Nimrod's creator comes even closer to the God of Genesis. He creates all things in seven days, and sun and moon follow their ordained paths in obedience to him. And suddenly this astronomer's universe takes on a blissful, almost sacramental quality: 'just as two animals or two birds belonging to each other, when they see each other, will rejoice with the joy of the heart, so too sun and moon rejoice when they face each other, as the creator ordains'.

The next two passages, (7) and (8), show Ioathon celebrating the quest for wisdom. A heart filled with wisdom is better than a house full of golden vessels – for if these are put out, the house is bereft of them, whereas learning fecundates the more, the more it is brought forth and perceived, like a fountain that emits more and sweeter water the better it is tended. Only the stream flowing from his master's heart can quench Ioathon's burning thirst. He is like those merchants who risk their lives in their search for precious stones, travelling into a distant region, not fearing robbers, spending their all, and at last, unafraid to die, plunging into the ocean to find the gems they long for. Yet Nimrod's wisdom, even if there is the same challenge of great distance and arduous effort (*gravitudo*) in order to attain it, is filled with 'a sweet sea' – he 'longs to save, not to destroy' those who learn from him.

It is here that the metaphors seem to take us close to Dante's imagery of the sea-voyage as the life-endangering quest for uncharted knowledge – 'the water I embark on has never yet been crossed' (see above, pp. 21–4) – and to Dante's expressions of the pursuit that is never assuaged till the supreme goal is reached:

> Indeed I see that our intellect remains forever
> unsated, if it is not irradiated by that truth
> outside which nothing true can range...
> It is for this that doubt is born, like a shoot
> at the foot of truth; and it is nature makes us
> clamber from hill to hill, right to the summit.[7]

In the next two extracts from the *Liber*, (9) and (10), the glorification of the unselfish pursuit of wisdom continues, on Ioathon's part as well as Nimrod's. Nimrod insists that material advantage is irrelevant to the acquiring of knowledge: 'without payment I found learning', he tells Ioathon, 'and so I shall give thanks to God, and all things that are mine are yours'. Learning can 'level mountains and build walls', but it can also 'free those who desire it from every evil ... for the life of those who are learned is their learning, and the death of sinners is their pride'. This Nimrod, that is, proclaims the exact opposite of what is exemplified by his namesake, the giant builder.

Ioathon agrees, and again his metaphors of building are strongly differentiated from the arrogant building of Babel: 'Master, everything that you indicate to me is true. Therefore with you goodness dwells. Roll forth the stones in your intellect, that we may build the city of wisdom, that we may escape the death of lack of wisdom . . .'. This leads him to a question about how the planets are distinguished, and again, near the opening of his reply, Nimrod alludes to 'the creator of all things', who creates in the sea 'the genera of all things that exist on earth'.

In the next passage (11), Ioathon exults in the blessedness that knowledge confers. Those who live at the end of time will take joy in all that the human mind – exemplified in Nimrod – has conquered and passed on to posterity. 'And now I have a great joy, a glorious crown upon my head, and am blessed unto the length of my life, for my ears have heard what no ear has heard before.' He affirms that he would gladly give his soul for his teacher's.

Nimrod soon afterwards (12) characterises further the absoluteness of the sage's quest: a bird, however high it flies, descends at last; a fish, if it plunges to the bottom of the ocean, comes to rest; only the intellect can both soar to heaven and descend below the earth, never resting in its effort to understand. He goes on to explain the relation of earth and water, in pointedly theistic terms: 'the might of the creator holds earth in place . . . light water bears the heaviness of earth, as the creator has commanded it'. This leads Nimrod to a beautiful perception of an 'argument from contingence' for the existence of God:

And the constancy of water below earth [shows] the might of the creator; and through his might we recognise that he is the creator of all things; and through his might we know that these things were not created of themselves (*a se*), but by the creator. And if those creatures had come into being of themselves, then earth would be better than heaven, the moon hotter than the sun, the stars greater than the moon – nothing that lives would die.

It is a series of impossibles (*adynata*), declaring that nothing in creation can have the self-caused, necessary existence (*aseitas*) which alone could render a divine creator superfluous.

The final passage (13) is one that Haskins found (in slightly altered form) in another context; not recognising its provenance, he suggested that it might be the record of an actual experiment performed by Adelard of Bath, during his sojourn in the East (before 1115).[8] But it is the mythical Nimrod, not the historical

Adelard, who tries to show the location of the centre of the earth, by making observations around the time of the summer solstice. He prepares himself in the manner of an ascetic:

Oh Ioathon, I did not find this measurement except with great anguish of body. At the time I took those measurements – thirty-nine years ago – I drank no wine, so that what I wanted to search out would not defeat me; my eyes never had their fill of sleep, but always others would stay awake and guard me, so that I should not err in [observing] the spheres. Thus I came to see that the midpoint of the world is Mount Moriah. For I experimented in many places, and set up a round piece of wood, twelve cubits long and one cubit thick, and suspended it by a rope, and I swung it from place to place in the middle of the day on June 25, till I suspended it over the spot where it was noon, and the splendour of the sun alighted on it from every side, and its shadow, underneath it, became round, like the roundness of the wood that I had suspended there. And from this measuring I discovered that the centre of the world is on Mount Moriah.

The *Liber Nemroth*, of which the Latin text[9] goes back to the tenth century or quite possibly earlier, has remained unpublished and in large measure neglected because its cosmology and astronomy are not 'advanced' for their time: they still belong, for the most part, to the world of Pliny and the two works *De natura rerum* of Isidore and Bede. The fascination of the book, however, seems to me to lie less in its scientific content than in its *montage*, in its portrayal of the dedicated pre-Christian seeker of wisdom, whose inquiry gradually leads him to understand the nature not only of the cosmos but also of its creator. What is unusual is the author's presentation of his conception of knowledge: not a lonely, haughty possession but a common pursuit, divinely bestowed, and embarked upon unselfishly by master and disciple together – 'I shall give thanks to God, and all that is mine is yours.' How different from the building of the tower of Babel! Here is a humanistic idealism that Dante, had he known of it, would have loved, and would assuredly have contrasted with the attitude of the coarse, overweening giant, the Nimrod with whom he was familiar.

(1)   Et dum recordaretur Nemroth formam celi, cognovit quod habuisset creatorem, set non cognovit quis esset.[1] Et vidit celum volvens in semetipso[2] non exiens de loco suo, et agnovit quod non erat de subtus[3] quod illud impedisset, nec desuper per quod suspenderetur, et in hoc non potuit dicere aliud nisi quia[4] virtus sit que hoc sustinet. Et nominavit eam[5] fortitudinem sustinentem celum et stantem sub nullo, ut ammiranda sit scientia Nemroth, quod mensurasset formam celi, et cognovit cursus[6] signorum, et circulos stellarum, et fundamentum terre, et non agnovit quod deus creavit eam.[7] Set et hoc cognovit, quia[8] desuper creatura fortis et dominatrix sit,[9] et nominavit eam creatorem, et depinxit et scripsit omnia secundum similitudinem suam,[10] ita ut qui tunc fuerunt voluerunt illum habere ut deum, propter suam virtutem et scientiam, dicente illo occulta in compoto astronomie. Et cognovit Nemroth quia[11] celum fuisset purum, et post hec[12] factus est sol, et luna et omnes stelle.[13]

(2)   Cum[1] vidisset Nemroth formam celi et commotionem ipsius, miratus est in virtute creatoris, et dixit quia[2] istud celum oportunum est ut a quatuor virtutibus regatur, et non moveatur de loco in alium.[3] Disposuitque in scripturis suis[4] dicens, quia[5] celum sustinetur a quatuor partibus per ordinationem creatoris, ne commoveatur.[6] Et non dixit de ipsis virtutibus ut sint sicut columne que sustinent edificia, set quasi ligamentum in edificio per partes coequales, et istos ventos[7] nominavit Nemroth – per loca, ventos, et in locis, virtutes.

(3)   Et dum intueretur Ioaton in celum, quod elevaretur et exaltaretur, et de occidente quod descendit usque deorsum, locutus est magistro suo et dixit: Magister et doctor, video celum exaltari in orientem et humiliari in occidentem. Per quam virtutem fit hoc?[1] Audiens[2] hoc Nemroth respondit[3] et dixit: Discipule meus, cognosce quia deus super celum posuit duas creaturas, virtutes firmissimas,[4] atque coniunctas[5] in elevationem vel descensionem[6] eius.[7] Et propter virtutes has depinxit in similitudinem duorum draconum, et vocavit eas ascensionem et descensionem.[8]

Et dum recordatus fuisset Ioathon cuncta que exposuisset Nemroth de rota celi, dixit ei: Magister doctissime, video

celum volvens die noctuque incessabiliter. Ergo qua virtute
volvitur miror. Respondit[9] Nemroth dicens: Ne mireris in
h<oc>[10] quod volvitur celum, set mirabilia magna de virtute
creatoris, quia[11] per virtutem eius precepit ei ut fieret et
factu*m*[12] est, et quievit et mandavit super ipsum.

(4) Axem celi itaque *ex*posuit[1] Nemroth, et in *dis*positione[2] eius
scientiam dei et suam fortitudinem esse, et obcecatum est
cor illius non cognoscens[3] deum. Et dum aspiceret ad celum,
vidit illu*d*[4] volvens et inclinatum in sua rotunditate,
exponens tunc illi duos cardines, unum a septentrion*e*[5] super
terram, et alterum a parte meridiana suptus terram, [et]
dixit: Cardines celi extreme partes sunt axis . . .

(5) Cum[1] videret Ioathan omnia que exposuisset Nemroth,
dixit: Magister meus,[2] quomodo <est>[3] oportunum ut
nominentur signa – super numerum mensium, aut alibi?
Quoniam cognovimus quia[4] primus mensis in quo creata est
omnis creatura fuit Martius, et signum in quo apparuit sol
prius fuit aries. Est itaque oportunum ut nominetur primo
in Martio aries,[5] et postea omnis mensis cum suo signo?
Respondit autem[6] Nemroth et dixit: Verum est quia[7] omnis
creatura in Martio fuit creata, et signum in quo apparuit
prius[8] sol fuit aries, et <non> nominamus in ipso Martio[9]
arietem, quia[10] die in quo apparuit sol in oriente transacte
erant[11] xxvi partes arietis. In xi kalendarum Aprilium creavit
dominus[12] omnem creaturam, et in viii kalendarum Aprilium creavit[13] solem et lunam et stellas. Nam signa fuerunt
creata cum celo, sed non apparuerunt in ipso, sicut et stelle
que ea ostendunt. Propterea damus unicuique mensi signum
suum.[14] Igitur Aprili arietem, Maio taurum, et cetera sic in
ordinem.[15]

(6) Cum[1] creavit creator creaturam, condidit in firmamento[2]
celi duo magna luminaria,[3] sicut superius diximus, solem in
oriente et lunam in occidente, in directura sua, et unumquod-
que eorum[4] pergit per semitam suam sicut pr*e*cepit[5] illis
creator, quia[6] omnia que creata sunt in his diebus vii, *seu*[7]
arbores seu herbe, vel quicquit terra producit, vel fontes
aquarum, et so*l* et lun*a*,[8] et cuncta que diximus, sursum ele-
vantur; et sicut duo animalia aut du*e*[9] aves pertinentes sibi,
dum viderint se invicem, letabuntur gaudio cordis, ita sol et

luna gaudent dum obviaver*i*nt[10] sibi per ordinationem creatoris.

(7) Et postquam exposuit Nemroth Ioanton discipulo suo
numerum Iovis, interrogavit eum et dixit: Magister, iam
cognovi quod cor quod repletum fuerit doctrina melius est
quam domus plena vasis aureis, quoniam domus plena vasis
aureis, dum eieceris ea, modicum et modicum minuentur,
usque dum veniet vacua; cor vero quod repletum fuerit doctrina, quanto magis illud perquires, tanto amplius fructificat,
sicut fons aque qui emittitur, quanto magis excolitur, tanto
amplius emittit aquam dulcissimam – ita est, nam et cor
quod repletum est doctrina, fluxerint ab eo flumina que
extingunt ardorem cupientium doctrinam. Nunc autem,
sicut exposuisti michi numerum annorum Mercurii, ostende
michi quoque Iovis annos . . .

(8) Et postquam exposuit Nemroth Ioanton discipulo suo
numerum Veneris in quo signo currit, interrogavit eum et
dixit: Magister meus, quando negotiatores qui cupiunt
lapides preciosos it*er*[1] agunt in regionem longinquam, et
apparet illis quod non prelongatur eorum ab itinere, et non
dubitant fures peregrinari in longinquam regionem, nec
dubitant dispensare res suas, nec mortem de animabus suis
[non] timent, et unusquisque desiderat ut habeat lapidem
preciosum atque alius non habeat meliorem, et si non
invenerint quod querunt in terra, intrant mergentes se sub
undas maris, et per cupiditatem lapidum preciosorum obli-
viscuntur mortem marittimam et pavorem bestiarum – ergo,
si negotiatores persecuntur necessitatem illorum in regione
longinqua, nos autem, discipuli tui, magis debemus per-
quirere doctrinam tuam, que est melior lapidibus preciosis.
Et si eis regio <longinqua>[2] et mare mortiferum dant quod
querunt invenire, illorum necessitatem, e<s>t[3] plus oportunum ut magister noster det nobis quam petimus ab eo doctrinam suam, qui est in regione longinqua plena fructu
magno et mar*i* dulc*i*,[4] qui cupit salvare non perdere, et si est
illic gravitudo, quod sine gravitudine non potest perficere
illum laborem.

(9) Ioanton ait: ergo ostende discipulis tuis doctrinam per quam
veniant ad honorem magnum, sicut dixisti, quod doctrina

modicum et modicum discitur; dum vero crescit doctrina, similis est favo mellis, cuius fabricamentum mirum est super omnia edificia, et dulcedo illius melior est quam sua edificia. Respondit Nemroth: sine precio inveni doctrinam, et gratias agam deo, et omnia mea tua sunt.

(10)　Respondit Nemroth dicens:[1] Discipule meus, doctrina melior est quam fortitudo, quia doctrina deprimit montes et edificat muros. Et qui cupit multum bibere vinum, advenit tremor in membris[2] et oblivio mentis, obsurdescunt aures,[3] et balbutit lingua. Et qui cupit doctrinam cupit honorem, et liberat se ab omni malo, quia doctor quod sibi non[4] vult alteri non faciat.[5] Et qui non facit alteri quod sibi non[6] vult, non peccat, quia vita doctorum est doctrina,[7] et mors peccatorum superbia est.

Respondit illi Ioathon dicens: Magister, omnia que michi indicas[8] vera sunt. Ergo tecum est bonitas. Evolve lapides *in* intellectu, *ut* edificemus[9] civitatem sapientie, ut evadamus[10] mortem insipientie,[11] quia prima perditio errantia[12] est, et prima errantia insipientia est, et prima insipientia elongatio doctrine. Et doctori est oportunum ut sit cor eius[13] paratum ad respondendum[14] hoc, quod eum prius quis interrogaverit. Superius ostendisti michi nomina vii locorum in quibus currunt vii errantia, per omnia divisa, et non michi ostendisti per quod sunt divisa. Nunc igitur ostende michi quomodo sunt divisa.

Ait illi Nemroth: Ipsa vii errantia loca nominamus planetas, et quia planete non se mutant de loco suo in ali*um*,[15] idcirco nominamus eas provincias, quia non sunt loca minima, sicut est vicus vel civitas, set sunt magna sicut provintie. ... Nominamus eas mare,[16] non ut sint sicut maria in quibus creavit creator[17] rerum omnium genera[18] que in terra sunt − bestiarum, volucrum, animantium, pisciumque − set per magnitudinem et latitudinem earum adsimilamus eas <ad> mare Oceanum, qui concludit omnem mundum.

(11)　Respondit Ioathon dicens: O magister et doctor, non ante fuit in seculo qui perscrutatus fuisset tantam scientiam, neque <ad> eam pervenisset sicut tu. Et beati qui in extremo tempore fuerint: qualis et quanta doctrina apparebit eis! Et si fuissent ossa eorum mortua, letarentur in dono[1] quod datum est mundo. Post discessum eorum exultabunt in se-

pulcris eorum, quia magnam doctrinam hereditabunt filii
eorum, et nunc habeo leticiam magnam, coronam glorio-
sam super caput meum, et beatificor in longitudinem vite
mee, quia aures mee audierunt quod non audivit auris
prius. Et si sors premium tulisset, dedisse*m*[2] animam meam
utique pro<pter> tuam. Respondit Nemroth dicens: O
Ioathon, animam tuam des propter meam? Hoc non
poteris.

(12)   Respondit <Nemroth>:[1] similis est sapientia avibus et pisci-
bus, et fortitudo sapientie potest quod nec possunt aves nec
pisces – quod avis volat et exaltat se usque dum superat
ardorem solis, et sic descendit; et pisc*i*s plumbit[2] in mare
usque dum perveniat ad fundum, et sic requiescit; et intellectus ascendit in altum usque dum perveniat ad celum, et
perscrutatur omnia que subtus celum sunt, et descendit
subtus terram et perscrutatur omnia que subtus eam sunt.
    Nam quod me interrogasti, quomodo est fundamentum
terre – terra stat super aquam et sustinet eam sicut navis, et
fortitudo creatoris tenet eam ut non se dispergat nec demer-
gat nec moveat se de suo loco, neque se volvat de una parte
in aliam. Et subtus terram est aqua conclusa sicut in vase
cum fortitudine occulta, et aqua levis[3] suffert pondus terre,
sicut precepit creator ei, et sustinet aquam inanis vacuitas
inanem. Et de facie terre usque ad aquam, mensura eius est
quanta est de terra usque ad lunam; et subtus aquam usque
ad celum subterius, est mensura ea quantum de luna usque
ad celum superius. Terre autem et aque mensura tanta est
quanta de terra usque ad lunam, et dum circuit luna de
subtus, iuxta aquam currit, et desuper currit in aerem, et per
hoc cognovimus quod mensura terre et aque ambarum tanta
est ut mensura aeris. Et constantia aque subtus terram fortitudo creatoris; et per suam fortitudinem cognoscimus quod
ipse est creator omnium, et per suam fortitudinem cognovimus quod ista non a se creata sunt, sed a creatore. Et si ipse
creature a se fuissent, melior esset terra quam celum, luna
calidior quam sol, stelle maiores quam luna – omne vivum
non moriretur.

(13)   Dixit autem Ioathon: Magister, adhuc video aliquit quod
michi absconsum fuit, et volo cognoscere quomodo fit, quia
omnes sciunt quod mundus habet quatuor partes et

quatuor angulos – et medietatem mundi unde cognovisti,
vel in quo loco est?

Respondit Nemroth: O Ioathon, et istam mensuram non
inveni nisi cum grandi angustia. In tempore[1] quando mensu-
ravi mensuras istas – est annus xxxviiii – vinum non bibi,[2] ut
non <me> exuperare*t*[3] quod inquirere volebam,[4] et oculi mei
non fuerunt satiati a[5] somno, set semper[6] alii me custodie-
bant[7] vigilantes, ut non errassem in circulis. Cognovi ergo
quia[8] medius locus est mundi mons Amorreorum, quia[9]
posui mensuras et probavi *per*[10] multa loca, et posui lignum
rotundum habens xii cubitos[11] longitudinis, et grossitudo[12]
illius cubitus unus, et suspendi illu*d*[13] per funem, et tantum
percommutavi[14] eum de loco in locum in medio *die*[15] vii
kalendarum Iulii, donec suspendi illum in locum medii diei,
et resedit super eum splendor solis ex omnibus partibus, et
facta est umbra ipsius[16] suptus eum rotunde,[17] sicut rotun-
ditas ipsius ligni qu*od*[18] suspenderam. Et de ipsa mensura
cognovi quia medius mundus est in monte Amorreorum.[19]

R: Rome, Vat. Pal. lat. 1417 (s. XI, copied in Germany)
V: Venice, Marc. lat. VIII 22 (2760) (s. XII ¾, copied in northern Italy)
P: Paris, B.N. lat. 14754 (s. XII ¾, copied at Chartres)

For clarity I have made the sigla correspond to the three cities where the MSS are
preserved today. I follow Livesey and Rouse's suggestions (*art. cit.*, n. 2) about the
date and provenance of the MSS. As they show, the Venice and Paris MSS are
closely related, but neither is a copy of the other. The first four folios of the *Liber*
are missing in the Paris one.

I use R as my base MS whenever it contains the passage edited, with a minimum
of corrections from V and P. (Even these could be reduced if we assume that the
author wrote a pre-Carolingian Latin – if, for instance, he confused accusatives and
ablatives, and made errors of concord, like Gregory of Tours – which left more
traces in the earliest MS than in the later ones.) I omit the chapter-headings, and do
not record purely orthographic variants, or the fitful alternation of ę and e in R.
Punctuation and capitalisation of names are my own. Letters emended are in
italics, additions are marked < >, excisions [ ].

(1) (R 1v, V 1r)   1 non agnoscens q.e. V   2 semetipsum V   3 erat de
subtus: *sic* R habuisset desubter V   4 quod V   5 eam nominavit V (RV *apud
Haskins*)   6 cursum V   7 ea V (RV *apud Haskins*)   8 et cognovit quod V
9 est V   10 suam similitudinem V   11 quod V   12 hec: *sic* RV (hoc
Haskins)   13 stelle celi V

(2) (R 1v, V 1v)   1 Dum V   2 quod V   3 alio R   4 scriptura sua V
5 quod V   6 a quatuor virtutibus per quatuor partes per ordinationem creatoris,
ne commoveatur de loco suo V   7 istos octo ventos V

(3) (R 2r, V 1v)   1 per qualem virtutem hoc V   2 et audiens V   3 r. ei V
4 cognoscas quia super celum posuit creator duas virtutes fortissimas V   5 evinc-
tas R   6 ascensionem R   7 es V   8 *Followed by heading* De xii fortitudinibus

que circumdant celum. R   9 R. ei V   10 h R   eo V   11 qui V   12 factus R

(4)   (R 2v–3r, V 4v)   1 disposuit RV   2 et in expositione R   sine expositione V   3 agnoscens V   4 illum R   5 septentrionem R

(5)   (R 4r, V 5v, P 203v–204r)   1 Dum V   2 meus *om.* VP   3 est *om.* R
4 quod VP   5 primo martius at a. V   primo martius ac a. P   6 autem *om.* VP
7 quod VP   8 p.a. VP   9 non *om.* R   non nominamus ipso martio VP
10 quod VP   11 sunt VP   12 dominus *om.* VP   13 aprilis creans VP
14 mensium signum (*om.* suum) VP   15 ordine VP

(6)   (R 6v, V 8v, P 206v)   1 Dum P   2 formam VP   3 l.m. VP   4 eorum
om. VP   5 precepit: *sic* VP   prius cepit R   6 quod VP   7 fuit R   *om.* VP
8 solem et lunam RVP   9 duo R   10 obviaverunt R

(7)   (V 18r–v, P 216v)   *No variants or corrections*

(8)   (V 19r, P 217r)   1 itiner (*sic*) VP   2 *om.* VP   3 et VP   4 mare dulce
VP

(9)   (V 20r, P 218r)   *No variants or corrections*

(10)   (R 13r–v, V 22r, P 220r)   1 N.d. *om.* VP   2 t. membri VP   3 obsur-
descit auris VP   4 quod d.q. non sibi VP   5 facit VP   6 alio q. non sibi VP
7 quod v.d. doctrina est VP   8 o.q. dicis VP   9 *sic* VP   evolvere lapides et
intellectus vite edificemus R   10 ut evademus R   et ut evadamus VP
11 m. ipsius i. VP   12 e.p. R   13 cor eius: *sic* R   eius os VP   14 *In* VP,
respondendum *is followed by*: qui (*sic* VP; *l.* cui?) prius eum interrogaverit. Et nunc
ostende michi quomodo sunt divisa loca vii errantium. Respondit Nemroth: Ipsa
nominamus loca que planete non semotant de suo loco in alium, et nominamus ea
provincias, que non . . .   15 alio R   16 Et n.e. maria PV   17 *In* VP, creator
is followed by: omnia, set per granditatem et latitudinem (et *l.* *repeated* P) eorum (eor
P) assimilamus eos mari occeano qui concludit omnem mundum.   18 generum
R

(11)   (R 14v)   1 donis R   2 dedisset R

(12)   (V 23r–v, P 220v)   1 *om.* VP   2 pisces V   plumbit: *sic* VP (*The verb is
not attested; the context requires the sense 'plunges', but the Late Latin* *plumbicare or
*plumbiare *postulated by philologists as the ancestor of Fr.* plonger – *cf. von Wartburg,*
Fr. Etym. Wört., *s.v.* *plumbicare – *does not appear to survive in written records*)   3
lenis P

(13)   (R 15r; *from* et istam mensuram *only,* V 26r–v, P 224r)   1 I.t. *om.* VP   2
istas mensuras xxxviiii annos vinum non bibi VP   vinum vi n.b. R   3 ut non
me exuperaret: *sic* VP   ut non exuperarer R   4 q.i.v. *om.* VP   5 a *om.* VP
6 semper *om.* VP   7 c.m. VP   8 *After* in circulis VP *have*: celi vel cursu
illius, et de umbra solis congnovi quod   9 quod VP   10 per: *sic* VP   pro R
11 cubitus VP   12 grassitudo V   13 illum R   14 commutavi VP   15
eius R   16 eius VP   17 rotunda VP   18 quem R   l.q.s. *om.* VP   19
Hec est enim figura eius. *add.* R

Notes

Abbreviations:

Works by Dante:

Conv.	*Convivio*
DVE	*De vulgari eloquentia*
Ep., Epp.	*Epistola(e)*
Inf.	*Inferno*
Mon.	*Monarchia*
Par.	*Paradiso*
Purg.	*Purgatorio*
V.N.	*Vita Nuova*

Journals and series:

GCS	Griechische christliche Schriftsteller
JWCI	*Journal of the Warburg and Courtauld Institutes*
MGH	Monumenta Germaniae Historica
P.L.	Patrologia Latina
RAC	*Reallexikon für Antike und Christentum*
REI	*Revue des Etudes Italiennes*
RF	*Romanische Forschungen*

Some standard abbreviations for classical texts and books of the Bible are also used.

Preface

1 *Nel mondo di Dante* (Rome 1944), p. 61.
2 *Ibid.*
3 *Prose Rhythm in Medieval Latin from the 9th to the 13th Century*, Studia Latina Stockholmiensia xx *(Stockholm 1975).*

1 The *Commedia* and Medieval Modes of Reading

1 I have in mind H. R. Jauss's concept *Alterität*, in the title essay of his *Alterität und Modernität in der mittelalterlichen Literatur* (Munich 1977).
2 Details of the six early commentaries I have used – those of Jacopo Alighieri, Graziolo de' Bambaglioli, Guido da Pisa, Jacopo della Lana, Pietro Alighieri, and Boccaccio – are given in the Bibliographical Note below, p. 148. Cf. also F. Mazzoni, 'Per la storia della critica dantesca 1: Jacopo Alighieri e Graziolo Bambaglioli (1322–1324)', *Studi danteschi* xxx (1951) 157–202; B. Sandkühler, *Die frühen Dantekommentare und ihr Verhältnis zur Kommentartradition* (Munich 1967); L. Jenaro-MacLennan, *The Trecento Commentaries on the Divina Commedia and the Epistle to Cangrande* (Oxford 1974).
3 Some of the detailed problems concerning the *Epistle* to Cangrande are discussed (and I hope oriented in profitable new directions) in Excursus 1 below.

Specialists will recognise how deeply the approach in the following paragraphs is indebted to Bruno Nardi's studies, in particular to his *Il punto sull'Epistola a Cangrande* (Florence 1960). It would overburden the present argument to analyse the contributions made to the debate *de Epistola* since Nardi's publication; briefly, it seems to me that such discussions as those in A. C. Charity, *Events and their Afterlife* (Cambridge 1966), pp. 200–7, R. Hollander, *Studies in Dante* (Ravenna 1980), pp. 39–89, and G. Padoan, *Il pio Enea, l'empio Ulisse* (Ravenna 1977), pp. 30–63, while they contain many points of interest, have not invalidated the central observations that Nardi made. In introducing the fine recent edition of the *Epistola*, in Dante Alighieri, *Opere Minori*, ed. P. V. Mengaldo *et al.*, II (Milan–Naples 1979) 512–21, G. Brugnoli summarises the principal questions of controversy, inclining in the main towards Nardi's solutions.

4 See particularly the appendix of 'Texte über den vierfachen Sinn der Schrift' in E. Garin, *Geschichte und Dokumente der abendländischen Pädagogik* I (Hamburg 1964) 257–82.

5 *Ep.* XIII (*Opere Minori* II (cit. n. 3) 598–643), II, 33–4.

6 For a conspectus of medieval otherworld legends and visions, see esp. C. Fritzsche, 'Die lateinischen Visionen des Mittelalters', *RF* II (1886) 247–79, III (1887) 337–69 (suppl. by E. Peters, *ibid.* VIII (1896) 361–4); A. Rüegg, *Die Jenseitsvorstellungen vor Dante* (2 vols., Einsiedeln–Cologne 1945); E. Cerulli, *Il 'Libro della Scala' e la questione delle fonti arabo-spagnole della Divina Commedia* (Vatican City 1948); and *Nuove ricerche sul 'Libro della Scala'* (Vatican City 1972); H. R. Patch, *El otro mundo en la literatura medieval* (= *The Other World* (1950), with suppl. by M. R. Lida de Malkiel (Mexico–Buenos Aires 1956)); U. Ebel, 'Die literarischen Formen der Jenseits- und Endzeitsvisionen', *Grundriss der romanischen Literaturen des Mittelalters* VI 1, ed. H. R. Jauss (Heidelberg 1968), pp. 181–215; C. Segre, 'L'*Itinerarium animae* nel Duecento e Dante', *Letture Classensi* XIII (1984) 9–32 (with excellent recent bibliography).

7 Cf. the fine observation of G. Contini (*Varianti e altra linguistica* (Turin 1970), p. 376): 'La sua protesta "Io non Enëa, io non Paulo sono" significa *e contrario*, anche in accezione stilistica, che suo paradigma è la perentorietà e imprevidibilità del "famoso saggio" e delle Scritture.'

8 Many scholars have quoted Pietro Alighieri's words (*Commentarium*, p. 8): 'Some things cannot be understood literally, for, taken literally, such things would induce not instruction but error ... For what person of sound mind could believe that Dante descended in this way, and saw such things, except allowing for my distinctions among modes of speaking figuratively?' For Pietro, the choice was between an account of the beyond told figuratively, for instruction, and a literal account by one who was a prey to hallucinations. Evidently he wanted his father to be remembered as a great imaginative writer and not as someone who had been 'abnormal' – and he saw these possibilities as mutually exclusive.

Similarly in our century, in a famous passage, Benedetto Croce (*La poesia di Dante* (Bari ²1921), pp. 6of), arguing that the *Commedia* was a 'theological romance', looked ironically at those who thought the work to be anything other than fiction. In a dichotomy which is something of a caricature, Croce sets on the one side an imagined group of early readers of the *Commedia*, so struck by the precision and coherence of Dante's descriptions that they believed he had really visited the otherworld, on the other the early commentators, who were compelled, because of those naïve readers, to insist that Dante was writing 'as a poet'. A brief aside, on 'the moderns, who do not need such *caveats*', points Croce's contrast between medieval manifestations of simplemindedness and the self-evident assumptions of twentieth-century man.

For Croce, the alternatives were plain: either Dante 'was deceived by his own imaginings', or else he made everything up. The first alternative would be unfair to Dante's genius – it would suggest 'a great admixture of madness' in him, and would be inconsistent with the limpid, lucidly aware quality of his mind and spirit. Dante, that is, if he was not a deluded fanatic, was a man who conformed to Crocean standards of enlightenment. He is too great a poet for the first possibility, therefore only the second remains. *Tertium non datur.* Besides, Croce adds, all 'theological, scientific and socialist romances' aim to be precise and meticulous in their detailed imaginings.

In my view, the *Commedia* cannot helpfully be classified with romances of any of these kinds: in its central intentions, it seems as far from, say, Ramón Lull's *Blanquerna* as from William Morris' *News from Nowhere*. What the alternatives imposed by Croce cannot comprehend are the literary realms of the prophets and sibyls, or the apocalypses of late Antiquity, or again, nearer to Dante's time, the writings of prophetic and visionary inspiration, such as those of Hildegard of Bingen, Joachim of Fiore, Mechthild of Magdeburg, or Marguerite Porete. Any attempt to categorise Dante's *Commedia* in a literary genre that fails to take these diverse affinities into account cannot be adequate.

The majority of scholars since Croce have continued to think of the *Commedia* in terms of fiction. Thus C. S. Singleton, for instance, speaks of 'the make-believe of his poem' (*Dante Studies* I (Cambridge Mass. 1954) 16; on Dante's 'fiction', cf. also *ibid.* pp. 62f). More recently, Hollander (cit. n. 3), p. 63, cites with approval Singleton's dictum, 'The fiction of the *Divine Comedy* is that it is not fiction', and claims that 'we can ... almost all agree that Dante's poem is a *fictio*' (p. 64); 'Dante creates a fiction which he pretends to consider not to be literally fictitious, while at the same time contriving to share the knowledge with us that it is precisely fictional' (p. 86). Hollander produces no evidence that Dante contrived this, let alone *how* he might have contrived it. Again it is salutary to recall that the great prophet-visionaries of the twelfth and thirteenth centuries – Hildegard and Joachim, Mechthild and Marguerite – made unflinching claims to truth. I believe it is their kind of claim that Dante makes.

One key passage which relates to this problem is that in the Cangrande letter, where the *forma sive modus tractandi* of the poem is characterised, among other things, as *poeticus, fictivus* (*Ep.* XIII 9, 27). Can this mean 'semplicemente che di volta in volta sono usate nella *Comedìa* espressioni poetiche, fittive, descrittive, digressive ecc., senza dare ad alcuno di quegli aggettivi importanza preminente o generale' (thus Padoan (cit. n. 3), p. 51)? There would seem to be two objections: first, *forma sive modus tractandi* suggests something more fundamental than simply an inventory of diverse kinds of expressions found in the *Commedia*: it should refer to the expository method as such, rather than just to sporadic occurrences. Second, the series of adjectives would be less troubling in relation to the *Commedia* if *fictivus* were not placed immediately after *poeticus*: if it were mentioned separately, one might plausibly argue, for instance, that it referred to the use of such devices as mythological allusions. As it is, one cannot easily escape the impression that for the author of the Cangrande letter poetry and fiction were in some essential way united, and that the *forma sive modus tractandi* was a rhetorical and philosophical way of communicating instruction, on the consequences of good and evil actions, rather than a way of truthfully narrating visionary experiences. And if that was the author's view, then Nardi and Padoan are agreed on this at least, that such a view belittles the claims Dante himself makes in the *Commedia*.

On the development of the concept *forma sive modus tractandi*, and its subdivisions, see most recently A. J. Minnis, *Medieval Theory of Authorship* (London 1984), pp. 119–45. In the passage Minnis cites from Ulrich of Strassburg (p. 140), however, the poet is called not *philomicos* but *philomites* ('myth-lover'); he does not 'excite to admiration', but 'to wonder', and it is through this wondering that philosophical inquiry arises (cf. Aristotle, *Metaphysics* 982b).

9 While detailed allegorisations such as these are clearly 'feigned', I would still argue that the central underlying perception is not an allegory, but has the reality of a *figura*. The Donna Gentile does not exclude the girl who consoled Dante for Beatrice's death (*V.N.* 35–6), but presupposes her. Because she was first perceived as alive and human, she can figure something more. At the same time, Dante's *expositions* in the *Convivio* rely on an allegorical method which he carefully compares with that used for Scripture (*Conv.* II 1).

10 All the principal passages in which Dante insists upon the veracity of his visions are cited and discussed in B. Nardi's 'Dante profeta', in his *Dante e la cultura medievale* (Bari ²1949), pp. 336–416; cf. also Padoan (cit. n. 3), pp. 33–42.

11 Or at least the first two *cantiche*: it is not absolutely unequivocal, from the wording of the *Epistle*, that *Paradiso* was complete when it was written.

12 Singleton (cit. n. 8), p. 1, rephrases: 'allegorically, it is (to reduce his longer statement of it) God's justice as that may be seen in the state of souls after death'; he goes on to suggest that this means, for instance, that in *Inferno* v lust is imaged in the storm, and that the allegorical meaning, therefore, is that 'it is proper, it is just, that the condition of the lustful after death should be the condition of lust itself'. This is a valuable observation as such, yet I cannot see how it can correspond to, or be derived from, the wholly conventional and unilluminating Latin words in the *Epistle* (25): *homo prout merendo et demerendo per arbitrii libertatem iustitie premiandi et puniendi obnoxius est.*

13 As Sandkühler (cit. n. 2), pp. 235–9, pointed out, Graziolo de' Bambaglioli, commenting on *Inf.* II 53ff, already (in 1324) speaks explicitly of a historical Beatrice, the daughter of a *dominus*, who had died. But immediately afterwards, paraphrasing II 76ff, Graziolo continues: *O domina virtus, hoc est o summa virtus . . .* So, too, the *Ottimo* commentary (*ca.* 1334) affirms of Beatrice: 'Ella fu il primo suo amore in carne, e la teologia è il primo amore allo spirito.' Nonetheless, even when the historical reality of Beatrice is acknowledged, the early commentators also invariably hold her to represent an abstraction. Graziolo is unusual in that, after a detailed allegorêsis of the first two cantos of *Inferno*, he continues in the main with a simple literal exposition (cf. Mazzoni (cit. n. 2), pp. 190f).

It should also be noted that there is no unanimity among the first commentators about particular allegorical significances. Thus for instance, while the *lonza* of *Inf.* 1 32 is usually identified with *luxuria*, Jacopo della Lana (p. 109) and at one moment Graziolo (p. 2), identify it with *vanagloria*. And while Beatrice is most often identified with *theologia*, Guido da Pisa (pp. 31f) says that she *tenet typum et figuram vite spiritualis*, and only sometimes (*aliquando*) can be taken as theology, while Jacopo Alighieri (p. 51) claims that throughout the *Commedia* Beatrice means the Bible: 'la qual per tutto questo libro la divina scrittura s'intende'.

14 They are conveniently assembled in E. Auerbach's *Gesammelte Aufsätze zur romanischen Philologie* (Berne–Munich 1967), pp. 43–160 ('*Figura*', ibid. pp. 55–92); a longer version of one of these essays was published separately: *Typologische Motive in der mittelalterlichen Literatur* (Krefeld 1953).

15 '*Figura*' (cit. n. 14), p. 77. This is not to deny that it is possible to use the concept allegory itself in a flexible and sensitive way, or that there are medieval allegorical poems (and moments in poems) of great imaginative 'reality'. But I do not know a *medieval* exposition of allegory that is adequate to such allegorical poetry (see my discussion, '*Arbor caritatis*', in *Medieval Studies for J. A. W. Bennett* (Oxford 1981), pp. 207–53). Nor, again, do I know any examples of allegorical exegesis in the thirteenth or fourteenth century that even approach the intellectual stature and richness of those found in Philo or Plotinus, or Scotus Eriugena, in earlier periods.

16 '*Figura*', p. 86.

17 On the relations between the poetry of Alan of Lille and Dante, see esp. E. R. Curtius, 'Dante und Alanus ab Insulis', *RF* LXII (1950) 28–31; A. Ciotti, 'Alano e Dante', *Convivium* XXVIII (1960) 257–8; P. Dronke, *The Medieval Poet and his World* (Rome 1984), pp. 101f, 431–8.

18 Alain de Lille, *Anticlaudianus*, ed. R. Bossuat (Paris 1955), p. 56. This figurative sense of *emblema – abundantia –* is attested not only in glosses (*Thesaurus Linguae Latinae* V 2, 450, 73), but also in Carolingian and Ottonian poetry; in the early twelfth century, Thiofrid of Echternach († 1110), *Serm.* I, 1, speaks of Ecclesia's breasts as filled with *gratiae caelestis emblemate*. (I am indebted to *Mittellateinisches Wörterbuch* for this information.)

19 *Anticlaudianus* V 265–305. The invocation is placed at the centre of the central book of the epic – the fifth of the nine.

20 In the course of the poem she is also often called Prudentia, and at times Sapientia or Sophia. Her helplessness in the highest heaven makes clear that she is not to be identified with divine Wisdom (Hagia Sophia).

21 I think it chronologically unlikely, however, that by 1182, when he was composing the *Anticlaudianus*, Alan could have known any of Joachim's writings directly. M. Reeves and B. Hirsch-Reich, *The Figurae of Joachim of Fiore* (Oxford 1972), give an illuminating account of the main lines of Joachim's thought, with extensive bibliography.

22 J. Huizinga, *Über die Verknüpfung des Poetischen mit dem Theologischen bei Alanus de Insulis*, Mededeelingen der Koninklijke Akademie van Wetenschappen, Afd. Letterkunde 74, B, 6 (Amsterdam 1932), pp. 65ff, first pointed out the (from an orthodox Christian standpoint) highly unusual selection of virtues and vices in the *Anticlaudianus*. Thus the *concilium virtutum* near the opening includes among the virtues not only Ratio and Prudentia but Copia, Favor, Iuventus, Risus, Largitas and Nobilitas; among the vices that they combat in Bk IX are Segnities and Stultitia, but also Senectus, Paupertas, Esuries, Sitis, Ieiunia, Fletus, Tristities, and Infamia. In his epic, we might say, Alan showed himself to be the Joachim of the scholastic and chivalric world.

23 *Inf.* I 101ff. C. T. Davis, *Enciclopedia Dantesca* s.v. *veltro* (V 908–12), has given a comprehensive and judicious account of the speculations concerning this prophecy.

24 *Purg.* XXXIII 37–45; cf. P. Mazzamuto, *Enciclopedia Dantesca* s.v. *Cinquecento diece e cinque* (II 10–14), and also the discussion below, pp. 75–7.

25 It is significant that, among the paintings in Natura's house,

> Aristotle depicts
> the wrestling-ground of logic, but, more divinely,
> Plato dreams the very mysteries of things,
> and heaven's depths, and tries to scan God's purpose.   (I 131–4)

Alan's contrast between logical thought and imaginative discovery of the *archana rerum* implies a clear value-judgment.

26 The passage in Dante (*Par.* II 127–32) where the spheres take up like craftsmen the images provided by the divine artist, and make of each image a seal, by which God's art is impressed upon the spheres below, is particularly close to Alan in inspiration.

27 Cf. my study 'Integumenta Virgilii', in *Lectures médiévales de Virgile* (Rome 1985), pp. 313–29. Insofar as there is the possibility of allegory in the *Anticlaudianus*, it relates not so much to the *dramatis personae* (whose names declare their significance) as to their actions – such as constructing, travelling, or fighting – which could also stand for experiences within an individual human mind.

28 In the thirteenth century William of Auxerre, in his commentary on the *Anticlaudianus*, and Adam de la Bassée, in his *Ludus super Anticlaudianum*, tried to identify the *puella* with Noys (the divine mind, the feminine divine emanation

that Alan knew from the *Cosmographia* of Bernardus Silvestris); yet this too is imaginatively unsatisfactory, because Alan explicitly states that *poli regina . . . haurit mente Noym* (V 166–9).

29 This point is particularly well brought out by Padoan (cit. n. 3), pp. 44–6.

30 J. A. Scott, 'Dante's Allegory', *Romance Philology* XXVI (1972–3) 573, however, rightly notes that, on at least two occasions, the techniques of biblical exegesis were applied to Ovid's *Metamorphoses* – by Arnulf of Orléans (s. XII²), and later by Pierre Bersuire (†1362).

31 He also differs from Dante in a number of philosophical expressions and tenets – cf. Nardi (cit. n. 3), pp. 31–40.

32 U. Krewitt gives a very full documentation of the tradition in his *Metapher und tropische Rede in der Auffassung des Mittelalters*, Beihefte zum 'Mittellateinischen Jahrbuch' 7 (1971). Cf. also M. L. Colish, *The Mirror of Language* (Lincoln–London ²1983). Colish's discussion of Dante's inheritance is unfortunately flawed by the concept of 'the decorative approach to poetry', 'the ornamental view of poetry' (pp. 168, 171, and *passim*). This contrasts markedly especially with the thought of Geoffrey of Vinsauf:

> First look at the mind of your word,
> then at its face – don't trust the face's colour!
> Unless the inmost colour is at one with the external,
> meaning there grows base. To paint a word's face
> is to paint scum, it is a falsification, a pretence
> at form, a whited wall, a hypocrite word,
> pretending to be something though it is nothing.

(*Poetria nova* 739–45; cf. *The Medieval Poet and his World* (cit. n. 17), pp. 28ff).

33 *Metaphorismorum* in the Latin text. I cannot trace the formation *metaphorismus* elsewhere: it does not occur in the *Novum Glossarium Mediae Latinitatis* or the other ancient and medieval Latin dictionaries known to me, and has not to my knowledge received comment from Dante scholars. In the writings whose authenticity is not disputed, Dante once uses *transumptive* to mean 'metaphorically' (*Ep.* III 2, 4), but never uses *metaphorismus*, *metaphora*, or any derivative from these.

34 *Ep.* XIII 18, 44, citing *Rhet.* III, 1414 b 19–20. His wording here is closer to the translation by William of Moerbeke (*Aristoteles Latinus* XXXI 1–2, *Rhetorica*, ed. B. Schneider (Leiden 1978), p. 308) than to the anonymous one (*ibid.* p. 149), but is not fully identical with either. In the passages cited and discussed below, I use William's version, giving references both to this and to the Greek text.

35 *Symbolic Images* (London 1972), pp. 165f.

36 *Rhet.* III 1410 b 12 (*Aristoteles Latinus* XXXI 298).

37 *Ibid.* 1404 b 7, 11–12 (XXXI 283).

38 *Ibid.* 1406 b 9 (XXXI 288).

39 *De oratore* III 152.

40 *Ibid.* III 155. Here Cicero was imitated by Quintilian, *Inst. or.* VIII 6, 6. Quintilian goes on to elaborate a conception of allegories and enigmas as extended or continued metaphors. Among his examples are Horace's ode (I 14) about the ship of the state, and the riddle of Vergil's shepherd Damoetas (*Ecl.* III 104f). Quintilian's observations on allegory would apply particularly well to, for instance, Christ's parables in the Gospels; they are not readily applicable to Dante's *Commedia*, or for that matter to any of the pervasively allegorical poems – such as the *Anticlaudianus* and the *Roman de la Rose* – that Dante knew. These showed poetic possibilities which Quintilian could not, historically, have known or surmised. Again, Quintilian's somewhat unfriendly treatment of *aenigma* is less pertinent to Dante than is the Neoplatonic conception transmitted to the Middle Ages by Dionysius (cf. my discussion in *Fabula*

(Leiden–Cologne 1974), pp. 34–47), or indeed the observations of Isidore of Seville, who, unlike Quintilian, distinguished carefully between allegory and enigma (see below, p. 25).

41 *De oratore* III 157f.

42 *Poetria nova* 247–62, ed. E. Faral, *Les arts poétiques du XIIe et du XIIIe siècle* (Paris 1924), pp. 204f:

> Quae fit in occulto, nullo venit indice signo;
> Non venit in vultu proprio, sed dissimulato,
> Et quasi non sit ibi collatio, sed nova quaedam
> Insita mirifice transsumptio, res ubi caute
> Sic sedet in serie quasi sit de themate nata:
> Sumpta tamen res est aliunde, sed esse videtur
> Inde; foris res est, nec ibi comparet; et intus
> Apparet, sed ibi non est; sic fluctuat intus
> Et foris, hic et ibi, procul et prope: distat et astat.
> Hoc genus est plantae, quod si plantetur in horto
> Materiae, tractatus erit iocundior; hic est
> Rivus fontis, ubi currit fons purior; hic est
> Formula subtilis iuncturae, res ubi iunctae
> Sic coeunt et sic se contingunt quasi non sint
> Contiguae, sic continuae quasi non manus artis
> Iunxerit, immo manus Naturae.

The passage is discussed more fully in *The Medieval Poet and his World* (cit. n. 17), pp. 24ff. I have found no indication that there is any precise earlier analogue to Geoffrey's conception. E. Gallo, *The 'Poetria nova' and its Sources in Early Rhetorical Doctrine* (The Hague–Paris 1971), in his section on *collatio* (pp. 170–2, 228), does not adduce one; at the same time, he does not note the importance and originality of Geoffrey's insights here.

43 Ed. A. Gaudenzi, in *Bibliotheca iuridica medii aevi* II i (Bologna 1892) 252–97. The section 'De transumptionibus', which contains the passages discussed below, is on pp. 281a–285a. It is tempting to speculate whether Boncompagno's title, *Rhetorica novissima*, may have been his 'riposte' to Geoffrey's *Poetria nova*: this work, which was dedicated to Innocent III and which had a rapid and wide diffusion (more than eighty manuscripts are still known), will have reached Italy in the years immediately preceding Boncompagno's treatise.

44 *Transumptio est quedam imago loquendi in qua unum ponitur et reliquum intelligitur* (p. 281a).

45 *Transumptio est quoddam naturale velamen, sub quo rerum secreta occultius et secretius proferuntur (ibid.).* There is a certain analogy to this conception in the philosophical discussion of 'veiling' by the early-twelfth-century Platonist William of Conches: cf. *Fabula* (cit. n. 40), esp. i (iii): 'Mysteries and how to cover them' (pp. 47–55).

46 The citation is from Ps. 22[23]: 4.

47 *Europäische Literatur und Lateinisches Mittelalter* (Berne ²1954), ch. 7, sect. i.

48 On Dante's addresses to the reader in the *Divina Commedia*, see Auerbach, *Gesammelte Aufsätze* (cit. n. 14), pp. 145–55; L. Spitzer, 'Gli appelli al lettore nella *Commedia*', in his *Studi italiani* (Milan 1976), pp. 213–39.

49 *Par.* I 67–9; Ovid, *Metam.* XIII 944–50.

50 *Par.* IV 124–32. On Dante's expressions of his thirst for knowledge, see esp. P. Boyde, *Dante Philomythes and Philosopher* (Cambridge 1981), pp. 54–6.

51 While one might, following Auerbach, speak of a figural relationship between Ulisse's voyage and Dante's, it seems to me that, both historically and critically, it would be still more appropriate to call it a symbolic relationship: see the discussion of *symbolum* in sect. iv.

52 *Par.* IV 139–42.
53 *In Apoc.* I i (P.L. 196, 686f). On the Dionysian background, see my discussion in *Fabula* (cit. n. 40), pp. 43–6.
54 *Etym.* I 37, 26:

> Inter allegoriam autem et aenigma hoc interest, quod allegoriae vis gemina est et sub res alias aliud figuraliter indicat; aenigma vero sensus tantum obscurus est, et per quasdam imagines adumbratus.

On the significance of Goethe's distinction, and its medieval analogues, see *Fabula*, pp. 119–22.

55 E. Jeauneau, 'L'usage de la notion d'*integumentum*', in his *Lectio Philosophorum* (Amsterdam 1973), pp. 127–92; *Fabula*, pp. 23–8, 48–52.
56 Gombrich (cit. n. 35), pp. 150ff; *Fabula*, pp. 44–7.
57 Whom Plato also calls gods (*Dii deorum*, 41 A, in Calcidius' Latin version, ed. J. H. Waszink, p. 35). The passage cited below is from *Timaeus* 41 D–42 B; my translation follows the Latin of Calcidius (ed. cit. pp. 36f) rather than the Greek.
58 *Par.* II 131f; VII 64f. The poem, *O qui perpetua*, is *Cons. Phil.* III m. 9. While some of the ninth- and tenth-century commentators on this poem were troubled by its Platonism and questioned whether the author could have been a believing Christian, Dante had no doubts whatever about Boethius' faith (see below, pp. 96ff).
59 On the (Alexandrian) origins of this principle in relation to Scripture, cf. Charity (cit. n. 3), pp. 185f.
60 The passage given below is translated from the version printed by T. Gregory, *Platonismo medievale* (Rome 1958), pp. 98–102; cf. also Guillaume de Conches, *Glosae super Platonem*, ed. E. Jeauneau (Paris 1965), pp. 210ff.
61 This is not found in Scripture, but is an inference made by Jerome; William of Conches himself, in his later work, *Dragmaticon*, attributes the notion to Augustine (see the texts cited by Jeauneau *ad loc.*).
62 *In Aristotelis librum de Anima* I, lect. VIII 107, ed. A. M. Pirotta (Turin–Rome ³1948), p. 31. Cf. *Fabula* (cit. n. 40), pp. 3–5.
63 Bruno Nardi, *Saggi di filosofia dantesca* (Florence ²1967), p. 70, has also adduced a notable parallel to the more positive Dantesque interpretation of Plato's myth, in Albertus Magnus, *De natura et origine animae* II 7.
64 *Purg.* XXX 109–12.
65 *Conv.* II xiv, 14; IV viii, 1. Dante, like Thomas, will have read the *Ethics* in the version of William of Moerbeke, which is edited along with Thomas' commentary by R. M. Spiazzi, *In decem libros Ethicorum Aristotelis ad Nicomachum expositio* (Turin–Rome ³1964).
66 *Par.* IV 73f; *Ethica* III, 1110 a 2 (Spiazzi, p. 111).
67 *Ethica* III, lect. II 395 (Spiazzi, p. 115).
68 Livy, II xii, 13. It is not wholly certain whether Dante knew this passage at first hand, or only indirectly, through Aurelius Victor or Florus: cf. A. Martina, *Enciclopedia Dantesca* s.v. 'Livio' (III 673–7).

In turning to Dante's further problem: how can Piccarda's assertion have been true, that Constance – even though she never returned – kept her love for the nun's veil, Beatrice's answer is once more profoundly Aristotelian, and again Aquinas' words and thought are perceptible in it; at the same time, Beatrice's emphasis is neither that of Aristotle nor that of Aquinas. Aristotle mentions the Theban prince Alcmaeon's murder of his mother Eriphyle – it was the subject of a tragedy by Euripides – as the kind of action so terrible that we should face death and the harshest torments rather than let ourselves be forced to do it (1110 a 27). Here, for Aristotle, even the slightest degree of complicity with the one who compels would be culpable. In the *terzina* describing Alcmaeon's deed –

> come Almeone, che, di ciò pregato
> dal padre suo, la propria madre spense,
> per non perder pietà si fé spietato.

> as Alcmaeon, who, when his father implored him
> to do so, slaughtered his own mother –
> not to lack piety, made himself pitiless.   (IV 103–5)

– Beatrice strangely combines the calm expository statement drawn from Aquinas (*coactus fuit matrem occidere ex praecepto patris sui*: loc. cit.) with Ovid's impassioned paradox (*natus erit facto pius et sceleratus eodem*: *Metam.* IX 408).

With the next two *terzine* (106–11), however, Beatrice (or Dante) moves away from the thought of the *Ethics*. Aristotle had just said, 'on some actions praise indeed should not be bestowed, but pardon, when someone does what they ought not to, when it is a thing that overstrains human nature and that no one could bear.' Earlier, he had spoken of actions prompted 'by fear of greater ills', saying that these are mixed actions, yet more like voluntary than involuntary ones. Beatrice here (106ff) reverts to the question of deeds prompted by fear – not, like Aristotle, to deeds made necessary because the alternative is humanly unbearable – and she says in effect that deeds prompted by fear are the same in kind, though not in degree, as the unspeakable ones such as Alcmaeon's: when she claims that these 'offences cannot be excused (*scusar non si posson l'offense*)', it is almost as if she were directly contradicting Aristotle's words, 'there should not be praise, but pardon (*laus non sit quidem, venia autem*)' (1110 a 24; Spiazzi, p. 114).

69 Cf. *Ethica* III, lect. I 390 (Spiazzi, p. 112):

... operationes, quae ex timore fiunt, sunt mixtae ... (operatio) potest dupliciter considerari. Uno modo *absolute* et in universali, et sic est involuntarium. Alio modo secundum particulares circumstantias ... et secundum hoc est voluntarium.

2 The Giants in Hell

1 'Sul XXX dell'*Inferno*', in his *Varianti e altra linguistica* (Turin 1970), pp. 447–57, at p. 456.
2 *Remedia amoris* 44; on medieval expressions of the thought (e.g. *Carmina Burana* 77, st. 10: *quod ille qui percutit melius medetur*), cf. my *Medieval Latin and the Rise of European Love-Lyric* (2 vols., Oxford ²1968), I 325ff.
3 Line-references, here and below, are to *La Chanson de Roland*, ed. Joseph Bédier (Paris 1937).
4 'Dante e la prospettiva', *Studi Fiorentini* (Florence 1958), pp. 19–51.
5 *Perspectiva* IV 155; this passage is reproduced in the selection from Witelo given by C. Baeumker, *Witelo, ein Philosoph und Naturforscher des XIII. Jahrhunderts* (Münster 1908), p. 178.
6 *Perspectiva* IV 16, ed. F. Risner (Basle 1572), p. 123.
7 Cf. A. Pézard, 'Le chant des Géants', *Annales du Centre Universitaire Méditerranéen* XII (1959) 53–72, at p. 57.
8 Cf. my 'Bernard Silvestris, Natura, and Personification', *JWCI* XLIII (1980) 16–31; M. R. Lida de Malkiel, 'La dama como obra maestra de Dios', in her *Estudios sobre la Literatura Española del Siglo XV* (Madrid 1977), pp. 179–290.
9 Johannes de Hauvilla, *Architrenius*, ed. P. G. Schmidt (Munich 1974), I 244ff.
10 Cf. J. Terlingen, 'Dante e il mito dei Frisoni', *REI* n.s. XI (1965) 422–38, who cites

Bartholomaeus Anglicus, *De proprietatibus rerum* XV 56, De Frisia: *est autem gens viribus fortis, proceri corporis, severi animi et ferocis* ... Terlingen did not realise that the identical sentences about the Frisians can be found in Guido of Pisa's commentary on *Inf.* XXXI, ed. V. Cioffari (cit. n. 56 below), p. 663 (though with the variant *magni corporis*).

11 Gen. 3: 7; Isidore, *Etym.* XIX 22, 5.

12 In the Vetus Latina of Genesis (ed. B. Fischer) we read:

10:8 Chus autem genuit Nebroth hic coepit esse *gigans* super terram   9 hic erat *gigans* venator ante dominum deum propter hoc dicunt sicut Nebroth *gigans* venator ante dominum   10 et factum est initium regni eius in Babylon...

Chus begot Nimrod; he began to be a giant on earth; he was a giant, a hunter, in the presence of the Lord God; because of this people say 'like Nimrod, a giant, a hunter in the presence of the Lord'; and his empire began with Babylon...

It was Jerome who, in the Vulgate, replaced the word 'giant' in each case, by 'mighty' and 'robust' (*potens, robustus*).

13 *De civ. dei* XVI 4; cf. also Orosius, *Hist. adv. paganos* II 6. Brunetto Latini, *Li Livres dou tresor* I 23f, ed. F. J. Carmody (Berkeley–Los Angeles 1948), p. 35, while he too presents Nimrod as *le jaiant* and as builder of the tower, does not specify the tower's purpose. On the other hand, Brunetto adds that Nimrod promulgated idolatry and fire-worship (a detail derived from the pseudo-Clementine *Recognitions* I 30).

14 *DVE* I vii, 7.

15 Vergil, *Aen.* VI 577–84; Ovid, *Metam.* 151–5.

16 *Comm. in Somn. Scipionis* I 3, 7.

17 *Aen.* VI 287 and X 565–8 (Aegaeon, as Servius explains *ad loc.*, being another name for Briareus).

18 While commentators have related Dante's expression *smisurato* to Statius (*Theb.* II 596: *immensus Briareus*), I do not know if it has been remarked that his term for the giants' chains, *le ritorte* (XXXI 111) is likewise Statian (*Theb.* IV 534f: *intorta ... vincula*).

19 *Aen.* VI 595–8.

20 See the excellent discussion by W. Kranz, 'Dante und Boethius', *RF* XLIII (1951) 72–8.

21 While the Greek and Latin word for 'giant', γίγας, is probably of pre-Greek provenance (see W. Speyer, *RAC* X 1247, s.v. 'Gigant'), it was already in antiquity derived from Γῆ, so that the *gigantes* are the γηγενεῖς or *Terrigenae*, the sons of Earth. This etymology was transmitted to the Middle Ages by Isidore (*Etym.* XI 3, 13) among others.

22 See Lucan, *Pharsalia* IV 601f, 656–9.

23 *Ibid.* IV 596f ('Earth spared the gods, in that she did not raise Antaeus on the plain of Phlegra').

24 *De planctu Naturae*, ed. N. M. Häring (*Studi medievali* 3a serie XIX (1978) 797–879), VIII 137–9.

25 *De civ. dei* XVI 4.

26 S. J. Livesey and R. H. Rouse, 'Nimrod the Astronomer', *Traditio* XXXVII (1981) 203–66.

27 'Le Nemrod de l'*Enfer* de Dante et le *Liber Nemroth*', *Studi danteschi* XL (1963) 57–128. I discuss some details of this study in Excursus II below.

28 'Intorno al Nembrot dantesco e ad alcune opinioni di Richard Lemay', in his *Saggi e note di critica dantesca* (Milan–Naples 1966), pp. 367–76: 'In tutto ciò non vedo ombra di ribellione a Dio' (p. 372).

29 Thus Beryl Smalley, *The Study of the Bible in the Middle Ages* (Oxford ²1952), p. 179.
30 The Latin text is edited by E. Sackur, *Sibyllinische Texte und Forschungen* (Halle 1898), pp. 59–96
31 On the *Hebraei* cited by Peter, see Smalley (cit. n. 29), *loc. cit.* Livesey and Rouse (cit. n. 26), p. 234 n. 80, cite a passage from the Bible commentary of Nicolas of Lyra (*ca.* 1270–1349), where Nicolas preserves a Jewish legend in which Nimrod is a tyrant, an idolater and enemy of God, who commands men to worship fire. He throws Abraham, who refuses, into a furnace, but Abraham is preserved unharmed. This episode can be traced back to the (probably fifth-century) *Midrash Genesis (Noach)* XXXVIII 13 (*Midrash Rabbah*, trans. H. Freedman and M. Simon (10 vols., London 1939), I 311), a text which later (XLII 4, *ibid.* p. 346) also states that Nimrod 'incited the world to revolt'. But no mention is made of Nimrod's astronomy. In a version of this legend that became widely diffused as a Jewish–Spanish ballad, however, the plot begins with 'King Nimrod' seeing in the stars that Abraham is about to be born. Thereupon he commands the midwives to kill all newly-born male children:

> Cuando el rey Nemrod – al campo salía
> miraba en el cielo – y en la estrellería.
> Vido luz santa – en la Judería,
> que había de nacer – Abraham *abinu*.
>
> Luego á las comadres – encomendaba
> que toda mujer – que preñada quedaba,
> la que pariere hijo – que lo matara,
> que había de nacer – Abraham *abinu*.

Abraham is miraculously saved, and grows to age and wisdom with miraculous speed. He then charges Nimrod with holding himself to be God, and not wanting to believe in the true God:

> Di, raja, ¿por qué – te tienes tu por Dios?
> ¿Por qué no queres – creer en el verdadero?

Nimrod has Abraham cast into a fire, and claims he will believe in God if Abraham is preserved unharmed (as indeed he is). The ballad ends in praises of Abraham, but does not (at least in the versions I have found) mention Nimrod's change of heart. (Text in R. Gil, *Romancero Judeo-Español* (Madrid 1911), no. LVII; bibliography in S. G. Armistead *et al.*, *El Romancero Judeo-Español en el Archivo Menéndez Pidal* I (Madrid 1978), pp. 199–202.) For a wide range of Arabic and Hebrew analogues to this ballad, cf. H. Schützinger, *Ursprung und Entwicklung der arabischen Abraham–Nimrod-Legende*, Bonner Orientalische Studien XI (Bonn 1961). Schützinger does not, however, mention the Sephardic ballad itself.
32 *Hist. schol.*, Liber Genesis cap. 37 (P.L. 198, 1088).
33 *The Latin Josephus I*, ed. F. Blatt, Acta Jutlandica, Humanistisk Serie 44 (Copenhagen 1958) IV 2 (p. 137).
34 Lemay (cit. n. 27), pp. 78–84.
35 *Ibid.* p. 109.
36 According to Nardi (cit. n. 28), p. 376.
37 Ed. K. Young, *The Drama of the Medieval Church* (2 vols., Oxford 1933), II 68–72. There are also moments when the Semitic king seems to be trying – unsuccessfully – to say a few words in Latin: e.g. *i et o, iomo bello, o illa et cum marmoysen aharon, et cum cizarene ravidete*...
38 *Select Papyri* III, ed. D. L. Page (Loeb Classics, 1950), p. 338.
39 Ed. F. W. E. Roth, *Fontes rerum Nassoicarum* I (Wiesbaden 1880) 457–65.
40 Hildegard von Bingen, *Lieder*, ed. P. Barth *et al.* (Salzburg 1969), pp. 142f.

41 *Le jeu*, ed. A. Henry (Paris 1962), 1517–20.
42 *Le miracle*, ed. G. Frank (Paris 1949), 163ff.
43 See V. de Bartholomaeis, *Origini della poesia drammatica italiana* (Turin ²1952), pp. 172–6; *Le Polyptique du Chanoine Benoît*, ed. P. Fabre (Lille 1889).
44 *Le Polyptique*, p. 23.
45 *DVE* I vi, 5–7.
46 *Orac.* III 97–113; I follow the Greek text in *Sibyllinische Weissagungen*, ed. A. Kurfess (Tusculum, Munich 1951), pp. 76–8. V. Nikiprowetzky, *La troisième Sibylle* (Paris–The Hague 1970), pp. 195–225, suggests the date 42 B.C. for the main part of the third Oracle, and a date after 25 B.C for verses 1–96. On the syncretism underlying the passage cited, see *ibid.* pp. 115–26.
47 *De civ. dei* xv 9; cf. Vergil, *Aen.* XII 899f, and Pliny, *Nat. hist.* VII 16, 73–5.
48 *Liber monstrorum*, ed. F. Porsia (Bari 1976). On the date and provenance of the work, see M. Lapidge, *'Beowulf*, Aldhelm, the *Liber Monstrorum* and Wessex', *Studi medievali* 3a serie XXIII (1982) 151–92. Occasionally in medieval tradition, instead of integration, an opposition is set up between classical and biblical giants. Thus for instance in the widely read ninth-century *Ecloga Theoduli*, ed. R. P. H. Green, *Seven Versions of Carolingian Pastoral* (Reading 1980), pp. 26–35, the shepherdess Alithia counters her rival, the shepherd Pseustis, who tells of the giants' rebellion against Jove, with the 'correct' version of the story:

Feignwell: There arose men created from mother Earth:
            to drive out heaven's dwellers was all their will;
            mountain was piled on mountain, but Vulcan hurled all the foes,
            struck by lightning, down into his cave.

Verity: Adam's descendants, in Babylon's sovereign city,
            built a tower that would reach to heaven.
            Anger aroused God: confusion of tongues arose;
            there they were scattered; the city's name is not lost.   (85–92)

In terms of the poem, Alithia is telling Pseustis that he has his facts wrong; yet the poet's confrontation of the two stories is witty rather than polemical, and the point of the Eclogue, in which each pair of strophes sets a pagan and a biblical scene in parallel, is that the Graeco-Roman fables, though false in themselves, are always *umbrae veritatis* – adumbrations, in a feigned mode, of the biblical realms of truth. Compare also the treatment of the biblical and classical giants in the late-eleventh-century epic *Messias*, by Eupolemius, ed. K. Manitius, MGH (Weimar 1973), I 666–78.
49 *Alexandreis*, ed. M. L. Colker (Padua 1978), II 349–54, 498–503.
50 P.L. 198, 1228.
51 *Ibid.* 1089.
52 *The Latin Josephus I*, ed. Blatt (cit. n. 33), IV 2 (p. 138).
53 Also once called *angeli* by Peter (P.L. 198, 1089).
54 *The Commentary on the First Six Books of the Aeneid of Vergil Commonly Attributed to Bernardus Silvestris*, ed. J. W. and E. F. Jones (Lincoln–London 1977), pp. 109, 111. On the question whether Dante knew this commentary, see my article 'Bernardo Silvestre', *Enciclopedia Virgiliana* I 59–64.
55 Pietro Alighieri, *Commentarium* (the first redaction, *ca.* 1340), ed. V. Nannucci (Florence 1845), p. 262.
56 Guido da Pisa, *Expositiones et Glose super Comediam Dantis* (*ca.* 1328), ed. V. Cioffari (Albany 1974), p. 656.
57 *Ibid.* pp. 651f:

In the fable of Antaeus some things are feigned and some true. It was true that Antaeus was a king in Libya, and that he was a giant, and that Hercules killed him. But it is feigned to say he was the son of Earth, and that by touching the earth he regained strength . . . Morally, the fight between Hercules and Antaeus prefigures the fight between body and spirit . . . Allegorically, you can take Hercules as Christ, Antaeus as the devil . . .

. 58 Cf. A. Renaudet, *Dante humaniste* (Paris 1952), p. 179.
  59 R. Weimann, *Shakespeare und die Tradition des Volkstheaters* (Berlin 1967), pp. 111–21; the passage cited is on p. 116.
  60 Cf. Young (cit. n. 37), II 189, 194f: the ultimate source is again Josephus (XVII 6, 5), taken up, among others, by Bede and Peter Comestor.

3 The Phantasmagoria in the Earthly Paradise

  1 Many commentators have pointed to the 'dark utterance (*obscura . . . verba*)' of Themis in Ovid (*Metam.* I 347–415), when the goddess of justice commands Deucalion and Pyrrha to 'throw the stones of the great mother' behind them (i.e. the stones of Mother Earth, that grow miraculously into a new human race). But it has not been observed that more of Ovid's context is pertinent to Dante: what the primordial survivors had asked the goddess was: 'Tell us, Themis, by what art the loss of our race may be repaired' (379f). So, too, for Dante and Beatrice it is a question of repairing mankind's loss, through a heaven-sent intervention on earth (see the discussion of the *messo di Dio* below).
     The second allusion in Dante's verses was not fully clarified till 1932, in a remarkable essay by F. Ghisalberti (*Studi danteschi* XVI 105–25): whilst it was Oedipus, son of Laius (i.e. *Laiades*), who solved the riddle of the Sphinx and thereby caused her death, in Ovid's verses alluding to this (*Metam.* VII 759ff), all surviving manuscripts read *Naiades* in place of *Laiades*. Ghisalberti showed that, on account of this error, a new piece of mythography was fabricated by medieval commentators on the passage, in order to present the Naiads as expert solvers of riddles, and indeed as the rivals of Themis (who sent a monster to destroy the Thebans' flocks in revenge for the Sphinx's death – cf. *Metam.* VII 762ff).
  2 *Purg.* XXXIII 82–90; see also below, pp. 77f.
  3 *The Divine Comedy of Dante Alighieri*, trans. J. D. Sinclair (3 vols., London ²1948), II 429.
  4 'The Procession in Dante's Purgatorio', *Deutsches Dante-Jahrbuch* LIII/LIV (1978/9) 18–45; reprinted with some abridgements in K. Foster and P. Boyde (eds.), *Cambridge Readings in Dante's Comedy* (Cambridge 1981), pp. 114–37.
  5 *Poetria nova* 254f: see above, ch. 1, n. 42, where the Latin is cited in context.
  6 Cf. N. Mineo, *Profetismo e apocalittica in Dante* (Catania 1968); R. Manselli, 'A proposito del cristianesimo di Dante', *Letteratura e critica: Studi in onore di Natalino Sapegno* (Rome 1973), II 163–92.
  7 *Purg.* XXXII 17 (cf. *Purg.* XXIX 82–132).
  8 *Purg.* XXXIII 71f (see below, p. 78).
  9 The finest edition of the hymn (*Pange, lingua, gloriosi proelium certaminis*) is probably still that of A. S. Walpole, *Early Latin Hymns* (Cambridge 1922), pp. 164–73; on the use of the *dulce lignum* verse as a refrain, see *ibid.* p. 167.
 10 Ez. 4: 7–24 (*arborem . . . robustam*: 4: 17).
 11 Ez. 17: 1–24; 31: 3–14; Is. 10: 33–11: 1.
 12 *Sed contra* K. Foster, '*Purgatorio* XXXII', in Foster and Boyde (cit. n. 4), pp. 151f, who argues that 'the Tree originally bore flowers of the same hue as those that broke out afresh', and who would therefore link the purple of the tree's foliage with 'human nobility'. Nonetheless, it seems to me more likely that the tree in the earthly paradise would normally, as an apple-tree, have had pink or white blossoms, and that it is only on this one occasion, the renewal effected by Christ's sacrifice, that the blossoms show 'less of rose and more of violet colour', because of the blood he shed.

13 See below, pp. 96, 101.

14 *De eruditione hominis interioris* I (P.L. 196, 1230f). This work of Richard's was first mentioned in relation to Dante by C. G. Hardie, 'The epistle to Cangrande again', *Deutsches Dante-Jahrbuch* XXXVIII (1960) 51–74, and 'Beatrice's chariot in Dante's earthly paradise', *ibid.* XXXIX (1961) 137–72. In these essays Hardie also first indicated a relation between the *drudo–puttana* scene in *Purg.* XXXII and Dante's lyric *Così nel mio parlar* (see below, pp. 72–3). I have found both Hardie's suggestions most valuable, however much the detailed observations and the emphasis in the present chapter diverge from his.

15 *Purg.* XXVII 127–42.

16 'The Procession' (cit. n. 4), pp. 25–7, 39–44 (Foster and Boyde (cit. n. 4), pp. 120–1, 131–7).

17 See above, p. 26.

18 Cf. Jacopo della Lana, commenting on XXXII 40 (ed. Scarabelli, II 382): 'sua chioma, cioè le sue brocche' – that is, he rightly distinguishes the *coma* from the despoiled *altra fronda* of the previous verse.

19 Foster, in Foster and Boyde (cit. n. 4), pp. 148f, perceptively relates *Sì si conserva il seme d'ogne giusto* to Christ's phrase, of his baptism at the hands of John, *sic enim decet nos implere omnem iustitiam* (Matt. 3: 15). Hence Dante's *Sì* (corresponding to Matthew's *sic*) could also point to the self-abnegation and obedience – imitating those of Christ – implied in his own purgation.

20 See Ovid, *Metam.* 1 685ff.

21 The *splendor* (71) has been taken to be that of the procession which soon afterwards rises to heaven, or again as the light of the seven candelabras (cf. *La Divina Commedia*, ed. U. Bosco and G. Reggio (3 vols., Florence 1979), *ad loc.*, II 546); but Matelda is the focal figure in the present scene – Matelda who, from her first appearance in the earthly paradise, had been characterised by her luminousness: 'I do not believe so great a light blazed / beneath the lids of Venus...' (*Purg.* XXVIII 64f).

22 Matt. 17: 1–8; Mark 9: 2–8; Luke 9: 28–36.

23 She is encircled by her seven attendant nymphs (cf. 'The Procession' (cit. n. 4), pp. 33–6, Foster and Boyde (cit. n. 4), pp. 126–8), who here have 'in their hands those lights / that are secure against North wind and South' (98f). These lights should probably not be identified with the seven candelabras of Canto XXIX, as many commentators argue, since the candelabras, which paint flames in the sky, are too vast to be held in the hand. The image of the lights might rather have been inspired, I would suggest, by the seven lamps of Apoc. 4: 5 (*septem lampades ardentes ante thronum, qui sunt septem spiritus dei*).

24 Many commentators take verse 96 (*che sovra li altri com'aquila vola*) to qualify *altissimo canto* (i.e. epic or tragic poetry as such), rather than its 'lord', Homer. Yet while this is grammatically possible, in the *De vulgari eloquentia* passage that I cite in this connection the eagle is clearly a poet and not a poetic genre. It is noteworthy, too, that Graziolo de' Bambaglioli (alluding to Ez. 17) praised Dante as an eagle:

> De ipso etiam potest exponi quod dicit Eçeçiel: 'aquila grandis magnarum alarum, longo membrorum ductu, plena plumis et varietate, venit ad Libanum et tulit medullam cedri et summitatem eius evulsit, et transportavit eam in terram Canaan'. Quoniam sicut inter volatilia universa solius est aquile ad altiora transcendere, sic iste venerabilis auctor accessit ad Libanum, hoc est ad divine intelligentie montem, et ad omnium scientiarum fontem et intellectus sui profunditate pervenit ... Et huiusmodi sapiente tante medulla, et profunditate sublimi huius mirande inventionis, flores et fructus elegit, quos ad declarationem (*l.* delectationem) et doctrinam viventium, de prudentissimis et occultis materiis scienciarum translatos, in publicum voluit demonstrare.
>
> (*Proemio*, p. 1, with some modifications of the diplomatic text)

25 It was not until this book was in press that I saw H. Shankland's perceptive study of some of Dante's flight-imagery, 'Dante "Aliger"', *Modern Language Review* LXX (1975) 764–85. Shankland does not, however, discuss the metaphors of flight in the final cantos of *Purgatorio*.

26 Dante's choice of expression, *iuga transiliens*, even links Henry's coming symbolically with that of the Bridegroom in the Song of Songs (2: 8): *ecce iste venit, saliens in montibus, transiliens colles*.

27 *Comment. in Ezechielem* VIII 17 (P.L. 110, 699).

28 So too in *Par*. XII 106ff.

29 On the historical context of Dante's thoughts, see B. Nardi, 'La "Donatio Constantini" e Dante', in his *Nel mondo di Dante* (Rome 1944), pp. 109–59.

30 *Comment. in Cant.* (Rufinus' translation), ed. W. A. Baehrens, GCS, Origenes VIII (Leipzig 1921), pp. 235f. While *The Jerusalem Bible* (London 1966), p. 995, ascribes the verse (2: 15) to the Bride, Origen himself construed it as a command *ab sponso amicis suis virtutibus* (*Comment.* p. 240).

31 Compare Dante's expression – *lo carro e' buoi traendo l'arca santa* (*Purg.* X 56) – when he sees the ark of David sculpted on the first terrace of purgatory.

32 *Expositio in Apocalypsim* (Venice 1527; repr. Frankfurt a.M. 1964), fol. 156rb: *corpus Dyaboli non aliud esse dicimus quam multitudinem reproborum ... corpus vero draconis: reproborum omnium innumera multitudo*.

33 *In Apoc.* IV 1 (P.L. 196, 799).

34 Bosco and Reggio (cit. n. 21), II 553.

35 I cite the text from Dante Alighieri, *Rime*, ed. G. Contini (Turin ³1965), pp. 170f; the translation from my *The Medieval Lyric* (London–New York ²1977), p. 163.

36 *Deus, venerunt gentes* (Ps. 78[79]):

> God, the pagans have invaded your heritage,
> they have desecrated your holy Temple;
> they have reduced Jerusalem to a pile of ruins,
> they have left the corpses of your servants
> to the birds of the air for food,
> and the flesh of your devout to the beasts of the earth ...

Here, and in the citation of John 16: 25 below, I have followed the admirable translation in *The Jerusalem Bible* (cit. n. 30). Elsewhere I have modified this translation, or translated afresh, in order to bring citations in English as close as possible to the Latin of the Vulgate.

37 Apoc. 17: 8–12.

38 For an account of interpretations of the difficult verse, *che vendetta di Dio non teme suppe* (XXXIII 36), see Bosco and Reggio (cit. n. 21), II 559f.

39 This would seem to be implied by Dante's earlier choice of the expression *legno dolce* (XXXII 44 – see above, p. 59).

40 Ovid, *Metam.* IV 51ff; on the medieval Latin poetic versions of the legend, see esp. P. Lehmann, *Pseudo-antike Literatur des Mittelalters* (Leipzig 1927).

41 The four songs are nos. 43–6 in Contini's edition (cit. n. 35), nos. 77–80 in that of K. Foster and P. Boyde: *Dante's Lyric Poetry* (2 vols., Oxford 1967).

42 Here I think primarily of the songs nos. 34–6 (ed. Contini; = 64–6, ed. Foster–Boyde), though the expression *pargoletta* also occurs at the close of the first of the *petrose, Io son venuto al punto de la rota*.

43 I do not see, for instance, how it is possible to imagine that Dante's theory of the two paradises in *Mon.* III 16 exemplifies his estrangement from Beatrice, as Hardie argues ('Beatrice's chariot' (cit. n. 14), p. 167). For this theory receives full poetic confirmation in the earthly paradise itself, in *Purgatorio* XXVIII (see my discussion in *The Medieval Poet and his World* (Rome 1984), pp. 395ff). Again, I cannot see any trace of remorse in Dante at his own earlier fury – in

Inferno XIX – at the evils of Church and papacy (thus Hardie and others): the most extreme expression of that fury is put in the mouth of no less a personage than St Peter, in *Par.* XXVII 19ff.

44 Eunoe, unlike Lethe, is Dante's own coinage and invention. Dante's notion of the double stream was quite possibly stimulated by an episode in the *Livre de l'eschiele Mahomet* (see *The Medieval Poet* (cit. n. 43), pp. 402–4).

4 The First Circle in the Solar Heaven

1 Plato's epigram, and its much longer Latin adaptation (*Dum semihiulco savio*), were preserved both in Aulus Gellius' *Noctes Atticae* XIX 11, and in Macrobius' *Saturnalia* II 2, 15–17.

2 Cf. Aristotle, *Phys.* VIII 9; *De caelo* I 2, II 3–8; *Metaph.* XII 8.

3 Cf. A. Parronchi, 'Dante e la prospettiva', *Studi Fiorentini* (Florence 1958), p. 47, for a possible link with Witelo in this image.

4 Compare also the way the word *Valore* (x 3), designating the Might of God the Father, is echoed at 29, in the might (*valor*) of heaven, and again at 92, in *avvalora*: it is Beatrice who gives Dante the might to rise in paradise.

5 See especially the discussions by E. Auerbach, *Gesammelte Aufsätze zur romanischen Philologie* (Berne–Munich 1967), pp. 145–55, and L. Spitzer, 'Gli appelli al lettore nella *Commedia*', in his *Studi italiani* (Milan 1976), pp. 213–39.

6 *Par.* II 1–18. On the significance of the sea-imagery in this passage, see above, pp. 21–4.

7 For the elucidation of this allegory, both in *Par.* II and in *Conv.* I i, 7, see B. Nardi, *Nel mondo di Dante* (Rome 1944), pp. 47–53; and *Saggi e note di critica dantesca* (Milan–Naples 1966), pp. 386–90. Cf. also K. Lange, 'Geistliche Speise', *Zeitschrift für deutsches Altertum* XCV (1966), 81–122.

8 E.g. Richard of St Victor, *In Cant.* V (P.L. 196, 420): 'in his presence, the soul is made new, and as it were cleaving to him she senses the sweetness of the taste within (*interni gustus dulcedinem*)'.

9 On the astronomy of the opening of *Par.* X, see especially P. Boyde, *Dante Philomythes and Philosopher* (Cambridge 1981), pp. 150–5.

10 *De divinis nominibus* IV 4, 117–23. I follow the Latin version of Johannes Saracenus, printed in Thomas Aquinas, *In librum Beati Dionysii de divinis nominibus expositio*, ed. C. Pera *et al.* (Turin-Rome 1950), pp. 100f.

11 *Cons. Phil.* V m. 2. On the range of light-imagery Dante uses of God, cf. Boyde (cit. n. 9), pp. 207–14.

12 E. R. Curtius, *Europäische Literatur und Lateinisches Mittelalter* (Berne ²1954), pp. 375f ('Ist den so glorreich eingeführten Zwölfergruppen etwas gemeinsam, ausser dass sie Selige sind? ... Hält man sich die Personenkreise des *Paradiso* vor Augen, so stellen sie sich als eine persönliche Kanonbildung dar').

13 Cf. *'L'amor che move il sole e l'altre stelle'*, in my *The Medieval Poet and his World* (Rome 1984), pp. 439–75.

14 *Cons. Phil.* IV m. 6.

15 *De div. nom.* IV 15, 180, ed. Pera (cit. n. 10), p. 150: 'We shall understand love, whether divine, angelic, intellectual, animal or natural, as a certain unitive and concretive power, moving higher beings to care providentially for lower ones, moving equals to supreme mutual affection, and the lowest to revert towards better and higher ones'. Cf. Albertus Magnus, *Super Dionysium de divinis nominibus*, *Opera omnia* XXXVII 1, ed. P. Simon (Münster 1972), pp. 225ff; Thomas Aquinas, *In librum*, ed. Pera (cit. n. 10), pp. 151f.

16 *Metaphysica* I 3, 11, *Opera omnia* XVI 1, ed. B. Geyer (Münster 1960), p. 41.

17 *In XII libros Metaphysicorum expositio* I 5, 102, ed. M.-R. Cathala and R. M. Spiazzi (Turin–Rome ²1971), p. 29.

18 *Dante e San Tommaso* (Casa di Dante, Rome 1975), p. 20.

19 See above, pp. 30–1. Maria Corti, *La felicità mentale* (Turin 1983), pp. 110ff, has given good reasons for believing that Dante also worked with one of Albert's two commentaries on the *Ethics*, the so-called *Super Ethica*.

20 *Conv.* II xiv, 14; cf. Thomas, *Ethic.* II 1, 245, ed. R. M. Spiazzi, *In decem libros Ethicorum Aristotelis ad Nicomachum expositio* (Turin–Rome ³1964), p. 69.

21 *Conv.* IV viii, 1; cf. Thomas, *Ethic.* I 1, 1, *ibid.* p. 3.

22 *Ethic.* I 2, 30, *ibid.* p. 8.

23 *Ethic.* I 6, 77, *ibid.* p. 21.

24 'L'origine dell'anima umana secondo Dante', in his *Studi di filosofia medievale* (Rome 1960), pp. 9–68, esp. pp. 46ff. Of particular interest in relation to Dante, in my view, is a passage in Siger's *De anima intellectiva*, ch. VIII:

> Sentit ergo PHILOSOPHUS intellectivum seu potentiam intelligendi non pertinere ad eamdem formam ad quam pertinet potentia vegetandi et sentiendi. Si autem dicantur potentiae [unius substantiae], hoc non est simplicis formae, sed quodammodo compositae ex intellectu de foris adveniente et una substantia vegetativi et sensitivi educta de potentia materiae; unde PHILOSOPHUS *tertio De anima* intellectivum vocat partem animae.
>
> (Siger de Brabant, *Quaestiones in tertium De anima, De anima intellectiva, De aeternitate mundi*, ed. B. Bazán (Louvain–Paris 1972), p. 110)

On the question of the last phase of Siger's thought, see also n. 51 below.

25 See B. Nardi, 'Alberto Magno e San Tommaso', *Studi* (cit. n. 24), pp. 103–17, esp. pp. 108ff.

26 Albertus Magnus, *De anima* III, tr. 3, c. II, cit. *ibid.* pp. 115f.

27 I have discussed in some detail what will have attracted Dante about Siger's thought in my essay '*Orizzonte che rischiari*', *The Medieval Poet* (cit. n. 13), pp. 407–30.

28 See K. Foster, 'The Celebration of Order: *Paradiso* X', *Dante Studies* XC (1972) 109–24, at pp. 119, 123 n. 24 (with valuable references); H. Gmelin, *Die Göttliche Komödie: Kommentar* III (Stuttgart 1957) 204.

29 *Decretum*, dist. VIII, I. pars, *Corpus Iuris Canonici*, ed. E. Friedberg (Leipzig 1879), I 12.

30 *Sententiae* (Grottaferrata 1971ff) I, dist. XVII, c. 1 (I 2, p. 142). While the passage is indebted for some of its expressions to Hugh of St Victor and to Abelard (cf. D. E. Luscombe, *The School of Peter Abelard* (Cambridge 1969), p. 263), the identification of human love with the Holy Spirit appears to be Peter Lombard's own.

31 *Sententiae*, Prologus (*ibid.* I 2, p. 3); cf. Mark 12: 43–4; Luke 21: 2–4.

32 There is an outstanding modern edition, with French translation and commentary: *La hiérarchie céleste*, ed. R. Roques, G. Heil and M. de Gandillac (Paris ²1970).

33 The *Historiae* were available to Augustine from 417, i.e. for *De civitate dei* from Bk XI onwards (cf. P. Brown, *Augustine of Hippo* (London 1967), p. 284). Modern scholars, on the other hand, have shown that Augustine 'pointedly ignored' the work that Orosius dedicated to him (*ibid.* p. 296).

34 *Hist. adv. paganos* VI 22. Strangely, modern commentators on Dante's *Mon.* II viii and II x, such as G. Vinay (in *Monarchia, Testo introduzione e commento* (Florence 1950)) and B. Nardi (in Dante Alighieri, *Opere minori* II, ed. P. V. Mengaldo *et al.* (Milan–Naples, 1979)), while they mention expressions of comparable thoughts by authors nearer to Dante's time, do not signal this remarkable Orosian passage.

35 *In Cant.*, Prologus (P.L. 196, 406f).

36 *La Divina Commedia*, ed. U. Bosco and G. Reggio (3 vols., Florence 1979) III 169.

37 That of Bede is printed in P.L. 91, 1065–1236; the commentary which was widely

diffused in the Middle Ages under the name of Isidore (P.L. 83, 1119–32) is today recognised as a compendium by Alcuin: see E. Dekkers, *Clavis Patrum Latinorum* (Bruges ²1961), p. 275, no. 1220. Dekkers also (*loc. cit.*) mentions the possible ascription of an unpublished Song of Songs commentary, in a Fulda manuscript, to Isidore himself.

38 *Cons. Phil.* v pr. 4.

39 An excellent example of this conception can be found in the fragmentary Provençal poem *Boecis*, composed probably *ca.* 1070, ed. R. Lavaud and G. Machicot (Toulouse 1950).

40 Cf. Appendix III (*Praecipua quae de Boethio habentur testimonia*) in A. Fortescue's commented edition of the *Cons. Phil.* (London 1925; repr. Hildesheim–New York 1976).

41 *Cons. Phil.* I m. I, 15f (of Mors):

> Eheu, quam surda miseros avertitur aure
> et flentes oculos claudere saeva negat!

Maria Corti, *Dante a un nuovo crocevia* (Florence 1981), p. 101, compares the concluding words of Siger's own *De anima intellectiva* (ed. Bazán (cit. n. 24), p. 112) – *cum vivere sine litteris mors sit et vilis hominis sepultura*. But this phrase, which Siger adapts from Seneca (cf. Bazán *ad loc.*), is less close to Dante's thought than the Boethian one; besides, it alludes to a figurative rather than an actual death.

42 *Vala, Night the Second* (*Poetry and Prose of William Blake*, ed. G. Keynes, Nonesuch Library (London 1956), p. 278).

43 In a recent polemical essay, 'L'averroïsme latin au XIIIe siècle', in *Multiple Averroès*, ed. J. Jolivet (Paris 1978), pp. 283–6, F. Van Steenberghen claims that the term 'Latin Averroism' is not historically valid with reference to Siger of Brabant, Boethius of Dacia, and their colleagues. Even though Thomas Aquinas himself, in his *De unitate intellectus*, uses the expression *Averroistae*, Van Steenberghen refers to the 'partisans du monopsychisme d'Averroès', while deciding that 'Il faut donc cesser de parler d'averroïsme latin pour désigner l'école dirigée par Siger de Brabant' (pp. 284f). To me the word 'monopsychisme' – which has no medieval precedent – would seem rather more open to objection: it is a term by which Van Steenberghen and others have attempted to reduce a complex range of epistemological arguments and positions to 'la doctrine pernicieuse d'Averroès sur l'unicité de l'intellect humain' (*ibid.*). The adjective 'pernicieuse' itself indicates that Van Steenberghen is writing apologetics rather than history of philosophy. It is still necessary, in my view, to have an expression to characterise the wider ways in which the thought of Siger and Boethius of Dacia is similar *in orientation* to that of Averroes; for this, 'Latin Averroism' seems appropriate.

44 *Tractatus de unitate intellectus contra Averroistas*, ed. L. W. Keeler (Rome 1946); *De aeternitate mundi contra murmurantes*, ed. R. M. Spiazzi in Thomas Aquinas, *Opuscula philosophica* (Turin–Rome 1954), pp. 103–8 (where Thomas concedes, however, that there are no compelling philosophical arguments against Aristotle's thesis).

45 Cf. M. Grabmann, *Mittelalterliches Geistesleben* III (Munich 1956) 181.

46 Cf. P. Mandonnet, *Siger de Brabant et l'Averroïsme latin du XIIIe siècle* (2 vols., Louvain ²1908–11), I 260, who cites from *Martini continuatio Brabantina*, MGH, Scriptores in Folio XXIV 263.

47 See now Contini's edition, *Il Fiore e il Detto d'Amore* (Milan 1984), esp. pp. lxxi–xcv.

48 Cf. Mandonnet (cit. n. 46), I 265.

49 *Ibid.* I 282. It is significant in this connection that Mandonnet translates *quasi dementi* once (I 259) as 'presque dément' and once (I 281) as 'à moitié dément'.

50 I give some bibliographical details on Siger and Joachim in relation to Dante in *The Medieval Poet* (cit. n. 13), pp. 408f.

51 Here Auerbach's conception of *figura* would seem to me particularly apt: the earthly Thomas and Bonaventure are *figurae* of their heavenly counterparts; their reality, in Dante's solar heaven, is the perfect, celestial fulfilment of the existence they had adumbrated – imperfectly – on earth.

Dante's parallel presentation of the two 'unorthodox' teachers, Siger and Joachim, by the two established ones, Thomas and Bonaventure, precludes the possibility that he could have chosen to highlight Siger for another reason, as some scholars have alleged – namely that Siger, late in life, might have recanted his earlier ideas and come close to the thought of Thomas Aquinas. This view, which was based on an unfortunate attempt by F. Van Steenberghen to ascribe some anonymous (and theologically unexceptionable) *Quaestiones de anima* to Siger, was expertly disposed of in its time by Etienne Gilson, in his *Dante the Philosopher* (London 1948) (= *Dante et la philosophie* (Paris 1939)), Eclaircissement V ('Concerning the Thomism of Siger of Brabant', pp. 317–27). The notion of a Siger who recanted his more challenging Aristotelian teachings has recently been revived, however, by a historian of philosophy, A. Zimmermann ('Dante hatte doch Recht', *Philosophisches Jahrbuch* LXXV (1967/8), 206–17), as well as by Maria Corti in her book on Dante (cit. n. 41), pp. 99f. Once again a more 'Thomistic' treatise has been found and been claimed as the work of Siger's final years: the *Quaestiones super Librum de Causis* that were printed under Siger's name by A. Marlasca (Louvain–Paris 1972). Two questions arise: can this ascription be upheld? And if so, how does it affect the meaning of Dante's tribute to Siger?

In one of the two surviving manuscripts of these *Quaestiones*, they are preserved anonymously; in the other, Vienna 2330, a cryptogram, as well as an entry in the table of contents on the flyleaf, attributes them to 'Seierus' (Marlasca, p. 16). However, on the same folio as the cryptogram, another hand attributes these same Questions to none other than Avicenna: *Questiones Avicene super librum de causis* (Marlasca, p. 8)! This itself should prompt a certain caution concerning the 'Seierus' ascription.

If one considers the internal evidence, several points seem to me deeply problematic. First, that the author of these *Quaestiones* copies almost verbatim some extensive passages of Thomas Aquinas (cf. Marlasca, p. 26), though without naming him, whereas in Siger's known authentic works, when he discusses theses of Thomas, he mentions him by name (cf. Marlasca, p. 12, n. 6). Marlasca's claim, that in lectures Siger could 'se permettre de reproduire plus ou moins littéralement certains passages d'écrits peu communs à la Faculté des Arts, certain que ses auditeurs ne s'en apercevront pas' (pp. 12f), appears to me implausible. For if the *Liber de causis* Questions were, as Marlasca states, composed in Paris in the years 1272/6 and probably 1274/6 (p. 29), whose writings *de anima* and *de causis* would have been better known in Paris at that moment than those of Thomas? (Insofar as such writings, even if by a theologian, were on Aristotelian themes, it would be hard to imagine that they were read less in the Faculty of Arts than in that of Theology.)

Second, nowhere in the *Quaestiones* does the author – if he is Siger – make any allusion to his earlier position on Aristotle's and Averroes' theses about the intellect. Is it conceivable that Siger, if he were here dramatically abandoning his own long-cherished views, views that he had refined and qualified in the course of several works, would be completely silent about what he had espoused before, and about what had now persuaded him to reject this totally? In the key *Quaestiones* in the collection, those on the human soul (26 and 27), this author makes not even an attempt to cope with any of the important points raised in Siger's known writings *de anima*. He proceeds by mere assertion (e.g. p. 106, lines 115–18; p. 107, lines 149–57; p. 114, lines 196–204). At the vital moment when this writer wishes to show that Averroes' interpretation of the 'possible intellect' is not only 'heretical in our faith, but also irrational', he commits a glaring *petitio principii*:

Sed intellectus hoc modo unitur corpori humano quod sub unitate existens non potest pluribus hominibus seu pluribus corporibus humanis uniri. Ergo necesse est multiplicatione corporum humanorum quibus unitur ipsum multiplicari... (p. 112, lines 156–9)

The whole Scholastic controversy centred precisely on the *way* in which the possible intellect, as Aristotle conceives it, can be united to the individual. To claim the bald assertion just cited as a proof of the irrationality of Averroes, as this author does (*irrationalis etiam sic apparet: ibid.* lines 146–7), is unworthy of the authentic Siger. Siger could hardly, at such a moment, have ignored all the difficulties he had himself raised over the years – unless, presumably, he had been compelled to make a retraction in this form by the Inquisitor. But in that case, why do the records say nothing about Siger's having made such a retraction? Why, on the contrary, do they dwell on Siger's fleeing from France in 1276, in order to appeal to Rome?

The exact character of the *Quaestiones super Librum de causis* as they survive remains difficult to assess. They do contain some discussions that, in the light of Siger's acknowledged writings, could be genuinely Sigerian, whereas the essential questions on the intellect, 26 and 27, appear to be by someone who was quite unable to discuss Siger's major epistemological problems at a philosophical level. Provisionally I would suggest that this set of *Quaestiones* – like so many sets that survive in manuscripts – is an eclectic compilation, drawing on both Thomist and Sigerian material, a composite rather than a unified work.

At all events, while we cannot wholly rule out that Dante should have known some work which circulated under Siger's name and yet was close to Thomas in inspiration, the notion that only such a work could have motivated Dante's tribute to Siger remains preposterous. Central to Dante's recognition of Siger and Joachim is his awareness of the *opposition* shown to them on earth by Thomas and Bonaventure. (No one, to my knowledge, has yet tried to claim for Joachim a 'late work' that would similarly show Joachim in close agreement with his adversary!) Moreover, the words Dante attributes to his celestial Thomas are precise: what Siger 'syllogized' were ideas ill-received but true: *silogizzò invidïosi veri*. Many of the clergy in Dante's day – and some scholars in ours – would have been happier if Dante had mentioned Siger's theses not as true but as matter for repentance: if he had written, say,

silogizzò invidïose tesi,
e poi se ne pentì ...

But that was not Dante's thought.

On Siger's career see now R. A. Gauthier, *Revue des sciences philosophiques et théologiques* LXVII (1983) 201–32, LXVIII (1984) 3–49.

52 Cf. my study 'The Song of Songs and Medieval Love-Lyric', in *The Medieval Poet* (cit. n. 13), pp. 209–36.
53 *In Cant.* VI (P.L. 196, 421).
54 Gmelin (cit. n. 28), III 212. When I gave a talk based on this chapter at the Institute for Cultural Analysis, New York, a historian of science in the audience objected that the clock could not have carried associations of cosmic harmony for Dante, because mechanical clocks in Dante's time were notoriously inaccurate. Yet however interesting the actual defects of early fourteenth-century clocks may be historically, they can hardly be relevant to Dante's intention in choosing this image. In *Par.* XXIV 13ff, the wheels of the clock, revolving at different speeds, likewise have connotations of perfect precision. On the devel-

opment of clockwork in medieval Europe, see J. Needham, W. Ling, and D. J. de S. Price, *Heavenly Clockwork* (Cambridge 1960), pp. 192–8.

55 Compare especially *Par.* IX 73 (*tuo veder s'inluia*) and 81 (*s'io m'intuassi, come tu t'inmii*), as well as *Par.* XVII 13 (*t'insusi*) and XXXIII 138 (*s'indova*). I would also see a deliberate link between *etternalmente* in the second line of *Par.* X and *s'insempra* in the last, bringing the canto as it were full circle.

Excursus I

1 *Studien zum mittellateinischen Prosarhythmus. Seine Entwicklung und sein Abklingen in der Briefliteratur Italiens*, Studia Latina Stockholmiensia X (Stockholm 1963). On the medieval Italian and French theorists of *cursus* and their teachings, see pp. 13–26; on Dante's practice, pp. 76–87; for a bibliography of the chief earlier scholarly literature, pp. 202–4.

2 *Prose Rhythm in Medieval Latin from the 9th to the 13th Century*, Studia Latina Stockholmiensia XX (Stockholm 1975).

3 His substantial review, in *Studi medievali* 3a Serie XIX (1978) 701–18, adds particularly helpful details about the statistical procedures.

4 Dante Alighieri, *Opere minori*, ed. P. V. Mengaldo *et al.*, II (Milan–Naples 1979). All references to Dante's *Epistles*, *Monarchia*, and *De vulgari eloquentia*, and to numbers of sentences in them, are based on this edition. In his notes to the Cangrande *Epistle* (pp. 598–643), G. Brugnoli includes some valuable observations of instances of *cursus*; on p. 607 n. 12, however, *vidéri pótest*, adduced as an example of *cursus planus*, is in fact non-rhythmic (it is *p 2*, not *p 3p*, in Janson's notation). On the text of the *Epistle* see also E. Cecchini, in *Miscellanea A. Campana* I (Padua 1981) 213–29.

5 And also frequently at clause-endings within sentences, as in the longer examples in *DVE* II 6 mentioned above. But the cadences that are not at sentence-endings would require a lengthy separate documentation and analysis, which, though it would be of considerable intrinsic interest, would be only marginal to the questions discussed in this Excursus.

6 Lindholm (cit. n. 1), p. 78.

7 It is slightly misleading in this connection that Janson (cit. n. 2), p. 79, basing himself on Lindholm's analyses, writes of Dante's 'predilection for the *tardus*'. This is not incorrect in the context of Lindholm's comparison of Dante with someone such as Cola di Rienzo, who virtually avoided *tardus*: in a sample of 1377 cadences, Cola has 665 strict *velox*, 110 strict *planus*, and only 13 strict *tardus* (cf. Janson, *ibid.* p. 23). But the figures given by Lindholm (cit. n. 1), p. 87, for Dante's undisputed letters (*Epp.* I–XII in the *Opere minori* edition, cit. n. 4) are:

velox	97
tardus	45
planus	68
others	4 (2 of these being *trispondaicus*)
Total	214

If we adjust these figures to include only the variants mentioned as admissible by medieval theorists (see below, p. 108), they become:

velox	93
tardus	39
planus	63
others	19
Total	214

These figures thus provide a welcome confirmation of the small sample comparison in my Table 5 below.

Excursus II

1 C. H. Haskins, 'Nimrod the Astronomer', in his *Studies in the History of Mediaeval Science* (Cambridge Mass. ²1927), pp. 336–45 (cf. also p. xv).

2 S. J. Livesey and R. H. Rouse, 'Nimrod the Astronomer', *Traditio* XXXVII (1981), 203–66.

3 'Le Nemrod de l'*Enfer* de Dante', *Studi danteschi* XL (1963) 57–128; and 'Le cas des géants', *Revue des Etudes Italiennes* n.s. XI (1965) 237–79.

4 *Ibid.* pp. 272f. The passage deserves to be cited:

> l'idée de voir en Nemrod le chef de file des hommes de science, férus de savoir au mépris de l'humble soumission de l'esprit à la Révélation ... se trouve déjà nettement exprimée chez saint Bernard. Il est probable que c'est dans le *IVe Sermon* de Bernard sur l'*Ascension* que Dante a puisé l'idée de condamner en Nemrod la science naturelle trop sûre d'elle-même. Evidemment, Dante a enrichi ce thème à son tour ... en particulier, il est vraisemblable que saint Bernard ne connaissait pas le *Livre de Nemrod* dont les données ont servi à Dante pour étoffer le caractère de son Nemrod.

This is seriously misleading. Not one word about Nimrod can be found in St Bernard's *Ascension* sermon. There is nothing but a phrase of general import about the 'sons of Satan' – 'thus they build Babel, thus think they can attain the likeness of God' (P.L. 188, 311 C) – by which Bernard clearly castigates human presumption as such. He gives no indication that he has Nimrod in mind. That is, while Dante might have known this sermon of Bernard's, he could not possibly have read a condemnation of Nimrod in it. (The notion that in condemning Nimrod Dante was condemning natural science is equally far-fetched – see above, p. 45.) There is a similar lack of rigour when Lemay ('Le cas', pp. 241f) in all seriousness raises the possibility that Dante had direct acquaintance with the works of Homer and Hesiod.

5 'Le Nemrod' (cit. n. 3), pp. 68, 70 (cf. also 'Le cas' (cit. n. 3), p. 266).

6 There is no justification for the way Lemay construes this expression ('Le Nemrod' (cit. n. 3), p. 67): 'l'ancêtre ou fondateur de l'astronomie *et même de la magie* ("occulta in compoto")' (italics mine). To omit the word *astronomie* from the Latin phrase cited here is wilful: the reference is clearly to what is hidden in astronomical calculation, not to 'the occult'.

7 *Par.* IV 124–32.

8 'Adelard of Bath', in *Studies* (cit. n. 1), pp. 31f.

9 Livesey and Rouse make some perceptive points against Haskins' theory that there was a Syriac original of the *Liber Nemroth*, and suggest that the text might well have been composed by a western author, who knew some eastern works – such as pseudo-Methodius – that had already reached the West in translation, but who relied only on western astronomical material. At the same time, I should like to record my impression that the work *reads* like a translation. Many of the awkwardnesses in the Latin (where they are not due to corruptions – even the oldest manuscript, R, often gives a badly garbled text) seem best explicable as a translator's attempts to follow his source over-literally. Besides, there are some early eastern allusions to Nimrod as an author which, though I am not competent to evaluate them, cannot be simply dismissed. Thus for instance the eighth-century Georgian writer Leonti Mroveli mentions among his sources a 'Book of Nimrod', which the Magi consulted and found to foretell the birth of Christ. Such a prophecy does not occur in the extant Latin text; nonetheless, it is not easy to believe that 'the so-called *Book of Nimrod* is nothing other than one of the many recensions of the apocryphal *Cave of Treasures*', as M. Tarchnišvili (*Geschichte der kirchlichen Georgischen Literatur* (Vatican 1955), p. 93) maintained. For the sixth-century *Cave of Treasures* itself *cites* the same prophecy,

giving as its source a book it calls *The Revelation of Nimrod* (*The Book of the Cave of Treasures*, trans. Sir E. A. W. Budge (London 1927), p. 205). The genesis of the Latin text, it would seem, still deserves further investigation.

Dr Sebastian Brock, to whom I turned for advice on the question of a possible Syriac original for the *Liber Nemroth*, suggested that the last words of extract 13 below – *quia medius mundus est in monte Amorreorum* – might point to a Syriac background. He wrote: 'the centre of the earth is Moriah ... The *only* Old Testament version which renders Moriah of *both* Gen. 22: 2 and 2 Chr. 3: 1 by "of the Amorites" is the Syriac Peshitta'. Dr Brock also reminded me, however, that the Septuagint at 2 Chr. 3: 1 has ἐν ὄρει τοῦ Αμορια, so that it is at least possible that this influenced certain Latin authors. Where the Vulgate here has *in monte Moria* (variae lectiones *in montem oria*, *in monte oria*, ed. R. Weber *ad loc.*), the Vetus Latina rendering of the passage has, like the Septuagint, *in monte Amoria* (*Les anciennes versions latines du deuxième livre des Paralipomènes*, ed. R. Weber (Rome 1945), p. 5).

Bibliographical Note

Dante's *Commedia* is cited according to the edition of G. Petrocchi, *La Commedia secondo l'antica vulgata* (4 vols., Milan 1966–7); the Latin works, according to *Opere minori* II, ed. P. V. Mengaldo, B. Nardi, A. Frugoni, G. Brugnoli, E. Cecchini and F. Mazzoni (Milan–Naples 1979); the *Rime*, according to the edition of G. Contini (Turin ³1965), with reference also to that of K. Foster and P. Boyde, *Dante's Lyric Poetry* (2 vols., Oxford 1967); the *Vita Nuova*, according to the edition of D. De Robertis (Milan–Naples 1980); the *Convivio*, according to that of E. G. Parodi and F. Pellegrini, in *Le opere di Dante* (Società dantesca italiana, Florence ²1960); and the *Fiore*, according to the new edition of G. Contini, *Il Fiore e il Detto d'Amore attribuibili a Dante Alighieri* (Milan 1984).

Of the earliest commentaries on the *Commedia*, I have consulted: Graziolo de' Bambaglioli, *Il commento dantesco*, ed. A. Fiammazzo (Savona 1915); Guido da Pisa, *Expositiones et Glose super Comediam Dantis*, ed. V. Cioffari (Albany, N.Y. 1974); Jacopo della Lana, in *Comedia di Dante degli Allagherii col commento di Jacopo della Lana bolognese*, ed. L. Scarabelli (3 vols., Bologna 1866); Jacopo Alighieri, *Chiose alla cantica dell'Inferno*, ed. G. Piccini (Florence 1915); Pietro Alighieri, *Super Dantis ipsius genitoris Comoediam Commentarium*, ed. V. Nannucci (Florence 1845), and *Il 'Commentarium' di Pietro Alighieri nelle redazioni ashburnhamiana e ottoboniana*, ed. R. Della Vedova, M.T. Silvotti and E. Guidubaldi (Florence 1978); and Giovanni Boccaccio, *Esposizioni sopra la Comedia di Dante*, ed. G. Padoan (Verona–Milan 1965).

Among modern commentaries, I have most frequently consulted those of U. Bosco and G. Reggio, *La Divina Commedia* (3 vols., Florence 1979), N. Sapegno, *La Divina Commedia* (3 vols., Florence ²1968), and H. Gmelin, *Die Göttliche Komödie: Kommentar* (3 vols., Stuttgart 1954–7).

A number of writings on the *Commedia* by modern scholars are cited in the notes above. I have learnt most from those of Auerbach, Contini and Nardi, and from the entries in the *Enciclopedia Dantesca*. Often, in preparing documentation, it was a delicate decision whether or not to signal a range of divergent views on specific points – at the risk of overburdening the notes with scholarly allusions and controversy. My choice of references represents a compromise that inevitably will not satisfy everyone; but if secondary literature on Dante has been adduced sparsely, I hope that the documentation of primary sources, in particular of medieval Latin texts, is comprehensive enough to be helpful to specialists and non-specialists alike.

Index

149